"A Family Guide to the Grand Circ[ ]
and excellent guide for anyone wa[ ]
good guide book with or without a[ ]

"Loved it! We were planning a trip to three of the parks, but after picking up *A Family Guide..* we added on two others. Really helpful information and definitely helped us plan out a better vacation.. and the stories were a welcome plus! I want to do this trip again!" - Tanya and Trevor L.

"What a fresh approach to travel guides, I actually read it cover to cover!" - Ernest D.

"I absolutely love it!!! The pictures are beautiful and to be honest, what he wrote actually made me cry at one point. We all get so caught up with TV, Facebook, gadgets, etc that we forget to live our lives and enjoy what God has truly given us. It makes me want to change my life completely." - Heather S.

"*A Family Guide to the Grand Circle National Parks* made my once in life time vacation a once in a lifetime vacation! Awesome travel guide, great stories, a great book!" - Jenn H.

"Meticulously and exquisitely written, very informative, beautifully illustrated with photographs." - Terry T.

"You have a terrific guidebook here!" - Michael M.

"Bought it, read it, and decided to just follow the author's route. This book was perfect for us! Really streamlined our planning, great coverage, I could just pick up the book and decide what to do each day." - Eric B.

Also by Eric Henze

The Complete Guide to Wilder Ranch State Park

RVing with Monsters

The Complete Guide to Henry Cowell Redwoods State Park

The Grand Circle Hiking and Visitor Guide

All titles published by Gone Beyond Guides

Follow us on Facebook and Twitter!

 facebook.com/GBG.GoneBeyondGuides

 twitter.com/GoneBeyondGuide

A FAMILY GUIDE TO THE
GRAND CIRCLE NATIONAL PARKS

COVERING
ZION, BRYCE, CAPITOL REEF,
CANYONLANDS, ARCHES, MESA VERDE,
AND GRAND CANYON NATIONAL PARKS

Eric Henze

Gone Beyond Guides
Publisher

To Angela, Everest and Bryce, with love...

Contents

Acknowledgements

Writing books is a team effort. They may be crafted within the mind of the author, but they are never completed alone. First and last on this list, thanks goes to my family. To my wife Angela and our sons Everest and Bryce, a huge thanks. You were not only the full on inspiration for the main characters of the short stories in this book, in real life too you put up with the nightly weave of words that culminated as this body of work.

To the folks who gave both early and ongoing input, I couldn't have done this without you. Paula Rothe, George Trager, Caroline and Tom Mcguire, Dayna Lango, Heather Sepulveda and Ernie Doucette, thanks for giving honest feedback. Each of you contributed in your own way, providing insights that I was too close to see. Thanks!

Then there's the group collectively known as the "Book Cover Task Force". This group includes Teresa Lopez, Kelley Kinney, Mariana McCready, Victoria "Odd Soul" Yuan, Alex Yick, Patty Ross, Katherine Roth, Sandy Schmidt, Robin Marquis, Ashleigh Coffeng, Marty Chagrin, and Chris Henrick. Each of them gave insightful and honest feedback on the book cover.

A special thank you goes to Maggie Perkins. Once my high school mentor and English teacher, how we stayed in contact these many years is not hard to believe for anyone who knows you. Your depth of heart, honesty, integrity and warmth has been a shining light in my life and it was an honor to receive your feedback for this book.

A warm appreciation goes to John Eichinger for keeping my computer running, to Greg Hendricker for his voice and influence, and to Nancy Smith for reminding me that grammar is the science within the art of writing.

To Jeff Sowell, for wonder. You started out as my car mechanic, but underneath that salty surface, I found a true confidant and friend. For all of your contributions, I don't know what to say, thank you doesn't go far enough.

Huge thanks goes to the many folks who put their photos into the creative commons. I poured through thousands of pictures and deliberated on finding those that had heart and soul, the ones that captured the essence of these national parks.

I would like to thank the National Park Service. Your help in creating this book has been immeasurable. I was continually impressed with the depth of passion of the park employees. It is beyond knowledge or dedication to a job, it is a commitment to the service and protection of these national treasures. I am humbled and deeply thankful for all of your help.

A special call out goes to National Park Ranger Lori Rome, Barb Webb, Shirley Torgerson, Gail Pollock, Lillian "Lulu" Santamaria, Andy Nettell of Back of Beyond Bookstore in Moab, Utah, Laurie Frantz and Jill Burt. Each of you took time out of your day to help me with tips, suggestions and guidance that markedly improved this book! Thank you!

To my editor Meghan Ward, tough, to the point, at times brutal, but with a core of honesty and integrity. She took the rough slab of my manuscript and polished it, rounding the edges and adding a sheen that allowed for an all-around better read. Every writer needs a good editor and am thankful to have found Meghan.

I want to thank Molly Roy, who created all of the maps for this new updated edition. Her efforts really have helped make this guide book more useful for our readers, which is the primary goal! Thanks Molly!

A huge nod of gratitude goes to Michael S Malone whose guidance and mentorship helped put the book on the right trajectory.

Finally, to my readers, this book is for you! Thank you for your support and please let me know your thoughts.

Preface

The fondest memories I have of my family are not made up entirely of grand events. Every day I get little reminders of why I'm here, like being greeted by my sons when I come home with a hearty and unified "Hey, Dad!" There are others; seeing my kids lost in the innocence of slumber, quietly placing a cup of coffee on my wife's nightstand as her first moment of each day, or just sitting outside on a warm evening with my sons Everest and Bryce having "father/son talk." These are moments beyond mere happiness. They bring grounded and whole contentment.

Within the territory of large events that bring this feeling, there are likely to be bigger ones down the road as our children grow. To date, neither of our two sons has driven a car, gotten a degree, or brought us grandchildren. For now, the largest events are our vacations, times when we move as one into some unfamiliar territory, exploring, learning together, operating as a team. The entirety of each vacation becomes an imprint of contentment of the grandest of proportions. Each has its own special tastes, sets of visuals, sounds and emotion. They are never perfect. As I think back on each in writing this, there were moments in every vacation that could have gone better. For some reason, though, those negative realities all get shoved to the back of the mind, leaving only the warm, gentle memories of familial togetherness.

That said, when it came to picking a vacation destination, we were in a rut and our vacations had become a bit routine. The planning would start with my asking the question, "Forget how much this would cost us. Where do you want to go?" Angela, my wife, would answer the same each time, somewhere abroad, usually Spain or Italy.

We would look up airfare and upon noticing it pretty much consumed 300 percent of our vacation budget, we'd start lowering our standards a bit. We'd look for deals, cheap packages to closer but still far off places like Costa Rica or maybe Hawaii or Washington DC. Nothing would present itself.

We'd then look at nearby states or a less foreign country, like Canada. Still, nothing would stick. In the end, our plans would be pushed down to a destination we could drive to.

Then Ang would say, "I don't want to drive a long distance." She would swoop this in quickly for good reason because she knew I don't mind driving and that my thoughts were now turning to places like Carlsbad Caverns, Alaska and Cabo San Lucas. Given we lived in the San Francisco Bay Area, these destinations would mean very long drives and it doesn't matter how big you may think a Yukon XL SUV is, it gets very small by the fourth hour of driving for our family.

In previous years, this would lead us to land on the exact same two vacation destinations. It would come down to either a beach or an amusement park. Sometimes we'd really mix it up and go to both. Now don't get me wrong, we like beaches and the Happiest Place on Earth is well, just about the greatest place on Earth for young kids, but I was ready for adventure. There was no way I was going to belt myself into a dinghy and listen to "It's a Small World" again. Not this time, not this year. We—I—needed something different.

Then I had a realization and when I told my wife, she agreed, and before we knew it, this epiphany had transformed our whole vacation planning process. The realization was simple. Our boys were growing up. The oldest, Everest, would be out of the house in four years and that meant we only had four more great summer vacations left. Sure, it was possible that he would want to come along with us after he left home. After all, he rarely passes up free food and leisure, but we knew the reality of that thought. Everest would be a grown man in four years and thus free to say no. Realizing time was running out changed everything. We rethought the budget and most importantly rethought the vacation.

Angela and I arrived on four must-do vacations, those epic journeys that you imagine you someday will of course take with your kids when they are old enough, back when you thought you had tons of time ahead of you, before you realized just how quickly they do grow up. The three other vacations we chose will remain a mystery; however, the one we chose first was to travel through the seven national parks within the Grand Circle. The thought of doing it in an RV was added and the answer was a resounding "Yes!" because traveling in a modality we had never undertaken only added to the sense of adventure. I have been to these parks many times over and, in fact, that was why I chose it as one of my must-do vacations. I had to show my wife and kids what I had seen years earlier. These parks are that amazing.

Once back from the vacation, writing the book became a journey that started after work each night. By day, I'm an Enterprise Architect working for an awesome visual graphics company in Silicon Valley. The role of an architect, by the way, is simple. I receive a ton of emails, I answer some of them, and I go to more meetings than is probably natural.

Typically, I'm required to go to 2–3 meetings at the same time. Every now and then, they allow me outside the office walls to visit with vendors whose sole purpose is to send me more emails and set up more meetings.

After work, I'd come home, help the kids with their homework and then duck into the den to write a little. The sacrifice of this arrangement was mainly with my wife and our shared TV bonding moments. Her backlog of TV shows that we would watch together started to pile up, but she supported the effort, mainly by watching them without me.

The kids are pretty self-sufficient, which means that while they still enjoy "Dad" time, during weekdays they would rather chill out with their own activities. Bryce is nine and loves karate. He's one of those either on or off type of boys; there is very little middle ground with that kid. Everest is 14 and settling into his teenage years, mastering the art of pushing down his childlike tendencies and embracing whatever he seems to think is cool. Both are great kids, thanks to my wife who ended one career as a bookstore owner to start another as a super mom. Oh, and yes, our boys are named after landmarks and yes, we too are unable to explain how this happened. We started with Bob, moved through the biblical names and then somehow landed on Everest. There really is no way to explain how something like that happens. Of course, once we went down that road, it was hard to stop. Our second son had to be Bryce.

For someone using this guide, the Grand Circle is filled with a fair amount of driving. To give the users of this guide something more, I decided to weave several short stories into the book . These stories are embellished versions of actual events about our family and people we have met along the way. They are met to amuse, help shorten the drive and enrich the journey. This first pass of this book led with the stories under the title "RVing with Monsters".

As I looked for story lines for each chapter, one memory that occurred in 1991 came back to me. I had been traveling through Arizona, and while I normally didn't pick up hitchhikers, there was this one guy whom, for whatever reason, I offered a ride. On the trip up through the red rock canyon walls of Oak Creek, he and I were able to quickly connect at a fairly deep level. Conversation wound its way to his heritage and he confided in me that he was a Hopi Indian and a shaman. In high school, I had met his teacher once, the elder shaman Thomas Banyacya. My connection to his teacher became common ground, and a friendship was formed. The young shaman took me to his house and gave me maps to the Hopi Prophecy Rock and told me that his purpose was to pass on the prophecy. I loved the heartfelt nature of his words, and because I was so enthused about it as a young college student, he said that I would one day find a way to pass on their belief. He didn't make me promise anything; he simply said that one day I would "tell the people." I've been holding onto that thought for 23 years and the context of this book made for a perfect setting for finally telling the Hopi Prophecy in a way that I hope folks find palatable.

Beyond the short stories, there are also two chapters that have been added to help make this a more complete travel guide. Given Las Vegas is one of the main starting points for a trip to the Grand Circle, there is a chapter on travelling to this "city of indulgence" family style. It contains where to stay and what to do if you are travelling with children. The other additional chapter is on renting an RV. Now you don't have to rent an RV to explore the Southwest, but if you are thinking about it, this chapter is meant to help demystify the whole RV experience.

I hope you enjoy this book as much as a travel companion as it is a travel guide. It is meant to take some of the hassle out of taking a family vacation to the Grand Circle. I would love to hear your feedback and can be found at www.facebook.com/GBG.GoneBeyondGuides. Again, Enjoy!

Eric Henze

Notes for 2016 Edition:

This book's goal is to be an indispensable asset for those traveling the Grand Circle. Towards that goal, we've made a few updates. Updates included input from some of the park rangers on adding warnings to troubling hikes and other recommendations as well as pricing updates where appropriate.

The biggest change to the book is the addition of maps. We provided overview maps for all of the seven parks. In fact we included two maps to cover the larges park, Canyonlands. We also redid the Grand Circle Overview map. This is my favorite map now! The new map attempts to simplify and bring clarity to all of the parks within the Grand Circle, we hope you find it useful.

Looking for info on all the other parks within the Grand Circle?

We have a new book coming out in early March 2016! It is called *The Grand Circle Hiking and Visitor Guide.* The book covers every national park, national recreation area, national monument and state park within the Grand Circle or to put it another way - every park shown on the Grand Circle Overview Map on pages 2-3! It covers over 75 parks and areas of interest in total, all with a healthy amount of detail.

The Grand Circle is too big for one book. With *The Grand Circle Hiking and Visitor Guide* and this book, you oh great traveler, should have everything you need to have an amazing trip within the land with the highest concentration of parks anywhere in the United States. Go forth and vacation!

Introduction to the Grand Circle

Few vacations are so widely diverse in scope yet so universally received as the Grand Circle vacation. It is a bold journey, filled with hearty adventure and all the greatness that is the Southwest. For many, it is a bucket list item, one of those must do vacations that are done at least once in your life. It is also a great vacation for a family; there is something for every age. Both young and young at heart are continuously offered a succession of wonders that present themselves with humble majesty. These are mighty vistas, dramatic from the rock you stand on all the way to the far horizon.

The Grand Circle takes the wanderer through a large number of National Parks, all of them completely unique, yet with one common theme: the vastness of the Southwest. The journey is done almost always by vehicle and because some of the areas visited are outside the grasp of a conventional hotel, it is ideally done in a motor home. Here the pace is slowed to the safe traveling speed required of a large house on wheels. A family can bond because they are home—in a house that opens to a different front yard potentially every day.

The Grand Circle is one of the best vacations in the United States. This book is a true guide. You can follow it to the letter, taking the same route outlined, or borrow from it as you wish to create your own adventure. It is meant to be a companion, sidekick, friend and pocketbook ranger on your own Grand Adventure of the great Southwest.

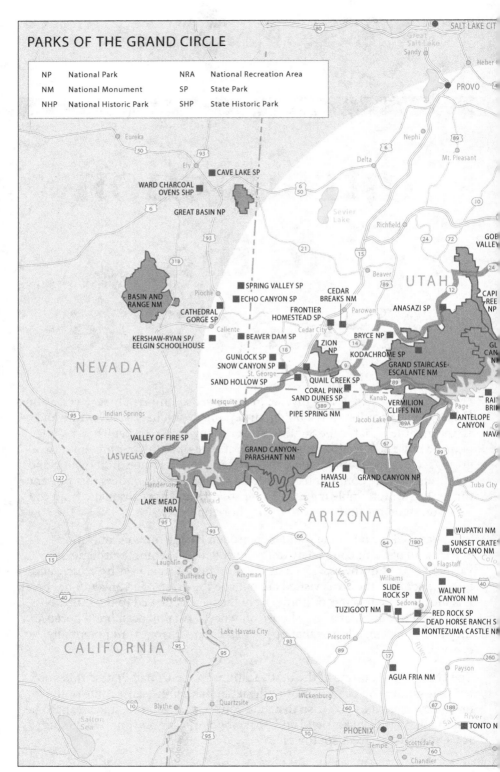

PARKS OF THE GRAND CIRCLE

NP	National Park	NRA	National Recreation Area
NM	National Monument	SP	State Park
NHP	National Historic Park	SHP	State Historic Park

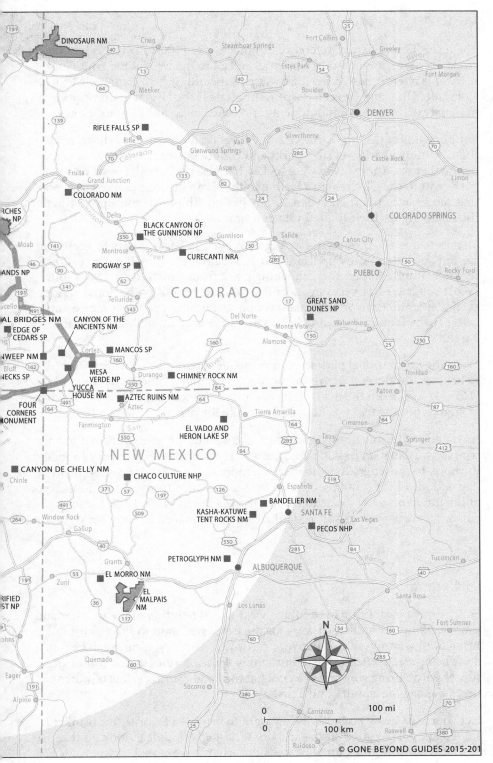

Getting Started

The term "Grand Circle" references an imaginary 1400-mile (2253 kilometer) circle drawn on a map in the Southwest offset to the west of the Four Corners. This circle is vast, covering five states including Arizona, New Mexico, Colorado, Utah and Nevada. Within the circle is the largest concentration of national parks, national monuments and state parks in the United States.

For purposes of this book, the Grand Circle has been trimmed down from the 12 national parks, 44 state parks and countless areas of interest to seven national parks. These seven were picked because they are the most popular parks within the Circle, and traveling to them can be done as one large loop that can be accomplished over a 10-day period. Thus, this route gives travelers the best bang for their limited vacation time.

The route described starts in Las Vegas. Why? Las Vegas is easy to get to by car or plane and, more importantly, if you are travelling by RV, has several RV rental facilities. It is an easy launching point from which to start your journey. If you leave Las Vegas by morning, you can be in Zion National Park or even the Grand Canyon by midafternoon. In addition, as Vegas increasingly caters to the family, it stands in its own right as a vacation destination for parents.

From the first national park to each subsequent park, the route is designed to balance the amount of driving needed. Each park is about 100-150 miles (161-241 km) from the next. There are longer stretches and shorter stretches, of course, but the trip was designed to make the driving distances fairly equal.

As stated earlier, the book is meant to take a lot of the guesswork out of your trip, so you can plan less and enjoy more. That's not to say you have to follow the book to the letter. There is so much more that can be done, even in a 10-day period, which is not mentioned in this book due to size limitations. Some of the fun of discovery is actually discovering the treasure. Look for state parks, scenic byways, dams, and other points of interest as you plan your trip.

What to Bring

In General:

For the most part, bring both hiking wear that is befitting of the weather and some walking-around-town wear for the times you want to shop or eat out. Bring books, family games and your favorite music. If you can at all help it, don't bring electronics. (One of our family vacation rules is electronics after sunset only). Bring sunscreen, a cool hat to shade your face, lots of water bottles, a big bag for laundry and a first aid kit.

Get your kids involved in what they want to bring—a favorite toy, blanket, stuffed animal is a good start—and do. We asked our kids to look up the places where we were going and help pick out what they wanted to do.

What age your child needs to be to enjoy this vacation depends mainly on what you want to get out of the trip. When it comes to exploring the parks on foot, most hikes are minimum of 3 -5 miles round trip and are rarely flat. Your child should be able to manage a hike of this length for the duration of the trip, assuming each day involves hiking.

Bring a positive attitude, the ability to slow down, and a sense of wonder. Bring lots of socks and underwear, and don't forget the toiletries. If you are going in the summer, bring anything that helps keep you cool. Conversely, if this is a trip in cooler weather, bring lots of layers, a windbreaker and a beanie. The weather changes drastically from day to night when it's cooler, especially at the higher elevations. Bring water sandals or shoes if you plan to hike in or near the water.

Lastly, bring fun little snacks that you don't normally allow yourself. If you are hiking every day, you can afford to eat something a little more on the naughty side and still feel good about it. You will certainly be burning it off.

What to Expect

In general, the less you expect, the more you will be amazed. If you go in the summer, it will be much hotter than you would like. Typically, most of us humans spend a lot of time inside, working, living and shopping in the comfort of a climate-controlled environment. As a result, it will take a few days to ramp up from mild to really hot temperatures. The good news is that the human body is amazingly adaptable, and within a few days you'll go from feeling unbearably hot to tolerably hot, even though the outside temps remain the same. Yay us for being able to adapt so quickly! During the first few days, though, drink a lot more water than you normally would to stay hydrated at all times.

Also, expect to hike early in the morning, relax through the midafternoon and head out again in the early evening. If it is exceptionally hot, expect to find yourself waking up even earlier to beat the heat. If you have a checklist of hikes you want to do, remember that you likely won't feel the same about hiking in triple-digit weather.

Don't expect to find any TV reception or even decent radio. Remote is as remote does, so choices are slim in this area of technology. We found the wireless connections across Utah were better than mobile phone connections. In general, don't expect that civilization is the same in Utah.

These towns are all small, some just outposts that became towns. If you need something, there is usually one of everything in most of towns if you are lucky and fewer choices if you aren't.

Expect to plan more than usual, given that everything is spaced apart. If you forget to buy milk, it is a long journey back to that store you drove past two hours ago.

Most of all, expect to be thoroughly blown away at least once during the trip. I realize that is a direct contradiction to expecting nothing, but it will happen. You will be visiting some of the most unique and incredible natural wonders on earth.

Weather

The Grand Circle as outlined here is hot in the summer, trending toward mild at the higher elevations. Bryce Canyon and the North Rim of the Grand Canyon are typically the coolest parks in the summer, and Canyonlands, Arches and Zion are usually the hottest. Temperatures do cool down at night in the summer, especially if you camp near the Colorado or another river. In general, water helps cool things down, so camping near it is a good idea.

During the cooler months, which are anywhere from October through March, you will find much colder temps and even snow in the high desert. Some of the roads, campgrounds and even some of the parks themselves will be closed. While the Grand Circle in the winter presents its own challenges, this also means having the parks to yourself and that wonderful juxtaposition of red desert rock capped with crisp white snow. The snow is usually light and melts quickly.

First Stop Las Vegas

What to Do in Vegas—Family Style

There are three principal ways to "do" Vegas these days. These three are defined as Adult Vegas, Conference Vegas, and Family Vegas. There are likely emerging new ways to interact with Vegas, such as Crowded Tour Bus Vegas, Strictly Shopping in Over Priced Stores Vegas and All You Can Eat Vegas, but for purposes of this book, let's stick to the first three.

Adult Vegas really doesn't need any explanation. It's what most people come to Vegas for—to have a good time and maybe have the guts to go a little bit outside of their comfort zone. For some, the veil of discretion gets turned off completely with the power of alcohol and well, anything can happen at that point, but for most folks, Adult Vegas is simply about maximizing fun in the myriad ways Vegas dishes it up.

Las Vegas View from the Paris Hotel

Conference Vegas has many similar attributes to Adult Vegas except one must adhere to that nearly forbidden word of moderation. Even though you are surrounded by dance clubs and bars of every conceivable nature, unlimited gambling, sports betting, and debauchery, you are still representing the company that shipped you out there. In the end, for those who value your careers, Conference Vegas is a level of hell.

Then there's Family Vegas. Family Vegas seems at first to be a bit of a misnomer. I mean, Vegas and kids? Come now. Honestly, though, it is completely possible to take your kids to Las Vegas and have a good time. Now, they might learn a thing or two along the way, but hey, didn't you kind of accept that when you decided to take them along? The hawkers are good. They only pass out the questionable entertainment postcards to your older kids and, let's face it, as a parent you've had to talk your way out of tougher questions than, "Daddy, why does that sign say 'Nude, Nude, Nude?'"

Seriously, dear reader, all the dangers you can think of when it comes to what could go wrong when you mix kids and adult entertainment typically only play out in the minds of the parents. The reality of the situation is far safer and gentler. If you stick to the same bedtime hours that you normally have for your children, the kids will thoroughly enjoy themselves, getting lost in the vast kid-appropriate indulgences Vegas has to offer. As the evening wears on, as long as the kids are safely tucked into their hotel rooms bouncing on the bed, the harm and foul that is playing out along the streets and within the clubs is hidden from their gentle eyes and ears. The bottom line here is that the two worlds won't mix because, for the most part, the Adult Vegas is sleeping when the Family Vegas is roaming the streets during the daylight hours.

Family Vegas Starts with a Great Pool

A kid's love for a hotel has as its foundation, two aspects. The first is something all hotels have… a bed you can bounce on. There is something universal about the hotel bed and kids. The children love to flop and roll around on the bed and the bed never seems to complain about the attention. The bed is your friend, too. Let it be the caretaker of your children's attention for that short moment that allows you to use the bathroom before anyone else does.

The bed is, however, secondary to one thing—the pool. If your kids are of the age that you could drive to any hotel in any town that has a pool and they would be happy as clams, then above all else, make sure your Vegas hotel has a great pool. Here are several hotels that make the grade both with delightfully awesome pools and, of course, beds to bounce on:

Mandalay Bay Resort and Casino

($$$) 3950 Las Vegas Blvd. South, Las Vegas, NV 89119 Phone: 702.632.7777

For our boys, Mandalay Bay is the best hotel because of the pools. With three pools and several hot tubs, the quantity alone is fun for kids to explore. But what really sets Mandalay Bay apart are the wave pool and the lazy river. The wave pool is 1.6 million gallons of artificial wave fun, though bodysurfing the small waves is best for the little ones.

8

The shore of this beach is lined with real sand. Yes, your kids can build sand castles in Vegas. There also is a wading pool for little ones off to the side of the wave pool area. The layout for this section is nice as it allows small children the ability to have fun without parents worrying about them drifting into the deep end.

Mandalay Bay Pool

The lazy river is almost a quarter mile (0.4 km) of gently flowing water. You can rent or buy an inner tube and float to your heart's content, which, if you are nine years old, is about four times around. There are a vast number of pool chairs to be had, though the ones closest to the "beach" and lazy river are prime real estate.

Monte Carlo Resort and Casino

($$) 3770 Las Vegas Blvd. South, Las Vegas, NV 89109 Phone: 702.730.7777

Monte Carlo

The Monte Carlo Resort pools are a close second to those of Mandalay Bay. The Monte Carlo also has a wave pool and a 400-foot long lazy river. In addition, there is a kiddie/ wading pool for the smaller children. A special treat for the kids in this area are lounge chairs that are right-sized for them.

The downside of Monte Carlo is its size. The lazy river is about 1/3 the size of Mandalay Bay's. This reduction in size is an overall trend for the resort's pool area but feeling cramped is perhaps its only complaint. If Monte Carlo has a resort pool, Mandalay Bay has a resort water park.

It must be said for both resorts, on a hot day the lazy river can turn into a "crazy river" by mid-morning. For us it was never so bad that the event became stressful, but be prepared to leave the notion of serenely gliding alone along blissfully cool waters at the pool gates.

The Mirage

($$) 3400 S. Las Vegas Blvd, Las Vegas, NV 89109 Phone: 702.791.7111

The Mirage breaks from the waves and lazy rivers, offering instead a combination of lush foliage and waterfalls. The feel is tropical and relaxing and yet still includes a separate family pool with a small waterslide. At the Mirage, the kids will thoroughly enjoy themselves at the pool while parents unwind amongst the illusion of island tropics. Two other pluses: the pools are heated and stay open an hour later (until 8 pm) than the pools at Mandalay Bay and the Monte Carlo.

The Mirage

What tips this over the edge as the choice for many parents are Siegfried and Roy's Secret Garden and Dolphin Habitat. Both attractions are favorites with kids. If you have a budding dolphin trainer or zoologist in your group, staying at the Mirage puts you closest to this attraction.

Golden Nugget Hotel and Casino

($$) 129 E. Fremont St, Las Vegas, NV 89101 Phone: 702.385.7111

GoldenNugget

There are two outdoor pools at the Golden Nugget, the Tank and the Hideout. As you may have guessed, the Hideout is for folks 16 years and older. The Tank, however, was made for kids and grownups who still have a bit of kid in them.

The Tank allows you to slide three stories down a transparent waterslide through a 200,000-gallon aquarium. While the biggest attractions within the aquarium are full sized sharks and rays, there are over 300 species within the ecosystem. The Tank is the centerpiece of the pool area; the pool sits around the aquarium.

The waterslide tunnel puts the Golden Nugget on the map for cool pools. The pool is heated year round and, like the Mirage pool, is open until 8 p.m., weather permitting.

The Flamingo

($$) 3555 Las Vegas Blvd. South, Las Vegas, NV 89109 Phone: 800.522.4700

If your child is a little adventurer, the Flamingo has 15 acres of pool and wildlife habitats webbed in a labyrinth of water slides and footpaths. The Flamingo's swimming area is like that of Mandalay Bay, a water park. There are pools, waterslides, waterfalls and creature comforts at the nearby Club Cafe. The lush picturesque grounds are home to silver pheasants, penguins and, of course, flamingos, which visitors discover as they walk among the mazelike layout of the pool area. The paths themselves are invitations to explore and, once done, there are ledges to claim and relax on within this multilevel area.

A Flamingo at The Flamingo

If your children love waterslides, finding every one of them is as much fun as sliding down them. The mazes and the waterslides provide hours of fun and the secluded grottos allow for equal time to just unwind and relax. There is a small but secluded wading pool for the little ones as well.

Okay—Now What? Family Attractions in Vegas

After a half day at the pool, there is a good chance your children will be looking for you to entertain them in a different way. The good news is there are more than 40 family friendly attractions in Las Vegas. When you combine the great pools with these great attractions, it becomes a wonderful family vacation destination. Here are some tips to get the kids and yourself out of the hotel for some Vegas fun—family style.

Visit what's close to you

Traveling on foot in Vegas is not only the easiest way to get around, but fun. By finding attractions close to your hotel, you can remove the need for taxis, rental cars and driving. This may not be suitable for all small feet, but if your kids can endure a walk from one hotel to the next, source out attractions that are within walking distance.

Near the South End of the Strip:

Tournament of Kings

3850 S. Las Vegas Blvd. Las Vegas, NV 89109 Phone: 702.597.7777

Excalibur: Home of Tournament of Kings

For our stay, we chose the medieval jousting and dinner at the Tournament of Kings. Held in the Excalibur Hotel, this is a cool dining experience ("wenches" serve up "dragon's milk" and you have to eat your three-course meal entirely with your hands). In addition to the tasty fare, you get to enjoy a very entertaining show. Your seat location doubles as the country you represent as you watch the knights of each territory battle it out for one victor and then rally their efforts against an invading army that has a dragon on its side. The whole event, with fireworks, swordplay and flamethrowers is quite a spectacle.

M&M's World

3785 S Las Vegas Blvd, Las Vegas, NV 89109 Phone: 702.736.7611

M&M's World is four stories of M&M chocolate paradise. Each story has a different theme, and there is something for everybody. Sure, there are logo T-shirts and, of course, there are M&M's themselves, but there is much more at M&M's World. We are talking logo Frisbees, dice, laptop covers, pens, socks, lip gloss, luggage, aprons, beach wear, and even

M&M's World Las Vegas

M&M's spatulas and measuring cups. You start wondering how your kitchen would look if you just went crazy with an "M&M's Everything" theme.

You can get your own personalized M&M's candy, up to eight characters and two lines on every one. You can choose from a wall of 22 M&M's dispensers and even watch the World's main characters, "Red" and "Yellow," in a free 3D movie that runs throughout the day called "I Lost my M in Vegas." The show combines live actors with a movie and runs about 10 minutes.

Titanic: The Artifact Exhibition

3900 S. Las Vegas Blvd. Las Vegas, NV 89109 Phone: 702.492.3960

This may not be your child's first choice, but it is a nice compromise that gives both kids and adults some entertainment. The intention of the exhibit is simple, to bring the history of the Titanic to life. With more than 300 artifacts and large replicas of portions of the ship, the visitor is swept back in time. The items include personal effects from the passengers as well as their emotional stories. The largest and most impressive item on display is the "Big Piece." Part of the ship's hull, this is the largest item retrieved from the wreckage. Weighing two tons, it took two days just to get the hull into its present location at the Luxor Hotel.

Titanic Exhibition

To make the journey even more interactive, both children and adults are given a keepsake that characterizes an actual passenger who was on the ship during its fated voyage. The keepsakes represent all manner of passengers both rich and poor. After the tour is over everyone can learn whether his or her passenger lived or were one of the 1523 who didn't make it.

Bodies...The Exhibition

3900 S. Las Vegas Blvd., Las Vegas, NV 89109 Phone: 702.492.3960

Okay, yuck right? Who wants to see a bunch of exhumed bodies stretched out in odd poses? Well, not so fast. The attraction displays a very tasteful and unique view of well, you. If you were ever the slightest bit curious as to what you might look like on the inside, then come see Bodies. More than just a science lab gone wrong, the many examples of the internal human in 3D are highly educational just by viewing them. Alongside the visual are equally interesting quick facts on the wall.

There are exhibits on the nervous system showing the extensive set of nerves that make up our body. There is also a smoking exhibit that shows the lungs of a smoker compared to those of a non-smoker. The smoking exhibit is so motivational, the Luxor put a bin to throw out your cigarettes next to it, should you choose. There are nine rooms in total, representing different parts of the body, including the circulatory, digestive, muscular, nervous, and respiratory systems. Off in its own private area is a section devoted to fetal development. Visitors can see the different stages of fetal development from eight weeks old to eight months. As this is a sensitive topic, the section is housed in a private area that can be bypassed at the visitor's discretion.

CSI: The Experience

MGM Grand, 3799 S. Las Vegas Blvd., Las Vegas, NV 89109 Phone: 702.891.7006, 877.660.0660

Have you ever watched a murder mystery on TV and thought you would have made a good crime investigator? CSI: The Experience puts that thought to the test. You are given forensic evidence and other clues to help you solve a case. This is a real hit with the younger kids; teenagers may find the clues a bit too straightforward.

Near the North End of the Strip

Adventuredome at Circus Circus

2880 S. Las Vegas Blvd. Las Vegas, NV 89109 Phone: 702.794.3939, 800.444.2472

Adventuredome

Adventuredome, the largest indoor theme park in the United States, should get your family's attention. The five-and-one-half-acre complex starts with a high-ceilinged dome with natural lighting that is itself impressive. The park has just about everything you would expect to find in a theme park, including thrill rides, laser tag, miniature golf, clown shows, bumper cars and other assorted carnival rides. Adventuredome recently opened a new ride called El Loco, which ascends 70 feet before diving downward and backward at 1.5 Gs.

Mirage Volcano

3400 S. Las Vegas Blvd. Las Vegas, NV 89109

The Mirage volcano operates nightly starting at 6 pm running until 11 pm on the hour. This attraction has been around since 1989 and it may seem a bit trite, but the Mirage has done a great job of keeping this free attraction relevant. In 2008, they did a $25 million redesign, leveraging WET, the same team responsible for The Fountains of Bellagio. They even hired ex Grateful Dead drummer Mickey Hart, who, along with composer Zakir Hussain, created a soundtrack made specifically for the event. It's well worth watching and still impressive after all these years.

Volcano Show at the Mirage

The Fountains of Bellagio

3600 S. Las Vegas Blvd. Las Vegas, NV 89109

Bellagio Fountain and Resort Hotel

This free attraction, located in front of the Bellagio Hotel, has become one of the most recognized and filmed attractions on the strip. It is not unusual to find yourself lost in the choreography of water as it shoots and dances in the air in unison to more than 30 songs. The lake itself is an impressive 375,000 square feet, equivalent to eight football fields. The amount of water in the lake could fill 2,000 swimming pools. There are 1,214 fountain shooters, capable of jetting higher than a 24-story building. At the peak of the fountains display, there are more than 17,000 gallons of water in the air. Impressive stuff and a must-see attraction. The fountain operates more frequently on the weekends, running every 15 minutes from 7 pm to midnight.

Just Park it Anywhere

While driving to Vegas ...

[Bryce]: Mom?

[Mom]: Yes?

[Bryce]: That billboard over there—what is that?

[Mom]: It's an advertisement for a buffet. That's where you can go and eat as much as you want from all the things shown on that billboard, plus a lot more. They even have a whole section just for desserts!

[Bryce]: Really? They actually have these things in Vegas?

[Mom]: Yep.

[Bryce]: My mind is so messed up right now.

We were closing in on Vegas! After months of planning and several near-cancellations, we were finally almost there. Around me was the darkness of the desert, but in the distance I could begin to see the glow of Vegas lights. I looked over at my wife Angela sitting in the passenger seat. She was taking a nap, as was our youngest, Bryce. Everest was playing with some handheld video console, with the volume turned off per my set of driving rules. You could hear the drone of rapid finger play as he tried his best to get to the next level of whatever game he was playing. Ang looked so content, so peaceful. Even in sleep she somehow exuded her Southern Bell charm. She was slumped over, yet still managed to look dignified. I took in this serene scene and realized fully and for the first time, we were finally on vacation.

This would be a good trip, it would be a trip we would talk about, laugh about and reminisce about for years to come. It took a lot of convincing, a tremendous amount of planning, but here we were, doing the Grand Circle, the vacation of a lifetime. Seven national parks, all in an RV. Each park would be a new experience for the family. I couldn't wait. Even the RVing part would be a first. Ang hated camping, but she was really getting into the idea of an RV. Bryce was ecstatic; we were going to his namesake park, Bryce Canyon. So what if we picked his name because of its Celtic origins and not because of the park. To him, this was major. He met the idea of traveling in an RV like any 9-year-old would, as if what we were doing was completely magical. Bryce was our wonder, our set of eyes to see things the way they should be seen. He helped us understand the true fascination of what we were doing simply because to him, this was all completely new territory.

Even our 14-year-old Everest was unnaturally buoyant and dare I say elated, though he showed it with the usual nonchalant composure of a teenage boy. Still, since the trip began, he was behaving a lot closer to the wonderful kid we had imagined having—less sarcastic, less cynical, less moody, less like us adults. He was behaving like a kid; it was great. All of this was great. Our first stop would be Vegas. It would help ease us into all that roughing it we were about to do, plus it was more cost effective to pick up the RV in Vegas as opposed to our home state of California.

It wasn't too late, but it was fully dark, about 9 pm. I had been tracking the glow of the distant Vegas lights on the horizon for the past twenty minutes. I knew to look for it and had been watching it get pleasantly closer as I made good time. We were maybe 40 miles from the "city that never sleeps." Another half hour or so, and we would be checked in and planning what to do next.

The Las Vegas Strip From a Distance

The serenity of this fine moment was disrupted by a subtle, disconcerting noise. It wasn't a loud noise, but it wasn't a good noise either. It was the sound of something metallic lightly bouncing inside the engine.

I gave a casual glance over at my wife. Still fast asleep, she wasn't hearing it. I was relieved. She didn't like car trouble. The car's care was put directly under my attention and she had very simple but tough standards in this area. If the car worked, I received neither accolade nor praise for I was simply doing my job. If however, the car didn't work, for whatever reason, my fault or otherwise, this was an entirely different matter. She never let the gas gauge get below halfway. Monitors and meters requesting the car be examined or maintained were

17

completed in quick order. The washer fluid was always filled, Purel was always available and country was always on the radio. These were her rules for the car. Follow them and life was good. Stray, and I faced certain peril.

That sound meant one thing: the car was no longer functioning properly. If she heard that sound, it would create a catastrophic series of events. Every missed oil change, every forgotten tire pressure check and every delayed maintenance of our 14-year marriage would come under scrutiny. Events that I couldn't possibly begin to remember would be recounted by her in the most minute detail, all building to an open and shut case putting me to blame for the car's misfortune Normally Ang was a quite dignified woman, but when it came to matters of motor vehicles, she took an altogether different tone. I gritted my teeth. "Come on, car, don't screw up on me now," I thought.

I carefully reached for the radio and turned it on with the silence of a ninja; setting the volume low enough so as not to wake her, but enough to try to drown out the rattle coming from the engine.

For about twenty minutes I listened for the sound through the music, waiting for pauses in the songs and trying to figure out what the heck that engine noise was. It was as if keys were being munched by the pistons, playing rhythmically with an undertone of cringe. I was starting to wince at the sound, looking like someone who had just opened a rank garbage can, but fortunately my wife still hadn't noticed. I kept looking over oh so casually, she was now half asleep, staring out into the darkness, the glow of Vegas off in the distance, its larger-than-life array of lights denting the night's sky. The crunching sound, on the other hand, was doing the opposite of what I wanted it to. It was getting louder.

During a pause between songs, the metallic sound was unmistakable. Clankity clankity, clankity clack. Clankity clankity, clankity clack. I glanced at the speedometer, then the rearview mirror, then my wife. She was no longer looking out the passenger window. She was now looking at me, with deep concern.

"What's that sound?" she asked.

"I don't know. It's been going on for a while now. We'll have to get it checked out in Vegas."

Ang turned the music down and focused her keen senses on the crunching noise. Her eyes narrowed in reaction to the mystery, her head cocked a bit sideways to hear the sound better.

"It sounds like the engine," she declared.

"What's that sound?" Bryce chimed in.

"I don't know, Bryce. Your mother and I are trying to figure it out," I said calmly.

"It sounds like the engine," Bryce declared. "Mom, do you hear it?"

"What's that sound?" Everest added.

"It's the engine!" Bryce said with a tone of impatience.

18

"Shrugs," Everest replied.

At this point I'm thinking, "Crap, there is no getting around this, everyone is hearing it. I'm screwed."

I turn off the radio completely and we all listen to this horrifying sound. It invades our wonderful little world like some sentient being. It now has a life of its own, commanding our attention. Clankity clankity, clankity clack. Clankity clankity, clankity clack. We fall under its spell. There is nothing we can do but listen to the terrifying yet peacefully rhythmic sound of the engine tearing itself apart.

I keep thinking the same three thoughts. "Should I keep driving? Should I pull over? We are so close!" Then, as if to show its displeasure at my turning off the music, the rhythmic sounds ceased and the car literally hopped, then sputtered and began making sounds that made those clankity clack sounds seem oddly pleasant and normal. The car was dying.

There was a thick air of concern as I pulled off I-15 and made a left onto an unnamed road. No one said a word. There were no streetlights, no house lights. We were out in the middle of nowhere. I could make out that we were next to a housing development under construction. I could see the vague silhouettes of half-framed houses and big construction equipment.

I figured we were somewhere near the town of Enterprise, Nevada and a mere 10 miles from our destination. The glow of Vegas was bright enough you could almost touch it, the lights an oasis of warm hospitality. I kept driving toward the light under some vain hope that driving slower would be enough to bring the car back to normal. The car was able to sputter another ten feet before the engine went into a virtual free fall of cacophony and then seized to a stop in one final gasp. In a heroic gesture, I quickly maneuvered the drive into neutral and coasted to the side of the road with our last vestiges of momentum.

For a brief moment, we sat in silence. I tried to turn over the motor, as if maybe it was just some bad gas. But I was only able to get as far as the grind of the starter. The car was dead, very much dead. We were in the middle of a hot dry desert night, far from anything that resembled civilization save the mocking glow of Vegas and some construction equipment. It was at that point that my sweet dear loving wife lost it completely.

"What the heck did you do?" Ang yelled.

"I think the car died." I replied, as if stating the obvious would help calm the matter. It didn't.

"You killed the car? Oh for the love of all that is green and golden, you killed the car! How did you kill the car? How are we going to get to Vegas? Our entire vacation is now ruined, just simply ruined! Oh my dear lord, I knew we should never have gone on this trip. Didn't I tell you we needed to have the car thoroughly examined before we went on this trip?"

"Well, I ah…"

"This is absolutely the last thing in the entire world that we could possibly want to have happened. We have reservations at the Mandalay Bay. They take your first night you know; it's nonrefundable! We will be sleeping in this dang car all night!" And so she went on asking questions that could not be answered, spilling accusations of malcontent and crafting worst case scenarios involving our having to somehow tow the car all the way back to our mechanic in California due to the shifty distrust of any mechanic that calls Las Vegas home.

At some semblance of a pause and with my impatience showing, I blurted, "Look, can you just call triple A? My phone died a few hours ago."

Her eyes brightened and she pulled out her iPhone as if it were her salvation. She unlocked it, held it in front of her face like a tri-coder and said in her most commanding voice, "Siri, I want you to call triple A." I was always impressed that Siri could understand Southern drawl.

"Triple A. There are 15 results that match that query. Which one would you like?"

"Fifteen results! Come on", she said to no one. She looked at her phone again. "Siri, call A-A-A".

Siri came back with, "Uh oh, I can't make that phone call." Siri was not helping.

"Let me see the phone," I said. I looked at it—the signal icon went from one bar to that cross through the bars stating you are completely screwed. Great, I thought. I got out of the car and tried twisting the phone around, walking in a circle, and holding the phone in the air while shaking it, which are all proper tricks to get a smart phone to function when all you have to work with is desperation. None of these tactics were working. We were not only stuck, we had no cell phone. This was not going to be good news to tell the wife.

Everyone was standing outside of the car at this point. They were following me around, watching me perform my cell phone reception ritual, waiting to understand the verdict of this dance to the cell phone gods. I looked over. Angela, my dear sweet wife, the love of my life, looked at me with the intent of a cobra ready to strike its victim. There could be only one answer that would calm her down at this point, and I didn't have it. The only thing I could do was state the obvious. I handed the phone back to her and said, "We are out of cell range".

"What!" she exclaimed before going into an uncontrolled fury that if channeled properly, could likely have powered a small casino. I envisioned people looking up from their gaming tables all the way back in Vegas, wondering what all that yelling could be about. I envisioned taxi drivers and pedestrians, shopkeepers and club bouncers, all stopping whatever they were doing to glance out into the desert with curious looks. I hoped one of them would perhaps get in their car to see what could possibly be causing this uproar, but alas, we were not so lucky.

Now mind you, this unchecked broken dam of ferocity that is my wife is a rare event. She is typically even tempered for the most part, but from her perspective, we were stuck, miles from help, it was dark, and the car was dead. Plus, who knows what was lurking out in the darkness, so factor in that the kids were in danger. The reality of the matter was we had been driving all day and our car was so close to a nice fluffy bed we could almost feel it. That was a lot for anyone to take in. The best thing for me to do was to let her do her thing. The dam had broken, and there really wasn't anything anyone could do but watch the churning waters of her vitriol engulf me.

I decided to have a look at the engine. Nothing but the calm steaming heap of a broken engine looking back, which is to say, I had no idea what happened to it. Ang was now alternating her argument with me and the completely useless Siri. It really wasn't Siri's fault that we had no cell reception, but I was thankful she was in this with me. I started feeling sorry for Siri.

At round four of Ang's torrent I said, "Look, honey. I am sorry, so sorry about the car. I'm not sure what happened. I'm sorry about your phone. I'm sorry about my phone. This all sucks, trust me. I'm sorry about everything here. I do, however, need a few moments to figure out what to do next. So I'm going over here to think." I pointed randomly into the darkness and then headed in that direction. For a while, I walked without thinking. I kept hearing Siri toying with my wife's patience, informing her of her now low battery life, that there was no cell reception way out here, that Siri was happy to occasionally find a phone signal and give directions to AAA plumbing in nearby Enterprise. I kept walking until I met up with a bulldozer. I stopped there at this beast and stared at it. The bulldozer stared back, in a welcoming kind of way. It seemed to understand what I was going through. And then I thought, "Maybe…"

I tried the door. It was unlocked! I found keys tucked into the ashtray compartment. Could these really be "The Keys," the heavenly keys to this bulldozer? I slipped the key into the ignition and turned it to the first position. The thing made a large warning beep sound. "No way!" I thought. "No Way! Salvation!"

I began to rationalize this new find in my head. What if we just borrowed this bulldozer? The folks who own it would understand. I mean it's in the middle of the night, we are stranded, and I'm not really stealing it, just borrowing it. I've got children after all; I'm just ensuring their safety. The owner of this bulldozer must be a father. Certainly he would understand if I drove his bulldozer a few miles to get us into cell range. This idea was a good one.

The more I thought about this, the more it made sense. And why stop at getting us to within cell range? Why not just take this thing all the way to the hotel? I imagined myself for a moment tooling down Las Vegas Boulevard. There was only the one seat but Ang and the kids could somehow cram into the cab with me. I couldn't just leave them while I drove off in a bulldozer. We could put the luggage in the scooped blade. I mean why not?

The idea distilled into sheer genius in my head. This could work! This could actually work! Besides, they say anything can happen in Vegas. This is certainly anything! We could even wave at the people as if we are in some type of bulldozer parade traveling slowly down The Strip! You there in that convertible, yes we are waving at you! You might be traveling in style, buddy, but we are traveling in a bulldozer!

I'd pull into the Mandalay Bay with the other cars, and man would I love to see the look on the valet's face when I pulled up. I would, of course, lower the scoop to make it easy for him to get to the luggage. Then I would get out of the cab as if I owned it and throw him the keys with a knowing smile and a correctly timed, "Here you go, fine sir. Don't scratch it!" We would enter Mandalay Bay like we owned it, in slow motion, just like in the movies. I'd feel like Batman. Batman in a bulldozer, going to Vegas with his family, in plaid shorts and a T-shirt. That's right. Batman. It was playing out so well in my head. How could we not make this our Vegas entrance?

I had no choice at this point. We had to do this. I turned the key further and the engine started. A huge plume of black smoke came out of the exhaust in front of me. Now to figure out how to operate the thing. Just then Everest and the rest of the family ran over to where I was.

"Dad! Dad! What are you doing?"

"I'm solving the problem, son. Get this, we are going to ride this bulldozer right here into Las Vegas! That is what we are going to do. Son, get the luggage."

"Dad, while you guys were arguing I used my phone and called a taxi. I was going to tell you but you ran off and we didn't know where you went. I told them what exit we got off. They said they'd be here in about 15 minutes."

Of course! Ev had his own phone and it usually got better reception. How could I have forgotten this? I slumped in the tractor seat dejected. "You mean, no bull-dozer?"

"Step out of the cab, Dad, before you hurt someone."

I turned the engine off; my dream had been killed by the pragmatic ways of my own son.

"Didn't he do good work?" Ang asked, nodding at Everest. "He called them all by himself. I'm so proud of you!" She gave Everest a tremendous hug and then looked at me inquisitively. "Were you really thinking you were going to drive that thing? Let me guess, you were thinking you could drive it to the hotel, I bet. My goodness, I'm not sure if your head is on straight sometimes." She laughed.

"Is that chuckling I hear? I'm glad to see you've come back to us," I said.

"I'm sorry for all that hollering. Thanks for letting me get it all out. I just kind of lost it for a bit I guess."

I looked back at the bulldozer as we walked to our car. "You know, guys, someday I will drive a bulldozer down Las Vegas Boulevard."

"We all have our dreams, Dad," Bryce stated matter-of-factly. "But if you do, I'm calling shotgun."

Considering an RV Rental

Why RV in the First Place

My wife and I tossed around the idea of RVing for years. In fact, when it came time to think about the summer vacation, renting an RV was always an idea that was put on the table by both of us. What stopped us was the cost coupled with the unknown of driving a house on wheels down a narrow highway. The price of renting an RV isn't too bad in itself, but you have to add on the mileage fee, the camping fee and the cleaning fee. Then there's gas. As I mentioned before, these things get about 10 miles per gallon (4.25 km/l), so gas costs need to be factored into the whole "Should we RV?" equation. My wife checked around and the answer was always the same, it would cost us about $300 a day counting all expenses to rent an RV. This is what stopped us because; let's face it, that's the price of a decent hotel. For us, the argument was, if we were going to spend that kind of money to rough it in an RV, why not just spend the money on a nice hotel with maid service and not rough it?

To be fair, the gas cost is a bit of a gray area in doing an apples to apples comparison. (The cost breakdown is detailed in the section below). If you think about it, you typically aren't just staying in your hotel; you are driving around and see the sights as well, which involves buying gas. Still, the economics were close enough that even if we removed the gas costs, it was expensive. It was a hard argument to win, so every year the "RV vacation" was put on the shelf for another time.

There was another aspect of RVing that kept us from pulling the trigger. We had done plenty of hotels and we had done our fair share of family camping. These modes of vacationing were known commodities. RVing, on the other hand, was something neither of us had ever done. As a result, we assumed it was kind of like camping and not at all like staying in a hotel. We thought RVing would be a form of roughing it, a much more expensive and completely foreign form of roughing it. Given that my wife had an aversion to camping in the first place, why in the world would she spend a boat load of money doing it? We also worried we would end up the lone family in an RV park full of aging snow birds and leathered desert rats one beer away from a fist fight. It was easy for my wife to close any discussion on RVing by bringing up these mythical stereotypes.

What we found is that we had formed a tremendous number of assumptions that simply weren't true. RVing isn't like staying in a hotel or camping, nor is it a hybrid of the two. The magic of RVing is that it is a completely new way of vacationing. It is more like being home, yet every day your home has landed in a different place. There is comfort knowing the bed is yours, knowing who has used your bathroom and knowing that the food on the table is consistent with the home cooking you are used to, because it is the same home cooking. Yet when you walk out the door of your home, you are surrounded by the natural transcendent beauty of wherever you parked your RV. Your doorstep is the threshold of a new memory, every day, something you can cherish and remember in a way that you can't get stepping out of a hotel room, no matter how nice the resort is.

Finding a Good Rental Place

Newer is Better

The most important thing to remember about an RV is that it is a house on wheels. Both aspects play a huge factor. Just as your house or apartment has a dozen major components that need to work correctly every time, so does your RV. Cars don't have toilets, kitchens and running water. RVs do. The other aspect, the fact that the house is on wheels, is the other huge component. Unlike the place you usually call home, you will be driving your RV home over potholes, dirt roads and not-so-smooth highways. The home will be going up hills and down hills, speeding up and slowing down, all things that aren't part of a stationary home's wear and tear.

Also, many of the components in an RV are either new to the first time RVer or engineered so differently that they may as well be new. You probably don't have a water pump at home or a refrigerator that works on propane. This means that for all but the handiest, they will seem a bit foreign to you. As these components will make up your home for the duration of the vacation, they had better work.

With that, it pays to find a rental place that rents high quality, well-maintained RVs and does a good job of ensuring everything works before you leave the lot. The good news is a number of rental companies take a lot of the worry out of the equation by only offering newer RVs. The place we used only rented out RVs that were fewer than six months old. Some offer their RVs based on number of miles. While things go wrong even with newer RVs, in general, newer is better.

RV Rental Agencies in Las Vegas

Apollo RV:

5837 Boulder Hwy, Las Vegas, NV Phone: 800.370.1262

We've had a good experience with Apollo RV. All RVs are brand new or close to brand new, which is a huge plus. The company is actually based out of Australia, but don't let that deter you; they have a solid footprint in Las Vegas. Their selection is good, as are their prices. If there is one downside, the sales side is short staffed, which makes getting a hold of them is a challenge at times. We did find the roadside customer service to be responsive, however.

Cruise America

551 N. Gibson Road, Henderson, NV Phone: 888.980.8282

Cruise America has a national footprint and is a great choice if you are planning to tour a larger swath of the United States. The website is well designed to help you plan your trip and choose an RV.

El Monte RV

3800 Boulder Hwy, Las Vegas, NV Phone: 866.303.1057

El Monte is listed as they have been around since 1970 and are a common go-to rental agency for the Grand Circle. That said, they tend to get poor marks on customer service and overall pricing. Their website isn't as well designed as some of the others listed.

Road Bear RV

3800 Boulder Hwy, Las Vegas, NV Phone: 702.269.8000

Road Bear gets high marks all around. Good prices, new RVs, great customer service. They have a national footprint and are doing a fairly decent job at building themselves into the number one national RV rental agency.

Sarah RV Center

1518 W Scotland Ln, Las Vegas, NV Phone: 702.384.8818

Sarah RV gets decent marks from customers. They rent and sell RVs. Positives are with the customer service. Negatives are with the RVs not being as new as advertised. Our own experience was poor but limited. We got a fantastic rate over the phone but when we called back, they wouldn't honor it, stating that their own employee had misquoted the price. Don't let this discourage your decision; other customers have given them high marks.

Customer Service is Key

You are driving a pretty complex vehicle. Lots of moving parts, some of which will be very new to most first time RVers. Most rental companies are pretty thorough in going through a decent education session, but it's a lot to take in and, more importantly, they are really only walking you through how to operate things, not how to fix them. If you read RV insider blogs, you find that owners of RVs are constantly complaining about how they have to fix something or another on their RV. These are complex integrated units, all of which must work right or else your family dream vacation will turn into a nightmare.

Given this complexity, it's important to have help when you need it. Find a rental agency that has 24-hour roadside service. Make sure that the rental agency themselves are on call to help troubleshoot the problem you are having. They know their own RVs better than a third-party tow service. Most problems are solvable over the phone. We had a problem 40 miles (64 km) outside of Vegas with the fridge. It wasn't getting cold. I called and they talked me through to a solution. (There's a little red button that resets the circuit breaker. It was a simple button to push but one so hidden that I would never have found it on my own). This one call turned our trip back around from the bummer it was becoming. Having a great customer service there for you is huge.

This isn't to say that something will go wrong with your RV. Most RVs work as they should, every time, for the duration of the trip. It's more that, as these are more complex than a car, the odds of something failing are simply greater. Also, unlike a hotel, you can't just switch rooms if something goes wrong. You need to find a way to get whatever has failed working again.

Costs

When you look at the total costs of renting an RV, it's by no means the cheapest way to travel. Most rental companies do offer discounts for renting for longer periods of time, off-season discounts and other hot deals. However, if you are looking to take the typical two-week family vacation during the summer, finding a deal will be tougher. This is peak RV season and if you don't rent it, someone else will.

That said, it is possible to negotiate with the rental agency. They want your business and there are plenty of rental agencies to choose from, so if they feel you are serious and you ask, they will sweeten the offer to close the deal. Do make sure you get the deal in writing, though.

Other tips:

- Act quickly. If you see a great deal, take it, because if you don't, someone else will. Assume the RV you are looking for is in high demand and they don't have many of them.

- Book early. Like booking an airline ticket, if you book well before you go, you will get up to 15% off versus booking at the last minute. Make sure you understand the cancellation policy and put a trigger on your calendar to remind you are about to hit the point of no return on getting a 100% refund if you think you may change your mind.

- Go offseason. It costs less to go during the winter months in some locations because the demand is less. Be a contrarian to the demand.

Our Average RV Rental Costs

To show a total cost per day you do need to include gas costs, which vary each day depending on the cost of gas and miles driven. We averaged about 150 miles (241 km) per day and gas cost about $4 per gallon, so that is what is used for the below calculation. Also, the campground fee represents the amount we paid at the majority of the campgrounds. Here's how it broke out for us, in rough averages, per day:

Cost Item	Daily Cost
RV Rental Cost	$ 150.00
Mileage Cost	$ 48.00
Gas Cost	$ 60.00
Cleaning Fee	$ 20.00
Campground Fee	$ 15.00
Total Cost per Day	$ 293.00

The mileage we were quoted was for $0.32 cents per mile. The cleaning fee was a total of 200 clams, which for a 10-day trip is $20 per day. We took this trip in June 2013.

Bored math nerd or budding economist standing at the pump? Try this on. If your RV gets say 10 miles per gallon and the mileage fee is say 32 cents per mile, you can roll the mileage cost into the gas price. (You really don't need to know this, but if you find yourself standing at the pump, bored silly watching the gas tank fill up, you may find this mildly helpful to relieve the boredom). For us, the cost of gas was about $4 per gallon. That gallon would get me 10 miles, of which the RV rental place is tacking on an additional 32 cents for each of those miles. That means that for every gallon we bought, it was like paying $7.20 per gallon. There is really no good reason to look at your RV costs this way, but it may help pass the time.

Selecting your RV

There is a lot of personal preference in selecting an RV. The choices them-selves are endless, well, numerous anyway, so this section is meant to cover aspects in choosing the right RV that bubble up to the top of the priority list.

Sleeping

The biggest thing to think about is sleeping arrangement. Take a look at the RV layout and mark out where your family will likely end up sleeping. The beds can be untraditional in size, they are meant to fit into an RV and do not always follow the single, twin, full, queen sizes we are used to. If kids are bunking together in the over-the-cab section (the most coveted sleeping spot for most kids) and you are unsure your kids will be able to fit in that space, you can measure out the area in your living room and put your kids in the mockup. Our two boys, (nine and thirteen at the time), fit fine in the over the cab area.

The only concern on over-the-cab and children is whether they can manage the stairs and the height. If they are really small or have height concerns (fear of falling out of the bed), then find a plan B sleeping arrangement.

For many RVs, the dining area converts to a bed if needed, so keep that in mind as you look for the right RV. While it does convert to a full bed, re-member that you will continually be converting it while on the trip. Also, it's usually the spare bed, which means it's not the most comfortable of the bed choices. It does, however, make an excellent Plan B for little ones.

Size

For most folks that start on the RV journey, their first RV is the smallest unit that comfortably fits all travelers. For folks that have been RVing before, they often will opt for a larger unit. The reason to go small is the fact that even the small units can be intimidating to drive. Over time, the RV will become quite comfortable as you get accustomed to it. The other nice aspect of the smaller RV is convenience. It's easier to park and easier to fit into a camp spot.

With the larger RVs, you will get more amenities, such as more sleeping areas, bigger home areas, a bigger kitchen and a bigger bathroom. Along with this will, of course, come a bigger cost. Find the right balance for your family's needs and if in doubt, go smaller. A 27-foot RV will comfortably fit a family of four.

Bathroom

The most impacted room in the smaller RV is the bathroom. It is only a little larger than a restroom on an airplane. If a larger bathroom is important, look for RVs that are bigger in this area. The other thing to think about is a changing area. In a hotel, the bathroom is the go-to place for privacy when one needs to change. In a small bathroom, this becomes a challenge. Some RVs have a privacy curtain that comes in very handy if you are in mixed company of any kind.

To Drive or Tow

This is really a matter of availability—whether the RV rental agency even offers towable RVs and whether your car or truck can tow a travel trailer or fifth wheel.

If you tow, the biggest advantage is that you can detach the home unit from the traveling around unit. This opens up the ability to go four wheeling or into congested cities and other areas that you simply can't do in a typical motor home. The other advantage is you can level the detached RV, which isn't an option for some motor homes. The biggest disadvantage to this option is you won't find them at rental agencies, so you will need to buy your own. This is because they require more experience to drive and, in the case of fifth wheels, a sturdy truck outfitted with a hitch placed into the bed of the truck. The other disadvantage of travel trailers and fifth wheels is that passengers cannot ride inside the unit while it is moving.

This leaves the motor home as the best and typically only option offered by rental agencies. The advantages here are that the family stays connected to the driver but has room to stretch out. They can play cards at the dining table and still be strapped in. The biggest disadvantage is that you are limited to where you can meander. If you see a cool high clearance dirt road up ahead, best to put it out of your head and keep driving; your RV can't go there.

Picking up and checking out

This section will help you fill in the gaps on the checkout process that you may miss while listening to the agent. She or he will, after all, cover a lot of information. One thing we did our first time is video tape the agent walk-through. This way, if we forgot something that the agent said, we had it recorded.

If you Read Nothing Else, Read This

For most of us, finding the right RV and the right vendor to rent it from is pretty straightforward. The Internet makes this part of the process easy. Just go to a search engine and type in "RV rental Las Vegas" or simply go with our favorite, Apollo RV.

It's a different story when you step into your RV for the first time. There are two things working against the first time RVer here. The first is excitement. The only thing preventing you from embarking on your perfect vacation is the checkout process. You want to listen, but there is a big part of you that just wants to get behind the wheel and get going. The second thing standing in your way is the fact that this is an unknown.

For us, we had never even stepped foot inside an RV, and that lack of experience put us into a situation where we didn't know what we didn't know. We were a couple of doe-eyed noobs, standing inside a home that doubled as a vehicle, about to share the road with folks who, for some reason, trusted we already knew what we were doing.

This section helps to remedy this situation. If you read the following paragraphs, you will go from looking like a tourist that just got off a cruise ship in Guadalajara to looking like the captain of that cruise ship.

The Three Most Important Things to Check

The Water Pump

It is said in survival books that you can live 3 weeks without food, 3 days without water and 3 minutes without air. Water is more than kind of important; it is essential to life. Having a big tank of the stuff on board is great, but without a properly functioning water pump, that big tank is pretty much useless. Add the fact that this is all going to be desert travel means you need to make sure your water pump is working correctly. Fortunately, this is pretty easy to do and can be done during the checkout tour.

The water pump does one thing: it adds pressure to the water line so water comes out of the faucets and shower. There are two styles of water pumps—those that operate on demand and those that operate regardless of demand. If you have the on-demand kind, the pump is always on, running off the auxiliary battery. It has the ability to know when it has pressurized the water lines sufficiently and will then go into standby mode. It may have an on/off switch, but this is mostly to save the aux battery from being drained when the pump isn't being used.

The less fancy water pumps don't have a pressure sensor. These will continue to operate as long as they are turned on, building up pressure until the pump overheats or the plumbing lines burst. With these pumps, you also need to turn the water on first, then the pump. While you should clarify with your RV renter which kind your RV will have, these types of pumps are typically found on older models.

Test the water pump during your checkout. Your RV rep will likely walk you through the process. Typically, there is a switch at the control panel and another one at the bathroom sink. (The control panel is a panel of switches and will be described in more detail further on). Don't be afraid to test it yourself. Turn on the water and listen for the pump, making sure water is flowing well out of the faucet. Feel free to test all faucets and shower heads.

Water is such a crucial element, and having it just be at the turn of a knob is one of the key reasons you opted to rent an RV. Make sure that your water pump works. One more point: make sure your RV comes with a water hose specifically for potable water. This hose will be needed for two reasons.

You will use it to fill the water tank and, if you are able to connect to city water at the RV Park, you will need the hose for that as well. The city water connection will use the city's water pressure and bypasses the need for the water pump.

The Toilet

At one RV park at which we stayed, a couple with a newborn baby camped next to us. While we were having the time of our lives, they were faced with a problem that was having a very negative impact on their vacation: a malfunctioning toilet. While the rental company offered to help walk them through fixing the toilet, that wasn't something they had signed up for when going on vacation.

The toilet is one of those things that should just work. If it doesn't, the impact could be something as little as having to use public facilities to as big as having to endure living in something that smells like a moving outhouse. Make sure the toilet works. Test it by flushing it fully and then watching for the presence of water in the bowl after the flush has completed. That little bit of water is creating an odor barrier. If it's not present, it means you have a broken bowl seal. If you have a broken bowl seal, all those nasty smells down in the tank can waft up into your home sweet home.

The best thing to do is ask to flush the toilet at the beginning of the checkout. Look for the water barrier in the tank and then check it again at the end of the checkout process. If it's not there, then you have a small leak and will want it remedied before leaving the rental agency.

Make sure you buy the RV toilet treatment liquid or dry pucks. These products contain enzymes and chemicals that help break things down in your black water tank. RV toilet treatment is your friend and is cheap. Ask your rental agency about what they offer and how much to use.

A side note on black water tank capacity. The black water holding tank is typically 36 gallons. Under normal use, the grey water tank will fill up first due to shower and general water use. Since both tanks are dumped at the same time black water tank capacity isn't usually an issue.

The Refrigerator

Like running water, having cold and even frozen foods on hand is one of the main perks of traveling by RV. Especially in the desert of Utah, an ice-cold soda can be an almost incomparable paradise on a hot day. Without a fridge on hand, that soda will likely be at body temperature or even hotter. You may still drink it to quench your thirst, but it will be a sad experience you will want to quickly forget. Make sure the fridge works.

RV refrigerators are unique pieces of machinery in the fridge kingdom. They run on propane, have no moving parts and use heat to cool things down.

The whole process involves water, ammonia, hydrogen, heat and simple chemistry. While you don't need to know the exact science behind this process, it is useful to know that your RV fridge is different from your fridge at home. It doesn't handle heavy loads and hot weather as well as the home fridge. That's not to say it doesn't work well; these fridges work well enough, even in the blistering heat of summer. Do be mindful, though, that this fridge is not well equipped to cool down a 12 pack of sodas, so minimize what you put into it so as not to overload it.

The problem with the fridge at checkout is you will likely not know if it's working. The rental place doesn't run the refrigerators when the RV is sitting idle and will likely not turn it on until right before you leave. This will give you no chance to see if it's functioning properly. The best advice here is to ask to have it turned on right when you arrive. While you are going through the paper work and outside checkout, the fridge will have some time to cool. Test it by opening it. It should feel noticeably colder.

The Rest of the Important Things

The Stove and Oven

The stove is pretty straightforward to test, but be sure to do so. Ask your rental agent to show you how to ignite the stove. Most are fairly intuitive, but seeing it done once should resolve any training issues.

The oven is a bit different. For ours you needed to ignite the pilot with a long match or lighter and then turn on the oven itself. Not only watch your agent do it, but also ask to do it once yourself with the agent there to walk you through it. The trick is finding the pilot and making sure you have gas coming out of the pilot rather than the main oven gas line.

One more note about the oven: ours did not come with any ventilation. This meant that any smoke coming from the oven would go straight into the RV. We announced ourselves to the entire RV park through our smoke alarm a few times during the trip. Opening windows does help a little. Also, given that most of the Grand Circle is at a high enough altitude to affect cooking times and ingredients, make sure you adjust for this.

The Shower

Nothing feels better than being able to shower off the trail dust at the end of the day. Make sure you test that the showerhead operates, that the water gets hot, and that the water drains out correctly before you leave the rental agency.

Kitchen and Bathroom Sinks

You have likely tested one of these in your water pump test. Make sure both deliver both hot and cold water and drain properly.

Microwave and Other Appliances

If your RV has a microwave, iPad dock, or any other device, test what you can as appropriate. The one thing that doesn't work on the trip will be the one thing you will wish did. Also, make sure you open the microwave to confirm it has been cleaned.

Kitchen Utensils

Utensils are either provided as part of the rental package or offered separately. Slow down enough to take a mental inventory of all of the things you think you will need. Open every cupboard. Inspect for cleanliness and be sure everything you think is there is actually there. Check for the little things, like a can opener, corkscrew and bottle opener. If the RV comes equipped with Teflon-coated pans, check to make sure they are on the newer end. You don't want to feel you are adding shreds of Teflon to your breakfast. You aren't roughing it. These utensils are part of your home, and you should be comfortable with them.

The Beds

With the beds, do the same things you would do in a hotel. If you check for bed bugs like my wife does, then check for bed bugs. Make sure the mattresses aren't lumpy and otherwise up to par. You will be spending a good percentage of your trip on those beds, so be sure you are comfortable with them. If one of the bed areas has to be put together, have the agent walk you through how to do it.

The Slide-Out

Like the ammonia fridge, black water system and water pump, the slide-out is something you probably don't have in your house. This now common feature allows for an RV to become roomier when parked. The user simply depresses a button and one or more portions of the RV will extend outwards. It is one of the nicer but more mechanical features of your RV. For the checkout process, make sure you know how the thing works. It's pretty straightforward on most RVs; a switch pushes it in and out.

On the road, the slide-out is one of those devices that can cause the happy renter a lot of grief. Before engaging the slide-out button, step outside the RV and make sure the area you are expanding into is free of any obstacles. It is very difficult to gauge this while you are inside the RV. This means you won't be able to see low hanging branches or other obstacles. If you don't ensure you have enough clearance, you will do serious damage to the slide-out and your vacation.

Pulling the sectional back in is very straightforward, but make sure the entire path it is going to pull into is clear of shoes, toys, paper or anything else that can get swallowed up by the sectional. If you do consume a toy, don't assume that pushing it back out will reveal the toy you just swallowed. The footing of these slide-outs are full of nooks and crannies that love to eat your children's favorite things. Every time you use the slide-out, the toy will make some horrifying crunching sound as it gets further crushed into oblivion. You do not want to be that parent. Also, make sure the ladder to the top bunk is set away from the glide path.

I created a little checklist before I started setting up the RV for the day and a reverse checklist for when I wanted to start moving the RV. The slide-out is one of those checklist items. One more tip: if you are an early morning driver, pull in the RV (and generally prepare it for takeoff) before everyone goes to bed. Having the sound of a slide-out be the first thing your family wakes up to will not endear them to you or future RV trips.

The Driver's Area

My personal opinion on what to ensure works before you drive off is the AC. The air conditioner on RVs is typically worse than the AC in a car. Here's why: While there is a main air conditioner that does a faithful job of restoring coolness to the entire RV, it only works when you are either plugged into electricity or running your generator. When you are driving, unless you are running the main AC unit, the only air conditioning for the entire RV is the one in the front cab. This means that the only comfortable folks in the RV are those sitting up front, (at least at first; it does cool off everyone else over time). Since you are reliant on the front AC while the RV is in driving mode, make sure that thing works. Turn over the motor and turn up the AC full blast if you expect to be driving in any heat whatsoever—which you will be if you tour the Grand Circle in summer.

One thing to note here. While the RV agent may tell you that you can't run the generator while driving, you can. Therefore, although it is possible to cool things down with the main AC while driving, if you are paying for the generator by the hour, you may find yourself relying on the front cab AC.

The rest of the checkout is fairly intuitive: do all the things that typically work on a normal car work. That said, just as you don't test the windshield wiper blades when you rent a car, it may seem silly to test everything in the driver's area.

The Main AC

You chose the RV route because camping was a bit too far on the roughing it side. You like the notion that you can get some of the creature comforts that renting a hotel offers in an RV. The air conditioner is one of those creature comforts. There is the driver AC and a separate main AC for the entire RV. Make sure it runs. Have the rental agent walk you through its operation and confirm that you can run it while driving.

The Generator

Have the agent walk you through how to turn on the generator, too. Typically, you prime it and then turn it on. Priming is simply done by holding down the power button to the off position for most RVs. If you are offered an all-inclusive deal on the generator, take it. The other option is paying by the hour, which can cost more. Here's why. For our trip, we preferred the campsites closer to the park versus closer to a town. The problem is the campgrounds inside or just outside the parks do not typically come with electrical hookups. On our last trip, there were only two nights out of our 10-day journey where we could just plug in.

An unlimited generator brings peace of mind. Hot spouses (the other kind of hot) and hot kids will not be happy you are having to meter out the generator usage. ACs can be run, electronics can be charged, and toast can be made, all without feeling you are going into overage minutes. The generator is the backbone of convenience, so make sure it works and get the unlimited package. Ours cost $5 per day.

One other thing to note here: The wall outlets only work when you are plugged into electricity, either directly or through the generator. They do not run via the aux battery and, thus, don't work when you are driving unless you run the generator. Another good reason to go with the unlimited package.

How the Electrical Works

The electrical on most modern RVs is fairly straightforward, but different enough from the way you manage electricity at home to make it worthy of pointing out. Your RV should be equipped with a long 30- or 50-amp electrical extension cable that typically is plugged into the RV. This cable is plugged into the generator, which you can turn on at your discretion. If you are at a campsite that has electrical hookups, you simply unplug the cable from the generator and plug it into the hookup. Most rental RVs run at 30 amps, while some of the hookup sites run at 20 amps. This is okay; just don't run a bunch of things at one time or you will blow the circuit. On the topic of circuits, if you plug into your hookup and nothing works, typically you just need to trip the circuit breaker on the hookup itself. Each hookup has one, and some campsites turn the electricity completely off when not in use by turning the circuit breaker to off.

The Control Panel

I always call this part of the RV the Command Center because that sounds way cooler than the Control Panel. That said, while it's fine for you to use the term Command Center as well (and earn that increased respect from your younger children), it's probably best to stick with Control Panel when hob-knobbing with fellow RVers if you don't want them to look at you as if you are an idiot.

The Control Panel is simply a bank of switches that allows you to monitor tanks and other aspects of your RV. It also contains the switches for the generator, slide-out, auxiliary battery, water pump and other amenities that need switches. Each panel is different, and your RV agent will usually walk you through what each one does.

Filling up the Water

This may seem as easy as turning on a hose, but as you will be drinking this water, there are certain steps to ensure you don't contaminate your water supply. First off, the drinking or potable water station is often at the same location as the gray and black water dumping station. It is possible to fill up the drinking water tank while dumping the wastewater at the same time. Don't do it. You don't ever get a glass of water while going to the bathroom at home and you will certainly not become any sort of hero by saving a little time if you give your family some stomach bug. It's not worth it.

Wash your hands and fill the drinking water tank before touching the wastewater area. You should have been given a hose that is only used for drinking water. Only use it for drinking water. Store it away from other hoses. Find the potable water faucet (there may be a non-potable water faucet in this same area; don't use that one), attach the hose to the faucet and then let the water run for a minute to clear out any possibility of something in the hose or water line. The rest is fairly easy, just put the other end of the water hose into the water tank inlet and let it fill. When water starts overflowing out of the water tank, you are done. Detach the hose, being careful not to let either end touch the ground. Use good hygiene practices here.

Dumping the Waste Water

Prior to their RV journey, dumping wastewater for most folks was something that was about as involved as turning a handle on the toilet. Dumping the wastewater from an RV will most likely seem pretty nasty and to that I say, you are in good company. It is nasty. Alternatively, if you are overfilled with joy at the opportunity to dump out your family's biologically created waste, you may want to question that feeling.

That said, RV manufactures have made it fairly straightforward to dump your waste to the point that, if done properly, you never come into contact with any of it. Here's how it works:

There is a gray water tank, (all the shower and sink water) and a black water tank (all the toilet water and toilet treatment chemicals). They combine underneath the RV into one spot that opens to a wide outlet. The RV comes with a long dump hose (stored usually in the back bumper). This hose connects in an easy to lock configuration by lining up eyelets with the outlet and turning until it locks.

Once you are sure the hose is on the outlet, connect the other end to the disposal site inlet. Most of these have a metal cap on them that you can step on to raise up the cap. Once both ends are in place, pull on the black water valve and discharge. The black water valve will always be associated with the larger of the two pipes. You should hear the water come rushing down and out of your tank and into the disposal tank. Fill a bucket half-full of water and flush that down the toilet after the black water has drained out.

Next pull and discharge the gray water. Always empty the gray water last. This will rinse out the black water as well as the dump hose. Once done, close both valves, unplug the dump hose and store it back where you found it. Overall, this process may smell a little but if done right, you won't detect too much of an odor or have to touch any of the unsanitary bits. Even so, wash up. That was a nasty job you just did.

Getting Cable TV

Some of us could be satisfied with watching the passing convoy of desert cloud ships sailing softly against a deepening sea of blue sky. Others in your group may need a TV fix to fulfill their entertainment needs. For those, the modern rental RV comes with cable outlets, typically on either side of the unit. There is nothing more Christmas-like for those who love TV than to spend the night in a place that has cable as part of the full hookup service. There is nothing more deflating than realizing the rental company didn't include the cable that goes from the campsite hookup to your RV's outlet. The TV will continue to sit unused and unloved. Your family will despise you and sullenly return to their electronic devices. You will have failed to deliver Christmas.

This actually happened to us at the end of one trip. To avoid it, make sure you ask the rental agency if they can include the cable wire. Make sure it's long enough to span a good 20-foot distance.

Driving the RV

Driving the beast vehicle you have just rented may be the most or only intimidating aspect to RVing. If you have been thinking about renting an RV you have probably checked out RVs on the road and asked yourself, "Could I drive something that big"? Even the smaller RVs can seem large if you are used to driving around a sub-compact.

The good news is this feeling of intimidation will ramp to a more comfortable sentiment in a remarkably short amount of time. Rental RVs are basically a big truck with a home attached. So while it looks huge outside, behind the wheel, it won't feel that much different from a full size pickup. During the ramp up period toward operating the RV with full confidence, here are some tips to keep in mind.

Speed

Sure, the speed limit says 75 mph, but you are in an RV. Go the speed you feel comfortable driving. If you are on a road that has a high speed limit, there is another lane, and faster cars can go in that lane. You may find a comfort level that allows you to drive faster as you get used to the beast, but right now, you are on vacation. Think "slow the heck down" thoughts. The drive is part of the journey. Enjoy it.

Wind

Wind and speed go hand in hand. If there is wind, this massive box of a vehicle will certainly feel it. Gusts are especially noticeable. If it's windy, keep two hands on the wheel, 10 and 2. Especially in the deserts of Utah, the gusts can literally push you into the other lane if you don't hang on tight. There is less room for error in an RV, so up the safety.

The other type of gust comes from oncoming trucks. The two massive objects crossing each other at high speeds create a bit of a tug that can definitely be noticeable. The first couple of times it happens it's a little unnerving, but it is easy to learn to anticipate and self-correct for it.

U-turns

Contrary to popular opinion, it is possible to make a U-turn in an RV. It just takes more time and typically requires backing up to allow room to complete the turn. If there is no else around and it's simply the easier choice, then navigate yourself through the U-turn.

If you are in traffic, the cars behind you may not realize you need to back up, which makes for a bit of a mess because the other cars have to back up as well. The easiest way around U-turns for the first time RVer is to not do them. Make a circle around the block. Two wrongs don't make a right, but three lefts do! Again, you are on vacation, you have all the time in the world; there is no need to take the most efficient route. Take the least stressful one instead and enjoy the ride.

Switching Lanes

Welcome to the big league. You are now the size of those eighteen-wheeler cargo trucks. One of the perks is acting like one—in a good way. Anticipate getting into the next lane, use the blinker. People will pay attention to it and then get over. Don't think for a second that you can just zip in and out of traffic, however. You are driving something the size of a brontosaurus. The blinker is really crucial for RV travel. In a car, you can tell if a person wants to get over. They turn and look behind them, then slow down a bit or speed up. There are cues. In an RV, your fellow driver can't see you; they just see the RV. The blinker becomes the only means of communication. I'm not much of a blinker user in a car, but I use the blinker religiously in an RV.

Parking

At the campsite, there are two major ways to park the RV. The easiest and least available is the pull-through. This type is easiest enough, though make sure there aren't any low-hanging branches that you will run into.

The second type is the back in. Backing in an RV into a campsite parking space the first time can be fairly daunting; it's probably the top of the list of intimidating things you will have to face. Here are some tips.

Get an RV equipped with a camera in the back to help guide you.

Try your best to plan your first back-in parking journey in broad daylight. Trying to back into a campsite in the dark is more difficult.

Have your spouse or kids get out and help. Turn off the AC, roll down the windows and take your time. The first sessions are as much about teaching the copilot what works in terms of helping to navigate (such as standing close enough for the camera to see what the copilot is doing). Everyone comes up with his or her own vernacular on what works as the best form of parking communication. It may help to develop yours by trying to back into a space in an open parking lot to practice.

Don't rush it. You will not lose any points by pulling forward and trying it again. This isn't a competition. You will get great at it, just like you are at everything else. There is no shame in making five attempts to get the darned thing backed in right.

Parking in town is a little different. Parallel parking is pretty much impossible as the space available is typically meant for the length of a car. The best advice here is to think like an 800-pound gorilla while being courteous. People will understand if you need to take seven parking spaces to park your beast. They will be even more understanding if you take up those seven spaces in the empty regions far from the store.

Using the RV

Most of this section could have titles like How To Use a Stove or Flushing the Toilet. They're not really needed. Most of the use of an RV is very similar to home use. Most of the details have also been described in other sections. This section is about the stuff that is a little out of the ordinary.

Dirt

The best thing about the RV journey is that each morning your doorstep is parked in front of one breathtaking view after the other. With nature, however, comes dirt. That dirt, like the wonderful view in front of you, is just outside your front door. This means dirt can very easily come on into your sweet transportable domicile.

The easiest way of combating this is to take your shoes off each time you enter the RV, but this is easier said than done. The campsite is part of your home for the most part, which means you will be getting in and out of the RV a lot. Taking your shoes on and off each time becomes a hassle. There are probably myriad ways of getting around this, but here are the two I found to be most effective. The first is to bring a pair of sandals that can easily be put on and taken off. Sandals are great to bring along anyway.

The second is to bring an outdoor doormat or small utility rug. This isn't practical if you are flying to pick up your RV, but if you do have room, throw a small one in with the rest of your gear. Putting a rug out in front of the door does three things: It catches the dirt enough to minimize needing to take your shoes off at all. It can serve as a place to put your shoes and perhaps best of all, you will be the envy of the campground because everyone faces the dirt problem and only you will have the best solution for handling it.

Water

In a hotel, water is available to you in a theoretically unlimited amount. You can take long showers and fill up Jacuzzis or let the water run all day while you are out buying endangered Spotted Owl hats. You aren't required to conserve water in a hotel. In an RV, you have to pay much closer attention to how much water you use because supply is limited, and every drop will have to be dumped and replaced (and it won't always be free.)

Most of your family may not understand this, so make sure you help them realize that someone will have to do work at some point in order to get more water. Doing dishes and taking showers are especially high water-consuming activities. For showers, the best practice method for the least use of water is to get in, rinse off, then turn off the water and soap up. After getting all sudsy, turn the water back on for a final rinse.

The best practice for doing dishes depends on how many you have. It's a similar technique to showering but with one exception. If you miss a bit of grime on a knife or plate, you have repeat the process. Therefore, rinse the dishes, scrub them well with dishwashing liquid and make sure you have removed all the food particles. Once everything is scrubbed down, turn on the water to rinse. Make sure you don't use too much soap or you will spend a lot of water to rinse it off.

Doing dishes is tricky in an RV as there isn't much space. If you have tons of dishes to do, work in small batches. In addition, many campgrounds offer slop sinks in which to do your dishes. These are typically near the restrooms and for many are preferred over trying to do them in your small kitchen.

Being Level

When you park your RV for the night, it's best to choose the most level campsite you can find. Being level is not only how you normally live, it can be a problem if you aren't level. That said, there will be more than a couple of campsites in your journey that will not be level at all. Here are some guidelines to help choose among the best of the non-level sites.

Make sure the RV is parked such that your feet are lower than your head. When you sleep, having the blood travel downwards towards your feet, as it does when you are standing, will feel more comfortable than having the blood flowing toward your head. If needed, turn your bed orientation around. Even a small incline will become noticeable if your head is on the downside.

If you have a site that leans, park it with the kitchen in mind. If you are in this situation, it is best if you can find a different site, but there may be some cases where you are getting the last site and likely the worst site. The kitchen is the hardest hit in a campsite that causes the RV to lean.

Any pans on a stove will easily slide off. There is simply nothing to glue down a pot of boiling water to the stove. Park the RV so the pans slide into the RV wall rather than onto the floor, and use the back burners. Start thinking as if you are on a ship in stormy weather. Don't set the jar of spaghetti sauce down without being sure it won't slide off the counter. Gravity is an unwelcome guest in the case of a leaning RV; pay attention to that guest.

Moving the RV

Whenever you decide to move the RV, walk around the vehicle and make sure everything has been stowed and put away. Make sure the front door is completely closed; it has a habit of seeming as if it's closed only to come open on the open highway. Make sure the slide-out is pulled back in, that all cables have been removed and put away. Before starting the engine, ask for everyone's attention and make sure they are seated properly and securely. Make sure they aren't surprised by suddenly going from a stationary experience to a moving one by warning them first. I have my family sound off just to make sure.

Since we are on the subject of moving, a lot of people ask if you need to be buckled in while the RV is moving. By law, the same rules apply to being buckled into a car, including the use of booster seats, so yes, you have to be buckled in. It is very tempting to not wear the seat belt the entire time, especially for those not driving. Just remember that while it may seem safe, it is not at all safe, and serious injury may occur if you find yourself in an accident. You may wonder if we always used the seat belts. We did allow some limited roaming under controlled situations, such as driving slowly within a national park so they could get a better view, but it was a risk that we chose to take and not an endorsement. Wearing the safety belt is the law and is the safest approach to RVing.

Checking the RV Back In

Well, the trip is done and you need to return the RV back to its rightful owner. Checking in a motor home is different from checking in a rental car. There is a much larger security deposit at stake (ours was $1500), and since there are so many more things that can go wrong on an RV than on a car, the agency will check the RV back in with you. They will have a checklist and test a number of items such as the slide out, air conditioner and control panel. The check-in process feels a bit like an audit, and it helps to have the person checking you in on your side. Being nice helps. Don't rush them and let them do their job. Beyond that, here are some tips for getting your full security deposit check back:

Fill up the tank before you arrive or otherwise abide by whatever gas terms you agreed to when you checked out.

Dump the gray and black water. Once you you've completed your last tour of the dumping station, let your family know that "the onboard facilities" are now off limits.

Pack up before you arrive and be ready to leave. If you look disorganized this may be seen as a sign of someone who can't take responsibility for an RV. The "easy breezy audit" has now become the "check every detail audit."

Clean up some. We put all the packed luggage on the bed, cleaned off the dining room table, cleared out the cup holders, swept the place and generally tidied up. The rental agency had no knowledge we had been living like pigs for the previous 10 days and thought we were clean, upstanding citizens. As a result, the check-in process was a walk through the park.

Problems: Come Clean

Our RV was missing a few things, some of which were noted at the initial checkout and others we discovered only after we had checked out and were on our way. The person checking you back in may be a different person, so make sure they are aware of all the items. Start with the ones that everyone noticed during the initial checkout and first make sure they were noted correctly on the checkin. Then move to the new ones. For us, these were minor, such as a portion of the screen door was missing. The honesty helped in the end, and we weren't penalized for anything.

If you did break something, it's the right thing to tell your rental agent. They will likely find out about it anyway, which will only complicate matters if you didn't tell them right off the bat. Think of this moment as a test of your character.

The Security Deposit

Make sure you follow up on getting your security deposit back. Many of these companies have centralized accounting departments. This means that the memo to credit your deposit may get lost along the way.

On one occasion, we were told it would take 6-10 business days to receive our security deposit. For whatever reason, the process took about six weeks and required calling customer service. Once we contacted them, they refunded us in two days, so in the end, while we didn't get the refund in a timely manner, we did get the problem resolved quickly. The point here is to make sure the security deposit amount you are entitled to is in fact returned to you.

Oh Blackwater

Mom and Bryce at the Hard Rock Café in Vegas..

[Mom]: Son, why did you take so long to come back from the restroom? Your food is getting cold.

[Bryce]: Well, I had to go, you know, to the bathroom.

[Mom]: Bryce, I just worry about you when you go to the bathroom.

[Bryce]: Why mom? I don't worry about you when you go the bathroom.

The Vegas that most people know, the Vegas that exists along the banks of the river known as "The Strip," is like nothing else in the world. It is so unique an entity as to be foreign, as unworldly as going to another country. You come to be a different person, to be larger than life and, for a brief moment, this world allows you to achieve that goal. If then the "on strip" Vegas is like a foreign city, going outside the thin veneer of Las Vegas Boulevard is like venturing into a border town. The rest of Las Vegas exists as a transition zone, a manmade area of great turbulence where the overindulgent worlds of Vegas and normal society combine, leaving in its path the worst of both. Off strip Vegas is where you can still get $2.99 steak dinners and $8 buffets, but also where seediness mixes with shoe repair and you can buy lettuce at the supermarket while playing the slots. As you leave the strip, the rest of Vegas seems dodgy, run down, as if it is weary of trying to keep up with its more glorious self. You see people who are just trying to live a normal life in a normal town, but for whatever reason, they chose Vegas. For us, leaving our hotel and heading off the strip was a bitter realization that the world called Las Vegas was an illusion and that the ordinary day-to-day task we were driving into to pick up our RV was the reality.

RV rental places all seem to have one common rule that they live by: they are (for the most part) only open on weekdays. They do have a small window between 9am and noon on Saturday only, but as it takes about 90 minutes to complete the checkout process, it's a tight window. For us, we were on vacation and thus could have planned an RV pick up on a weekday, but let's face it, hotels in Vegas are cheap during the week. Conversely, they are expensive on the weekends so we opted to drive to the RV place on a Saturday, walk through the checkout process and somehow drive the darn thing off the lot in the three hours the rental company was open.

As we drew nearer, Ang said, "Now kids, I don't want any discussions about blowing each other up or bombing your dad or shooting anyone. I don't want any violent talk of any kind when we are at this place, do you understand? Sparkle ponies! I want you to think sparkle ponies!"

A quick note on "sparkle ponies." First off, our boys are not overly violent future mass murderers, they are simply boys. If they cannot wrestle to get the wiggles out, they will turn to verbal onslaughts, slinging at each other ever-increasing tales of doom, usually through means that are physically impossible, such as gathering up an army of alligators to attack the other's army of trained fire ants. At some point, one of them will cross a line, that line typically having something to do with the aforementioned alligators and the other brother's genitals.

Angela will then stop this unworldly war and try to reset their boyish brains with simple, pleasant terms. "Think sparkle ponies" was the current term in use. This phrase is actually a derivation from her previously used term, "Think rainbows and unicorns," which did at one time work to reorient their minds toward peaceful thoughts. For whatever reason, Ang wanted a new phrase and sparkle ponies was chosen. It was the mantra that somehow returned our children to the precious adorable cherubs that we thought we were getting when we first decided to conceive.

"This RV checkout process is bound to take a while, and I don't want you to get rambunctious while we are at the rental agency" she said.

"Your mom's right, you two are representing the Henze family." I felt like I was really adding value here.

"So no shooting my brodder?" Bryce grinned.

"Face palm," said Everest. "Bryce, did you not hear what Mom just said? Mom, Bryce is shooting me. You should punish him."

"I'm aiming right at your giggly puffs!" Bryce grinned, pointing his finger directly at Ev's nether regions.

"Mom! Now he's using bad language and pointing guns. Please punish him!"

"What? Giggly puffs isn't a bad word!" Bryce said, still grinning and quickly holstering his finger.

"Yea, but we know what it represents and that is an inappropriate area. No giggly puffs." I commanded.

"How about asphalt? Can we say ASPHALT?" Bryce asked.

"What? No! I think you know the answer to that. Look buddy, you need to reel it in and real quick," I said with some impatience. Bryce was acting like a true nine year old.

"Sure, Dad. Can I sing, you know, a song until we get to the RV place?" he asked.

"Depends." I said with a tone of distrust.

Bryce started to sing. "Giggly! Giggly! Giggly! Everest is one big Giggly Puff!"

"Bryce, that's enough!"

Both boys laughed heartily.

"What! I'm just singing a happy tune!"

"You're going to be singing the blues if you don't stop. Now reel it in, buddy. You know what happened to Fatima after all, right?"

"Okay, Dad. Sorry," Bryce said.

Fatima was my weapon. While Ang had sparkle ponies, I had a fictitious third son named Fatima. It didn't really matter that Fatima was a girl's name or that the whole premise was completely inappropriate, this simple story had a fantastic effect on calming the boys down. Pronounced "Fat – ee –ma", he was the son we had in myth and legend prior to Everest but because he was such a bad child, we decided to let him go. The story becomes incredibly vague from there for obvious reasons but in a slightly humorous off-color manner, it did put a seed of doubt in my boys and they cleaned up real quick so as to be spared the fate of this nonexistent fifth Henze. They knew he wasn't real but were only 99 percent sure. It was that 1 percent of doubt that I could be telling the truth that mattered.

Apollo RV is about 30 minutes outside of town, a tremendous distance for a family excited to get started on their first RV trip. We pulled in and parked among a sea of RVs, all of which looked exactly the same. Not knowing what to do next, we went inside the office and met Sue, a pleasant down-home redhead who seemed to be the brains of the operation. She answered phones, cued up other renters that came in, loaded up the RV with miscellaneous items, suffered through the mounds of paperwork and ran our credit card all the while keeping a smile on her face.

"Hi there!" I said with an exuberance found only by someone not currently at work. "We are here to pick up our RV!" Sue gets our name and does some lookup magic on the computer. After a tense 45 seconds, she finds us in the system.

"So, you excited about renting an RV?" she asked.

"Yes ma'am!" I said.

"Have you ever driven an RV before?"

"No ma'am, I have not," I stated as enthusiastically.

"Oh, you're fired then," she said. She was kidding.

Renting an RV is a process, especially the first time. There is the bit about going over the contract, the proof of insurance, the realization you're going to need to buy the toilet treatment, the discussion around anticipated miles and finally the review of all manner of possible additional side items you can rent. These include linens and towels, tables, iPad docking stations, solar bun ovens and about 100 other items. The list is seemingly endless but finally you get to the big moment, your first encounter with one of the actual RV units. You saw a bevy of them as you pulled in but up until now you didn't know which one was going to be yours. Finally, you get to meet your home for the next ten days. I was like a kid at Christmas.

Sue walked us past all the other less suitable RVs to ours, the shining pride of the rental company. It was certainly the finest RV on the lot, and I secretly felt sorry for all those poor tourists inside who would have to suffer with the lesser quality RVs they would certainly be given. Yes sir, though our RV looked exactly like every other one on the lot, I was confident without a doubt we were getting the best one.

We immediately asked if we could go inside. The door was open, after all. This beautiful home on wheels was practically inviting us to come inside, so I headed for the RV door. Sue stopped in her tracks and paused. She had seen this doe-eyed look before. We were a couple of noobs excited as heck to just get in and drive off on our amazing vacation, and unless she reeled us in quick, she knew we would likely only get about a mile down the road before we hit something. So she paused and, with a deep breath, changed her sweet behind-the-counter persona to the cold personality of a focused drill sergeant.

"No. We can't go inside until we've finished the exterior walk-through. This is your first time, right?" She walked us through the features of each side of the RV, opening every panel and explaining what each was for in careful detail. There were so many hookups, I thought. There were cable hookups, water tank hook-ups, city water hookups, electrical hookups. I struggled to memorize all of them.

Any time our attention strayed in the slightest, say to wipe the sweat forming on our brows in the 105-degree heat, she slowed down until she had our complete attention. "Now, this is important," she kept saying. So many things we had to keep track of. It was mind-boggling.

In the end, we found if we nodded as if we completely understood her, Sue moved on to the next thing. My wife and I quickly became trained to stand, listen, say nothing and nod every time Sue wanted our assurance. After a short time, my brain filled up to capacity and all I could say to myself were things like "City wa-ter hook up. Check. Must figure that out tonight. Electrical hookup with gener-ator bypass. Doesn't seem too hard, so check, another thing to fiddle with until I figure it out."

Then Sue came around to the gray and black water plumbing. She explained that the black water held the poo. Got it. I'm not a big fan of poo, so I'd better get this right. Perhaps if I listened carefully enough, I may not have to see, smell or god forbid touch poo. I could live comfortably not having any of these interactions, so I had better pay attention here. I somehow managed to carve out a bit more capacity to absorb what Sue was saying.

"Now this is the nasty part of the tour. This is where your gray water and black water are disposed of. The black water comes out first. The black water is the big pipe, and it connects to your toilet. The gray water is the smaller pipe and it con-tains your shower and sink water. Both the gray and black water pipes connect to one big outlet pipe where everything comes out." Sue pointed at the pipes.

"There is normally a cap on the bottom, but it seems to be missing. First time I've seen this." She paused to write down the missing item on her checkout list. "Not to worry, though, the RV has been emptied, so nothing's going to come out. Okay, you would normally remove the cap, clamp on and turn the hose I showed you on this end, put the other end of the hose into the dumping station inlet and use this valve to release the black water. Let the black water drain first and then run the gray water with this valve, which will help flush the black water. Get a bucket, which we provide, and fill it with some water and flush that down the toilet. This will ensure you flushed everything out. Any questions?" I liked Sue, she was all business.

I really didn't want to ask any questions. I wanted to get in and drive off. Howev-er, there was one thing she did that didn't make sense. As she went through the instructions, Sue kept pulling on the valve handle instead of turning the valve. Most valves I had worked with were turned to open them, not pulled. I needed clarification. This was, after all, an important task.

"So do you pull on the valve or turn it?" I asked sheepishly.

48

With full command of the situation, Sue stated, "No. You don't turn it. You pull on it."

To clarify further, she reached down to the black water valve and gave the handle a hearty tug. Without any warning, gallons of poo, toilet treatment fluid and well, all matter of hell flowed out of this valve, right in front of us, immediately hitting the hot pavement and burning into our nostrils.

We all stepped back quickly with eyes opened wide with horror.

"Oh! Oh! Nasty!" my wife exclaimed, reeling back from the stench until she bumped into the RV parked next to us. She was beginning to dry heave a little. It was certainly bad. Unworldly bad. It was poop in 105-degree weather bad. Demons could have flown out from that pipe and it would not have been worse.

Sue closed the valve as quickly as she could and, to her credit, calmly stood up and said, "Excuse me for a moment" and rapidly headed off to get help. I really admired Sue at that point; she was remaining composed against overwhelming odds. I pulled my shirt over my nose and looked at my wife with deep concern as to how she was taking all this. Her first impression of an RV was poop. Not a good start.

She looked me sternly in the eye and paused for a moment before speaking. "Well, honey," Ang said in what I call her "soft but firm" voice, "I'm just glad you're doing this because there is no way in hell I'm ever going near those pipes. That is just plain disgusting! It smells like, well I don't know... it smells like a beached whale covered in toilet bowl cleaner, that's what it smells like. For all that is green and golden I'm just disgusted." As she spoke, the wind changed direction, throwing a blow to our senses. We were forced to dry heave together back to the office while Sue made it go away.

The kids saw the look on their mom's face. "Mom, what happened?" Everest asked.

"Ask your father," she grumbled as she headed toward the air conditioning vent.

"Dad! What happened?"

"Well son. We learned that daddy's doing all of the dumping station duties on this trip," I said glumly.

Everest said, "Yeah, we knew that already, Dad. What the heck is that smell?"

"Son, we had an accident. The RV, umm, took a dump in the parking lot."

"It what?"

"The RV pinched a loaf. It dropped the kids off at the pool, laid a brick, made a deposit. I cannot make this clearer and I am more than a little traumatized, so let's not talk about it. You know how I am around poo."

"Yea, we know dad. Mom changed all the diapers."

"And god blesses her for it. I'm going to join your mom over there by the AC. I can still smell it. Ugh!"

"Take it easy, Dad. We're here if you need us."

"What happened to Dad?" Bryce asked.

"The RV couldn't hold it in or something and did a number two outside," Everest answered.

"Oh god! I thought I smelled something. I hope the RV can hold it in while we are on the trip!"

Sue cleaned up the mess, and we all pretended it never happened, as is the standard protocol of adults when bodily functions are concerned. For some reason the staff put up with our kids wrestling in their waiting lounge as she completed the tour. We drove off and since I had recorded the RV walkthrough so as to not forget anything, the kids watched the poo scene over and over, laughing each time as if it was the first time seeing it. We quickly put this little incident behind us, but one thing is for sure, I will forever know that one does not turn the black water valve on an RV. One pulls on it.

Zion

National Park

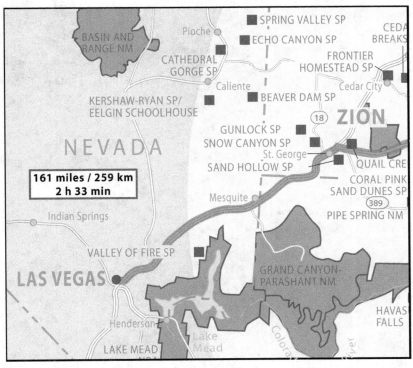

"The finest workers in stone are not copper or steel tools, but the gentle touches of air and water working at their leisure with a liberal allowance of time."

—Henry David Thoreau, early essays

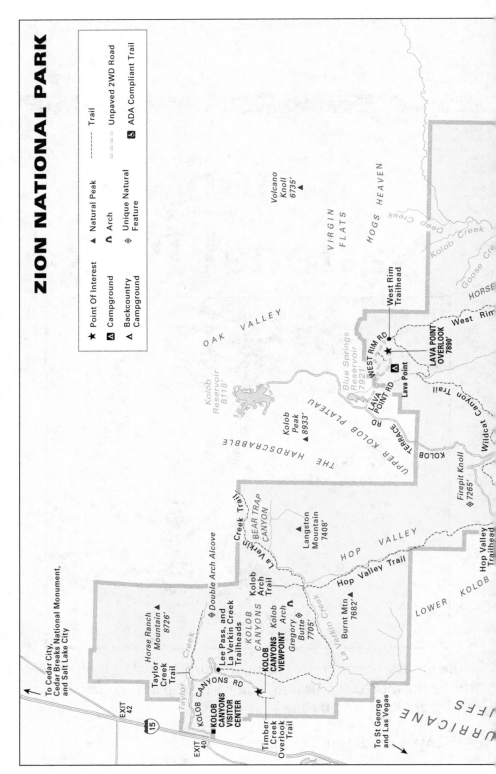

ZION NATIONAL PARK

Legend:
- ★ Point Of Interest
- ▲ Campground
- ▲ Backcountry Campground
- ▲ Natural Peak
- ⌒ Arch
- ◈ Unique Natural Feature
- ----- Trail
- === Unpaved 2WD Road
- ♿ ADA Compliant Trail

To Cedar City, Cedar Breaks National Monument, and Salt Lake City

EXIT 42

EXIT 40

15

To St George and Las Vegas

KOLOB CANYONS VISITOR CENTER

KOLOB CANYONS RD

Timber Creek Overlook Trail

Taylor Creek

Horse Ranch Mountain ▲ 8726'

Taylor Creek Trail

◈ Double Arch Alcove

Lee Pass, and La Verkin Creek Trailheads

KOLOB CANYONS VIEWPOINT ★

KOLOB CANYONS

Kolob Arch Trail

Kolob ⌒ Arch

Gregory ◈ Butte 7705'

Creek Trail

BEAR TRAP CANYON

La Verkin Creek Trail

La Verkin Creek

Burnt Mtn ▲ 7682'

Langston Mountain ▲ 7408'

Kolob Reservoir 8118'

THE HARDSCRABBLE

Kolob Peak ▲ 8933'

UPPER KOLOB PLATEAU

KOLOB TERRACE RD

Blue Springs Reservoir 7921'

LAVA POINT RD

WEST RIM RD

Lava Point ▲

LAVA POINT OVERLOOK 7890'

★

West Rim Trailhead

West Rim

OAK VALLEY

VIRGIN FLATS

HOGS HEAVEN

Volcano Knoll 6735' ▲

Deep Creek

Kolob Creek

Goose Cre

HORSE

Lava Canyon Trail

Firepit Knoll ◈ 7265'

Wildcat

HOP VALLEY

Hop Valley Trail

Hop Valley Trailhead

LOWER KOLOB

HURRICANE CLIFFS

52

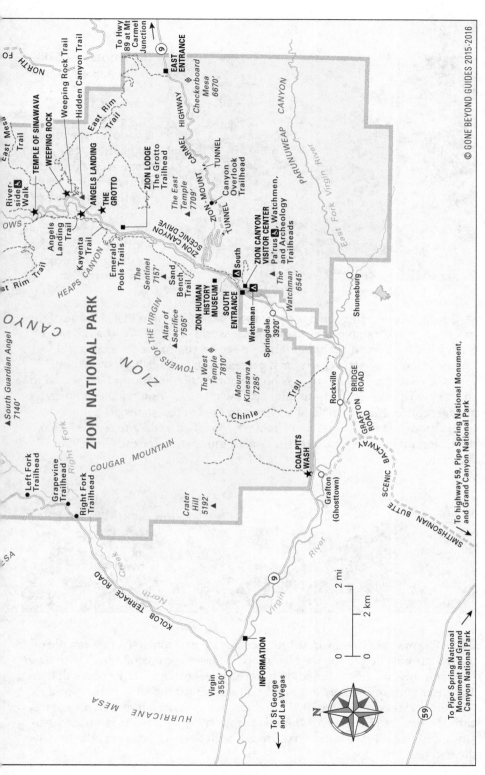

ZION NATIONAL PARK

NORTH FO

East Mesa Trail

Weeping Rock Trail
Hidden Canyon Trail

To Hwy 89 at Mt Carmel Junction

9 EAST ENTRANCE

Checkerboard Mesa 6670'

TEMPLE OF SINAWAVA
WEEPING ROCK

East Rim Trail

ZION-MOUNT CARMEL HIGHWAY

ANGELS LANDING

Riverside Walk

THE GROTTO

ZION LODGE
The Grotto Trailhead

The East Temple 7709'

TUNNEL
TUNNEL
Canyon Overlook Trailhead

PARUNUWEAP CANYON

East Fork Virgin River

OWS

Angels Landing Trail

Kayenta Trail

ZION CANYON SCENIC DRIVE

ZION CANYON VISITOR CENTER

Pa'rus & Watchmen, and Archeology Trailheads

st Rim Trail

HEAPS CANYON

Emerald Pools Trails

The Sentinel 7157'

Sand Bench Trail

South

Shunesburg

CANYO

South Guardian Angel 7140'

TOWERS OF THE VIRGIN

Altar of Sacrifice 7505'

ZION HUMAN HISTORY MUSEUM

SOUTH ENTRANCE

The Watchman 6545'

ZION NATIONAL PARK

NOIZ

The West Temple 7810'

Watchman 3920'

Springdale

Left Fork Trailhead

Grapevine Trailhead

Right Fork Trailhead

Right Fork

COUGAR MOUNTAIN

Mount Kinesava 7285'

Chinle

Trail

Rockville

BRIDGE ROAD

GRAFTON ROAD

Crater Hill 5192'

COALPITS WASH

Grafton (Ghosttown)

SCENIC BACKWAY

SMITHSONIAN BUTTE

To highway 59, Pipe Spring National Monument, and Grand Canyon National Park

MESA

KOLOB TERRACE ROAD

North Creek

Virgin River

HURRICANE MESA

Virgin 3550'

INFORMATION

To St George and Las Vegas

N

9

59

To Pipe Spring National Monument and Grand Canyon National Park

2 mi
2 km
0
0

© GONE BEYOND GUIDES 2015-2016

What Makes Zion Special

Ask the Park Ranger About "The Subway"

The journey to Zion National Park from Vegas starts at St. George, Utah. Before St. George, the land is wide open with an arid barren resonance that borders on melancholy. This is not a bad thing for the first time RVer as it allows you to get comfortable with your new vehicle on straight, distraction-free roads.

The journey starts at St. George because this town is at the foot of the Colorado Plateau, one of the most geologically stable landmasses in the world. This stability has allowed time, wind, water and perhaps divinity a canvas to produce majestic and immense works of natural art. Each presentation spreads itself over thousands of square miles, and each is both wonderfully unique and yet bound to similarity. This collection of natural art is why the Colorado Plateau holds the greatest concentration of National Parks in the United States. Roughly centered among the four corners of Utah, Arizona, Colorado and New Mexico, the Colorado Plateau makes up the overall foundation for the Grand Circle vacation.

Kolob Canyon

If one follows the Grand Circle tour per this book, Zion is the first temple of natural art unveiled to the traveler. It holds massive sandstone cliffs with deep hues and majestic lines, dotted with a green lush canopy of high desert plants. The sheer cliffs of Zion are among the largest sandstone cliffs in the world, reaching heights as high as 2000 feet. They are colossal and proud monoliths, bathed in colors of reds, browns and cream. At the canyon's bottom, the usually quite Virgin River meanders through with as much leisure as the tourists themselves.

Zion Lodge circa 1929

Zion Canyon itself is about 15 miles (24 km) long and is considered a box canyon, beginning with a wide mouth at one end and a cul de sac at the other. At the end of the canyon you'll find The Narrows, one of the best gems in the park. Here the Virgin River cuts like a surgeon into the sandstone layers, creating a thin slot canyon that winds itself slowly higher. During the summer when the river is lower, hikers can walk in the river with steeply cut rock walls on either side of them. The Narrows is a favorite with Zion hikers, both for the adventure of the journey and the ever-changing views.

The lesser-visited Kolob Canyon contains spectacular examples of the soaring red Navajo sandstone cliffs and is a short drive from the main section of the park. There are numerous finger and pocket canyons for hikers and backpackers to explore, including Kolob Arch, the third largest freestanding arch in North America. Kolob Canyon is a peaceful and stunning destination, presenting itself to the viewer more as oasis than desert, whether one explores it on foot or via the five-mile (8 km) scenic drive.

With the protection of the cliff walls and the Virgin River, Zion supports a relatively lush environment. Unlike its drier surroundings, the park is a sanctuary for plants and animals alike. Green vegetation is abundant and deer along with a host of birds are often seen within the park. The lush bounty of life combined with the towering red cliffs makes Zion magnificent. The word Zion itself was introduced by the Latter Day Saints as a reference to a place that is "pure in heart." There is a purity to Zion NP, a sense of peace and calm, but also a sense of adventure.

Staying in Zion

There is one lodge and two campgrounds within the main portion of Zion NP and one more campground about an hour's drive from Zion Canyon in the northern section of the park. Additionally, the town of Springdale, Utah is very close to Zion and there one can find several hotels, lodges, bed and breakfasts as well as privately owned campgrounds and RV parks.

If Zion NP is your first stop within the Grand Circle parks, it can be a bit misleading as there is a lot of choice in terms of places to stay for the night. Lodging amenities tend to ebb and flow with the popularity of the park itself. Given Zion is the second most visited park in the Grand Circle, there is a fair amount of choice for finding a room. The point is, this isn't the case with all of the parks, so planning is important.

Of the two campgrounds, Watchman is intended for RVs and has electrical hookups whereas South Campground is intended for general use and mixes tents with RVs.

Staying Inside the Park

Zion Lodge

Phone: 435.772.7700, E-mail: info-zion@xanterra.com

Zion Lodge was originally designed by Architect Stanley Gilbert Underwood in 1924 and carries much of the great Southwest character that went into many of his national park lodge designs. The original lodge burned down in 1966 and was rebuilt in 100 days with expedience in mind. In 1990 the lodge was renovated to return the grounds to the look and feel of Underwood's original designs. Today, despite the many visitors, Zion Lodge exudes a feeling of serenity and calm. The grounds are spacious and the interior is warm and inviting. The lodge is within walking distance of the Emerald Pools Trail, which is an excellent family friendly trail.

Zion Lodge offers twenty eight cabins with two double beds and twelve cabins with one queen bed. For most families, the cabin offers more privacy and containment than staying inside the hotel itself, thus they go quickly. All cabins have a private porch, full bath and a nice gas fireplace and scattered close to the lodge itself.

If double beds aren't cutting it, the lodge rooms may be a better option. Most of the rooms within the lodge have two queen-size beds and a television plus a full bath and private porch or balcony. The rooms are clean but as this lodge is well frequented, expect a little use. There are also second floor suites and accessible rooms available.

Watchman Campground

There are two campgrounds in Zion NP. Of the two, the Watchman Campground has the most amenities for RV travelers. What sets this campground apart is the ability to make reservations during the peak season. For many of the sites, electricity hookups are available. If you are following the route spelled out in this book and you are a first time RVer, this will be your first (and one of the few) times that you will hook up your RV to an electrical outlet. More on that in a bit.

The Watchman Campground is located just ¼ mile (0.4 km) from the South Entrance. There are 162 sites, two that are wheel chair accessible and seven group sites. Of these, 95 have electrical outlets. The remainders are tent and walk-in sites. The group sites are tent only as well. Campsites can be reserved at the Watchman from March through December six months prior to your date of arrival. Go to www.recreation.gov or call 877-444-6777. Camping is seasonal at Watchman, so check the Zion National Park Service for the latest information.

Before going into the other features of Watchman, if this is your first time in an RV and this is your first campground, here are a few tips that may help. Reserve the Zion campground beforehand and make sure your campsite has electricity. If you can't find availability for the dates you are looking for, keep checking, and check often. People do cancel, but those sites go quickly. Also, be flexible. We stayed in a different campsite each night in Zion, which is a minor hassle since you have to move each day but far easier than leaving the campground entirely.

The reason you want to reserve your site and get electrical is simply because this is your first time behind the wheel of a large motor home. Reduce the stress by knowing a site will be there to meet you. Make sure it has electricity so that the gang is comfortable on their inaugural night in the RV. You can run the AC if you have electricity. Since you are not allowed to run generators in the campground, the AC will help take the edge off of a hot summer's day. This little secret will help make your first night a pleasant one and hold the RV experience in the warm light of creature comforts-meets-the outdoors that you were hoping for.

The third tip for first timers is to allow enough time to get to the park before dark. You will be backing in your RV into the campsite. Doing this in the daytime is much easier than doing it at night, especially if you've never done it before.

Some of the sites are shaded but will only accommodate motor homes that are a maximum of 13 feet (3.69m). Electric campsites in loops A and B run $30 per night. Tent sites in loops C, D, and E are $20 per night. The campground does have relatively clean flush toilet restrooms as well as a slop sink to do dishes in and water stations. Watchman is within walking distance to the visitor center and the shuttle.

South Campground

South Campground has 127 campsites. All sites are first come, first served, and there are no electrical hookups. There are a good number of RV-friendly sites, though, and generators are allowed from 8:00 a.m. to 10:00 a.m. and from 6:00 p.m. to 8:00 p.m. Campsites here are a little less than at Watchman at $16 per night.

South Campground is otherwise the equal of Watchman with one exception, the walk in campsites. There are eight walk-in camp- grounds that are situ- ated along the banks of the Virgin River. For these, find your des- ignated parking spot, hoof your gear a short distance down to the river and then bask in the glory that you have

Mount Carmel Tunnel

secured one of the best campsites in the park. Please note that some of these sites do have red ants. There is certainly some consternation in seeing your site's best tent location surrounded by foraging biting fiery red ants. The fact is, these little guys will bed down for the night back at their home far away from your tent and are typically not a problem. Still, if you have small chil- dren, these river side sites might not be your best option.

Lava Point Campground

This is a first come first serve primitive campground with just six sites. There is no water and no fee to stay at these sites. Getting to this campground is an 80 minute drive from the main section of Zion so check at the Visitor Center to see if they have any update on availability before making the drive. The campground's primitive exclusiveness is a plus for many and offers trailhead entry points that are less frequented. Vehicles over 19 feet are not allowed.

Staying Outside the Park

The town of Springdale, UT is ideally located to serve the visitors of Zion NP. There are over a dozen hotels, plus vacation rentals, bed and breakfast nooks, lodges, and campgrounds. The best way to find the right place for you is to go to the Zion Canyon Visitors Bureau's site: www.zionpark.com. They list them all plus give a lot more information on dining and other things to do within and around the park. A few notable hotels are also listed here:

Cable Mountain Lodge

147 Zion Park Blvd, Springdale, UT, Phone: (435) 772-3366, cablemountainlodge. com

This is the closest lodge to the park's entrance. The rooms are clean with wood floors and a warm interior overall. They have single rooms up to suites with full kitchens, plus a swimming pool, though with the Virgin River right at the property line, there are plenty of options to cool off.

Cliffrose Lodge & Gardens

281 Zion Park Blvd, Springdale, UT, Phone: (800) 243-8824, www.cliffroselodge.com

What sets Cliffrose Lodge apart is the size and appointment of the rooms. They also offer one and two bedroom suites and even 1,250 square foot, three bedroom villas. There really isn't a bad room in this establishment. Cliffrose Lodge is literally on the border of Zion NP across from the Watchman Campground with the Virgin River acting as the boundary.

Driftwood Lodge

1515 Zion Park Blvd, Springdale, UT, Phone:(435) 772-3262, www.driftwoodlodge. com

Nice clean room and rooms of all sizes, including suites, check. Friendly staff, yep, they have them. So what makes the Driftwood Lodge different? The views from many of the rooms. With large grounds surrounding the property, the views are unobstructed and downright amazing. The room's themselves are relatively basic compared to some of the other lodges, but sitting on your porch with the view of Zion National Park in front of you makes this lodge a great value.

Majestic View Lodge

2400 Zion Park Blvd, Springdale, UT, Phone: (435) 772-0665, www.majesticview-lodge.com

Majestic lives up to its name as a clean, slightly larger than life establishment. Big logs, big view and a big pool make up this 69 unit lodge. No pets, most rooms have a balcony.

Ferber Resorts (Zion Campground and RV Resort)

479 Zion Park Blvd., Springdale, UT 84767, Phone: (435) 772-3237

Located just outside the park, this RV park offers full hookups with some sites next to the Virgin River. There are a host of amenities, including showers, a heated pool, Internet, a convenience store, a playground and laundry facilities. Rates are $39 per night with each person over two people running between $2 to $3.50 per person depending on age.

Zion Entrance Fee

If you are planning on doing the Grand Circle or portions of it, it may make sense to purchase the Annual Pass. This will save you money in the long run, but only if you buy it at the first National Park you visit. For example, the entrance fee at Zion is $30 for a private vehicle. The Annual Pass is $80 and allows you entrance to all National Parks. You will save about $45 for the trip described in this book if using the Annual Pass.

The Zion Tunnel Permit

At the same time you buy your Annual Pass or entrance fee, you will be asked if you are planning to go onward through the Zion Mount Carmel Tunnel, which you will need to do if you are going directly to Bryce Canyon National Park next. If you are and you are in an RV of any normal size, you will need to purchase a tunnel permit and be escorted through the tunnel. Specifically, if your RV is 7 feet 10 inches (2.4m) in width and/or 11 feet 4 inches (3.4m) in height or bigger, the NPS will require the permit. The tunnel permit costs $15 and is in addition to the park entrance fee. It will allow you two trips through the tunnel for the same vehicle within seven days of purchase.

The tunnel traffic is controlled by NPS rangers who will verify that you have a valid permit and cue you up for your one-way journey through 1.1 miles (1.8 km) of solid rock in a large moving house. Make sure you know how your lights work prior to going into the tunnel; it is pitch black in sections. Also, the tunnel control has operating hours, it is not a 24/7 service. The operating hours are seasonal and are posted on your permit. You will need the permit before being allowed to pass through, so keep it in a safe and memorable place.

Zion Geology

The geology section presented here and in other sections is not meant to provide detailed descriptions of all the different geological periods and layers of rock. While the study of geology itself is a fascinating one, it is also one of great depth, filled with foreign terms, a fair amount of complexity and an equal amount of debate. There is no textbook geology here.

Instead, these sections attempt to capture more of the wonder of geology by explaining the geological story using everyday terms. For a deeper study into the geology of Zion or any of the parks listed in this book, strike up a conversation with your park ranger or even just check out the visitor center. The fact is, most of the parks in the Grand Circle owe their uniqueness to geology, so to that end, these sections tease out the most amazing and salient geological aspects of the park.

Temples and Towers of the Virgin

What's amazing about Zion's geology is the journey it took to get here. Starting some 300 million years ago, all of Utah and Wyoming were situated near the equator on the western edge of the then massive super continent called Pangaea. At this time the area of Zion was covered by a shallow body of water referred to as the Kaibab Sea.

At around 200 million years ago, the supercontinent began to break up and the area of Zion continued in its journey northward towards its present location. Seas came and retreated over long, mind-boggling stretches of time, depositing sediments and plant and animal life. Sometimes tropical, other times arid, the area within the Colorado Plateau continued to change, each time adding a slightly different context to the layers.

One of the most notable layers for Zion anyway is the Navajo Formation. They make up the sky-high Navajo red monoliths that tower above you. At one time, for about 10 million years, these monoliths were sand. An area seemingly as vast as the Sahara Desert, some 150,000 square miles (338,500 km2) of sand dunes occupied this area around 176 million years ago. For 10 million years, much of the Colorado Plateau was nothing but a sea of sand and the thickest deposits of this sand landed where Zion is today.

How did all this sand become sandstone? Another sea covered the dunes about 150 million years ago. This sea flattened the dunes and slowly deposited more sediment on top of them. Through pressure, simple chemistry and a lot of time, the particles of sand cemented together to form sandstone. The red color is due simply to the presence of iron oxide, or rust.

The deposit from this shallow sea became the cap of rock called the Temple Cap and Carmel Formations. The most significant example of this formation can be seen as the top of the Altar of Sacrifice, the monolithic cap that can be seen from a great distance as you climb up to the park's entrance.

The present chapter of Zion started 13 million years ago when tectonic forces uplifted the whole of the Colorado Plateau. What makes the Colorado Plateau so unusual is that it was primarily lifted straight up rather than at an angle. This has allowed water to carve out deep gorges into the layers of rock. As the land rose up, water carved down into the layers, the battle resulting in what you see today. Water, wind and the patience of nature are what carved out the current version of Zion that lies before you. The Virgin River was at some points aided by the end of the glacial period of the Pleistocene Era. As the glaciers melted, water levels increased, carving into the layers at a faster pace. Most of what is seen today was not even visible 1 million years ago and the relatively recent slot canyons of The Narrows had not yet been formed.

It is hard to imagine such vast sand dunes, or Utah existing at the equator, or vast tropical oceans as the roots of Zion. It's even harder to imagine the amount of time involved that led up to the creation of this wonder. Even more amazing, the visual results that you see before you are relatively recent work. Perhaps harder still is to realize that even these monoliths are transient in nature, slowly eroding and evolving into something that may be completely different from what you see today. Think about if you could install a web cam that took a picture a day for a million years and then somehow could look at it in fast motion. While that sounds like an immense amount of time and amazing in its own right, it's a drop in the bucket for geology! The whole science really puts your life into perspective; we are viewers for such a short amount of time that it all looks like it is static and unchangeable. Pretty humbling this geology stuff.

Zion History

First Inhabitants

While it is not known exactly when people began occupying North America, the most suggested time frame is around 11,000 years ago. These people, known as the Paleo-Indian, were primarily nomadic hunter-gatherers. Early on, they hunted woolly mammoths, camels, and armadillo-like creatures that were as large as cars and known as glyptodonts. While there is no evidence of the Paleo-Indian culture in Zion, they are important to note as the forebearers of those who were.

The Paleo-Indian culture would evolve and advance into what is referred to people from the Archaic period. There is evidence that people occupied Zion from about 7,000 to 2,500 years ago. These people were still fairly mobile hunter-gatherers, but some groups settled and developed an ability to harvest from their location. They gained knowledge of all plants in the area, they understood what worked as food, what worked as medicine and what caused bodily harm. They learned the habits of the animals they hunted and of those that could hunt them. They formed an understanding of the resources around them, what rocks worked well for cutting and what worked as aids in processing and harvesting. The people of the Archaic period were likely the first visitors to Zion.

Park Poster circa 1938

Fast forward to about 2,000 years ago, the sophistication of the people took on elements of a complex culture and even political systems, similar to some degree to what modern people have today. This culture, referred to as the Anasazi, was now deeply rooted to the land. They had history that was tied to the land, and they developed their own languages and subcultures, but at the same time they shared their inventions and revelations through the process of trade. They learned how to farm the land, growing corn, squash and beans. Farming allowed for permanent structures to be built. They built homes, spiritual centers, and granaries. They were no longer limited to the possessions they could carry with them. This allowed not only for more utilitarian items such as pottery and basketry, but also for art and spiritual objects that had become a part of their everyday lives. They lived in a society with rules, customs, social classes and all the drama, love and heartache that we face in our own modern world. Don't let the fact that they didn't have smart phones fool you; these were a remarkably sophisticated people.

What is interesting to note is that Zion occupied the extreme west-northwestern boundaries of the Anasazi territory. Being on the edge cut them off from the major trade and cultural centers; however, the flip side was that this made the Anasazi of Zion a culturally unique group. Despite the lack of absence of large community structures and kivas, evidence of living structures, rock art, clothing, pottery, baskets and food granaries point to a smaller scale but significant society that inhabited the canyon.

At about 1200 CE, the Anasazi left the Four Corners region altogether. There are many theories as to why, but none can be irrefutably proven. The area was repopulated fairly soon after the Anasazi left by the Southern Paiutes.

Like the Anasazi, the Paiutes were a highly sophisticated culture. The Paiutes were seminomadic, following the animals as they migrated with the changing seasons and resources. Winters were at lower elevations, summers at higher elevations where the pinyon pine nut was a plentiful and a staple part of their diet.

Even when European settlers began to expand west, the geographic isolation of Zion Canyon allowed the Paiutes to live in relative peace. In 1849, the Gold Rush and the theme of Manifest Destiny started an occupation explosion of the western territories. California became ground zero for this westward surge. The state grew from a population of 15,000 to 300,000 in just three years after gold was discovered. However, the "spaces between" the east and west were not immune to occupation. Settlers traveled perhaps with the goal of California in mind, only to find a lovely spot in which to settle down on the way. By the 1860s, about a dozen settlers found their way to Zion mainly under the leadership of Brigham Young.

The influx of settlers caused a near extinction of most Native Americans. The Paiutes were no exception. With little knowledge of the land, the settlers overgrazed, overhunted and brought a cloud of disease that together irrevocably changed the culture of the Paiutes. Some communities lost 75 percent of their population, and with such a blow came a retreat toward survival at the expense of old ways. Many who survived became ranch hands for the European settlers.

The Crawford Ranch Near the Mouth of Zion

Pioneers

The modern history of Zion and all of Utah comprises two major historical events. One was the Gold Rush that created a general movement westward. The other, in Utah in particular, was the Church of Jesus Christ of Latter-day Saints, (LDS or Mormons for short). At the time of early migration, the territory of Utah was owned by Mexico. Between 1847 and 1890, some 70,000 pioneers made their way on foot or by wagon to Utah under the direction of their Mormon leader Brigham Young, creating settlements in what they called the Kingdom of Deseret, now known as Utah.

Mormon Nephi Johnson was the first pioneer to visit Zion Canyon in November 1858, using a Southern Paiute as a scout. Nephi settled farther down the Virgin River and with his settlement group founded the town of Virgin. Others came and built their own towns nearby, Rockville and Shunesberg around 1861 and Springdale in the fall of 1862. By 1864 there were 765 pioneers settled into the Upper Virgin Valley region.

One of the new Mormon settlers, named Joseph Black, explored the upper reaches of Zion Canyon and returned with marvelous tales of its beauty. Joseph's words of the wondrous canyon caught the interest of Isaac Behunin, who built the first cabin in the canyon, near the present day Zion Lodge. He dug a ditch from the river allowing irrigation to several acres of land, growing various fruit trees, corn, vegetables and tobacco.

The tranquility of the canyon drew a few other settlers, among them the families of William Heap and John Rolf. Isaac Behunin and most of his neighbors had two cabins. They summered in Zion and move in winter to the lower elevations of Springdale. Isaac had originally been asked by church elders to help settle the town of Springdale and had worked with the church on helping establish other settlements. He is cited, though not proven, as the person who named the canyon Zion. He even compared the impressive LDS Church in Salt Lake City to Zion stating, "These are the Temples of God, built without the use of human hands. A man can worship God among these great cathedrals as well as in any man-made church. This is Zion."

While the first years of settlement in Zion were peaceful ones, this was about to change. Increasing numbers of settlers created tensions among the Paiutes and Navajo, which ultimately led to bloodshed. The pioneers fortified themselves within Springdale and then Virgin, creating armed parties as lookouts. Additionally, Zion Canyon itself produced its own discord. During the summer monsoons the Virgin River flooded, wiping out the pioneer's crops. Poor soils didn't help matters. Isaac Behunin left Zion in 1874 to help found the town of Orderville, where he died in 1881.

The Birth of a Park

Word spread about the scenic and often unworldly sites of southern Utah. Much of the west had been tamed enough to allow thoughts of tourism to become the next chapter in Zion's story. In 1909, President William Howard Taft gave the canyon itself National Monument protection under the name of Mukuntuweap National Monument. By 1918, Mukuntuweap was expanded from the canyon floor of 5,840 acres to 76,800 acres and renamed Zion National Monument through the executive order of President Wilson. The next year Congress upgraded Zion to a National Park, making it the first in Utah.

Still, access to Zion was rough going. A road had been built into the canyon, even a railroad up to Cedar City, but getting to Zion via an easterly route proved to be a tremendous challenge. In 1927, the Zion-Mount Carmel Highway was started to create a reliable throughway. The road opened in 1930 and, as a result, park visitation increased. The most famous part of this highway is the Zion Tunnel, a 1.1-mile (1,711 m) testament to engineering.

The tunnel features side openings, called galleries, that provide light and ventilation. The galleries were also used to make it easier to dump the rock generated through the construction of the tunnel.

In the early days, the galleries held parking spaces to tourists to get out and look at the neighboring monoliths. As car frame sizes increased over the decades, however, parking and even walking in the tunnel were halted due to safety concerns. Today, with the advent of RVs, the tunnel is now a managed resource. RVs must be checked out prior to being allowed in the tunnel and for the duration of the motor home's journey, the tunnel is open in only one direction.

Waterfall at Emerald Pools

In 1937, the Kolob Canyon area was declared Zion National Monument and sits adjacent to Zion National Park. It was then added to Zion National Park in 1956. Another addition was the Zion Lodge, which was originally designed by the famous architect Gilbert Stanley Underwood. Gilbert designed a vast number of "rustic style" yet grand park lodges, including the Ahwahnee at Yosemite, Old Faithful Lodge at those at Yellowstone, Zion, Bryce, Cedar Breaks and the North Rim of the Grand Canyon. While the original Zion Lodge Underwood designed burned down in 1966, it was restored to look much like the original during a remodel in 1990.

The Contribution of the CCC

The Great Depression had few silver linings, the Civilian Conservation Corps (CCC) being one of them. As part of President Franklin D. Roosevelt's New Deal, an unemployed unmarried man aged 18–25 could get a job. The jobs required unskilled manual labor and their purpose was that of conservation development of natural resources. In the nine years the CCC was incorporated, 3 million young men found work. They received shelter, food and clothes plus $30 a month in wages. A full $25 of that wage had to be sent home as part of their terms of employment.

The CCC was applauded by Americans at the time both in its contributions to the nation and to the employees themselves. For the nation, the CCC planted nearly 3 billion trees, helping reforest much of America. They helped in the construction of 800

Trail up Angels Landing

parks nationally and in building remote public roadways and service buildings. With this focus came attention to conservation and overall awareness of our national and state park systems. The CCC employee left more physically fit with a strong sense of working as a team and was thus seen as a good candidate with future potential employers.

Some of the work done by the CCC in Zion has yet to be repeated. This was a period of engineering ingenuity combined with sheer audacity. Tunneling through solid rock, building trails up cliff faces, bolting in chains and carving steps directly into the rock were all signatures of the CCC era. They developed trails that delight the visitor and become part of the adventure as you walk them. When on a CCC-built trail, there is wonder not only in the surrounding nature but often in the creation of the trail itself.

At Zion, the CCC made additional improvements by removing invasive plants, creating campgrounds and building a measure of flood control along the Virgin River. It was all backbreaking work; however, from the journals of the workers, the time spent was one of joy rather than hardship.

The onset of World War II brought an end to the CCC, though it does make one wonder how much more they would have done on behalf of America's natural resource conservation if the program had continued to exist through the twenty-first century.

Modern Zion

By 1990 Zion National Park was reaching visitor capacity with each year receiving more than 2 million visitors. With the canyon roads congested with cars, the Park Service began a shuttle system in 2000. Today, the only way to visit the canyon floor past Zion Lodge is by shuttle. While the shuttle system may seem limiting, it is designed rather well. The shuttles are timely and offer the visitor the opportunity to slow down and take in the view. They do increase travel times significantly, especially if you are going deep within the canyon, say to the Narrows. However, the shuttle system offers something you came for in the first place—an opportunity to relax and slow down.

Today Zion receives more than 2.7 million visitors annually. While the shuttle has contained much of the congestion of years past, the struggle to offer up Zion as a national treasure for all to enjoy while preserving that treasure remains a challenge.

Hiking The Narrows

Things to Do in Zion

This section highlights some of the more amazing things to do in Zion, but is by no means exhaustive. You could spend a summer exploring all of Zion, but the reality is simple, you will be short on time, especially if you are planning to take in all seven of the national parks in this book. We stayed two days in Zion and managed to get in all the below hikes.

Of them all, there is one must do hike if the river is cooperative—The Narrows.

All hikes and things to do that are represented here are great for families, save for Angels Landing and downriver on The Narrows, which are both strenuous. The list is best for families who are active but may have younger members or do not regularly hike and need to ease back into the hiking scene.

Emerald Pool Trails

The Emerald Pool Trails are on the western side of Zion Canyon just across from Zion Lodge. They offer some pleasant walking and scenery with a shower fall of water that you can walk behind. The areas around the falls are mossy, green and heartwarming. This is a great hike to get to know some of the beauty of Zion.

Lower Emerald Pool Trail

Easy – (1.2 mi / 1.9 km), round trip, allow 1 hour

There are two trails described in the Zion hiking guide that make up the Emerald Pools, the lower pools and upper pools. Lower Emerald Pools is flat, is paved much of the way, is short in distance and provides incredible views of waterfalls and shallow pools. You do climb a bit on the lower trail, which allows for some nice views of the valley.

The two pools on the lower trail are nice enough, but as is almost always the case, the best pool is at the top. As the canyon is surrounded on both sides by steep cliffs, it will be well into morning before the sun hits the western side of the canyon. By midafternoon, the sun will have passed over the other side, providing more shade. In warm weather, plan on hitting the trail either in early morning or late afternoon to stay cool.

Upper Emerald Pool Trail

Moderate – (1.0 mi / 1.6 km), round trip from lower pools, allow 1 hour

Here the trail continues from the Lower Emerald Pool Trail for the final mile. The paved trail is now dirt and the trail climbs more steeply. If you are doing this trail in the morning, the sun may have passed over the monolith walls and is now part of the climb up. The views do get better as you gain elevation, and the pool at the top is by far the biggest, sitting at the base of the western cliff faces. It is well worth the effort for the views. These pools are not intended for swimming.

The Narrows

Imagine walking up a river flowing clearly and gently around your feet. At times there is no shore, only river and massive sandstone walls that run from the edge of the water and rise swiftly straight up 2000 feet into the sky. There are places where the canyon is wide enough to permit a view of distant sandstone monoliths and other places where the canyon is delightfully slender, only 20-30 feet wide. Each turn gives a different view, all wondrous and grand. For a bit, the river stretches out, allowing a chance to walk on soft sand. You see deer grazing on the banks. Waterfalls come sliding down curved walls from unreachable heights. There is no trail but the river. If you think about it, each step up and down is a step no one has ever taken before in exactly the same way.

Be warned, it is possible that you won't be able to hike the Narrows. If the Virgin River is running too high, either due to winter/spring runoff or to summer flash floods, you will not be able to go on this hike. That said, if the river is running favorably, then make it a point to add this to your itinerary. The park service actively controls access to the Narrows, which does take the guesswork out of the safety of hiking this trail.

Portion of The Narrows

Going Up-stream from the Bottom of the Canyon

Easy to Strenuous – (9.4 mi / 15.1 km), round trip, allow up to 8 hours depending on distance traveled

The Narrows is found by taking the shuttle to the very end of the canyon via the Riverside Walk Trail. It will take about 40–45 minutes from the campground to the end of the canyon via the shuttle. It will take another hour to 90 minutes to walk the 2.2 miles (3.5 km) needed to complete the Riverside Walk Trail. Make sure you add in this time when you plan your hike.

The Riverside Walk Trail is flat, easy and paved. The trail follows the Virgin River up along its banks, and there are plenty of places to drop off the trail to explore the river itself. At the end of the trail is a small set of steps down to the river where The Narrows begins and where the hike gets really interesting.

There are a few trails, but for the most part, you walk in the river itself. You will be walking upstream on uneven ground at times, so be prepared to get wet. Depending on how far up you decide to go, you will need to wade and even swim in some stretches. If you feel confident that the trail will be open, it's best to pick up water shoes beforehand and bring them on the trip for this hike. It will make your hike more enjoyable.

Depending on the time of year, the water may be swift and cold. In the summer, usually by June, the river slows down to a steady but not terribly swift pace, and the temperature is more refreshing than cold.

There are restrictions to how far up you are allowed to travel upstream without a permit. There is a tributary creek called Orderville Junction, which is a common destination for most hikers and is the limit of how far up you can travel without a permit. Orderville Junction is about two hours from the trail. That said, it is possible to never make it this far and still have an amazing hike. Each bend offers a different experience and new view with another bend at the end that beckons you farther.

Returning will take slightly less time since you are going downstream with the flow of water. If you are doing the hike in late afternoon, make a note of when you start the hike from the shuttle drop off and how much time you have left before sunset. If you have 3 hours, hike up for 90 minutes and turn around. The Narrows is not an easy hike in the dark especially if you don't have a flashlight.

Going Downstream from the Top of the Canyon
Strenuous – (16 mi / 25.7 km), one way, full day hike

Going downstream can be done with a National Park Service wilderness permit. Allow a full day for this 16-mile hike. You can find private jeep shuttles that regularly go up to the drop off spot. This is a strenuous day's hike. There are ample stories of folks that find themselves having to stick it out for the night because they thought it would be an easier hike. Hiking in streambeds is slow work and is more tiring than walking on even pavement. Underestimating this hike in the wrong conditions can be dangerous as well. Flash floods and exposure from the night's elements are serious considerations.

If You Hike the Narrows

- Have a full understanding of the weather before you go. Flash floods can originate from storms that aren't close to where you are hiking.

- Carry a gallon of water per person and some food, sunscreen and a first aid kit.

- Bring a pullover if the weather is temperate. It is colder in the canyon.

- Bring waterproof bags for cameras and other items that you need to keep dry.

- The only restroom on the hike is at the beginning of the Riverside Walk. There are no other places to go, even if you "have to." This is a popular destination and there are no discreet bushes. Make sure everyone goes prior to beginning the hike.

- Walking sticks are preferred by most folks for added stability, as are sturdy hiking boots. Water shoes and tennis shoes are okay for the casual hike up river. Sandals are not recommended though hiking sandals are okay.

- This is not a great hike for young children. My 9-year-old did fine, but keep in mind it is over two miles of walking just to get to the beginning of The Narrows. While the current is typically fine for adults, it may be too much for smaller ones.

Archeology Trail

Easy – (0.4 mi / 0.6 km), round trip, allow 0.5 hour

The Archeology Trail is a great hike if you are looking for an early evening stroll. The trail is short, less than half a mile (0.6 kilometers), but climbs fairly steadily to a 1000-year-old prehistoric storage site. While the site requires a fair amount of imagination to piece together the history, this is not the only reason for going.

The site is close to the Watchman campground and rises to a nice vantage point in a very short distance. One can take in phenomenal views both up and down the canyon. You will notice the green riparian corridor of the Virgin River as it meanders through an ever-widening canyon. In all, this is a short but worthwhile trek you can take if you are looking for something near camp.

Angels Landing Trail

Strenuous – (5.4 mi / 8.7 km), round trip, allow 4 hours

The views are unparalleled from the unique Angels Landing trail. Built during the wake of the Great Depression by the CCC, it comprises a series of switchbacks cut into solid rock. The final half mile is along a narrow knife-edged ridge that uses chains and carved footholds to assist you to the final destination. It is strenuous, but the end result is well worth it. You will have climbed from the bottom of the canyon to close to the top, giving you a view that will most certainly become a life moment. It is a world famous hike and one of the most popular in Zion.

The trail's name was coined by Frederick Fisher in 1916 when he looked up at the monolith and exclaimed, "only and angel could land on it." With the help of the CCC, (Frederick Fisher) forged a trail to the top.

The trail is composed of six distinct parts. The first follows a paved path along the river before dog legging west from the river toward a cliff wall. If you look carefully at this point in the trail, you will see the second portion of the journey, a series of switchbacks up this cliff wall. Even from a distance, the switchbacks are impressive if not audacious. The trail builders carved a fairly wide paved trail into solid rock and while you are indeed climbing up a cliff face, this portion is merely strenuous and no more dangerous than any well-established trail with exposure.

There is a reprieve at the third portion. At the top of the switchbacks, the trail goes between two massive monolithic columns through what is aptly named Refrigerator Canyon. The monoliths climb high enough to block out the sun and there is a cool breeze that greets visitors as soon as they reach the top of the switchbacks. This lasts for only a short half mile before you arrive at the fourth portion, called Walter's Wiggles. The Wiggles are a series of 21 short but consistently steep switch-backs that wind back and forth until you get to the next respite, called Scout's Lookout.

Angels Landing

The lookout is the fifth portion of the journey and a great place to take a rest. The Wiggles are be-low you and from the lookout, you can see the final half mile pitch ahead of you to Angels Landing. The area offers incredible views. There is also a pit toilet and plenty of places to relax before your final leg. Up to this point you have been on the West Rim Trail, so make sure you follow the signs to the top of Angels Landing, as the West Rim Trail does continue onward.

The final pitch is a bit exciting as it has the adventure of chains that you can grab onto to ensure you get up the last leg. This portion is a razor back ridge. It is fairly narrow with steep drop offs on either side. The trail is well marked by the chains and crosses the back of the ridge several times as you climb. Many hikers have made this journey and in the end, it is not as scary as it sounds. That said, this is not a place to test yourself; a handful of people have fallen to their deaths on this trail. I've seen teenagers on this trail but only two children who were in the single digit age bracket. Use caution, for both yourself and your fellow hikers.

Once at the top, there is a somewhat narrow but flat area to take in the lofty vista. To the north is a grand view of the end of Zion Canyon. You will find yourself gazing at an enormous cul-de-sac of towering rock. As the eye travels from the edge of Angels Landing down the canyon, the citadel of rock stands as one complete sentry extending to the horizon. The red cliff walls meet the green of the desert, culminating in a dense riparian snake of vegetation that surrounds the Virgin River. At times swallows soaring at incredible speeds up to 40 miles per hour (64 km/hour) can be seen. They will soar seemingly straight into the cliff walls only to stop at the last second and land in their nests.

Weeping Rock Trail

Easy – (0.4 mi / 0.6 km), round trip, allow 30 minutes

This is a short paved trail that ends at an alcove called Weeping Rock. True to its name, water seeps through the sandstone and then falls gently like a soft rain once it reaches the overhang. It is possible to stand underneath and watch the magic of water and stone, even on a sunny day. The trail is great for kids and casual hikers looking for a great view of the Great White Throne. There is about 100 feet of elevation gain and some trailside exhibits.

Left Fork Trailhead

Strenuous – (7.0 mi / 11.3 km), round trip, allow 5 - 8 hours

The Left Fork of North Creek is most popular for a stretch labelled The Subway, a short an rather amazing section of the creek that looks more like a worm tunnel than a streambed. This is one of the best hikes in the park and is more route than actual trail. The whole journey is alongside and often in the creek, which makes for slow going. Unlike The Narrows, which can be cooler in the summer heat, this hike is definitely a hot hike when temperatures are high. Start early if it looks to be a hot day.

It is possible to enter from the top and make your way down stream, but this is longer and requires a bit of rappelling and swimming (and carrying your rappelling gear). A permit is required no matter which direction you travel. From bottom to top is described here.

From the bottom, the trail starts by picking ones way down a 400 foot gully starting from the Left Fork Trailhead on Kolob Terrace Road. Once in the creek, head upstream for about two to three hours. The Subway section is a tight section of the creek with several twists and turns right above a cascading set of falls called Red Waterfalls. The Subway itself is spectacular with clear pools and an almost subterranean feel.

It is possible to continue upwards but be mindful of time. Shortly after The Subway you will be met with large black pools that you must swim to get across to continue exploring the slot canyon. Further up is a soothing little waterfall with a secret natural room behind a watery curtain. Journeying from here requires bouldering and rappelling experience. Enjoy and head back down before dark.

Like The Narrows, this slot canyon does experience extreme changes in water volume due to flash floods. The permit process helps provide education along the way for this route, but do enter well informed as to the weather for the day.

Springdale

Springdale was once a Mormon settlement at the mouth of Zion Canyon and is now a quaint little tourist town. The town has everything for a visitor, including gift shops, art galleries, restaurants, ice cream and gifts. The spunky little town of just 529 inhabitants even has a movie theater. It's a nice alternative to hiking if your family is just not the hiking type or has had enough of the outdoors for now. It is also where you can pick up

Shuttle Buses in Zion

alternative journeys via jeep tours and mountain biking. The NPS runs shuttle service to Springdale, which can be picked up near the visitors center. Check the visitors center for a schedule.

Visitor Center

The visitors center is located within walking distance of the Watchman Campground and is a great place to start your Zion journey. Here you can get a lay of the land, talk to rangers and, if your kids are interested, pick up a Junior Ranger Program. This is also the hub for finding a shuttle both into the park and out to Springdale.

If the center is closed or overly busy, the NPS has set up some very nice kiosks that allow you to get the information you need. The kiosks list out things to do based on how much time you have in the park and are definitely a great way to get started.

The visitor center is open every day except for Christmas Day. Hours are seasonal. Spring: 8:00 a.m. to 6:00 p.m., Summer: 8:00 a.m. to 7:00 p.m., Fall: 8:00 a.m. to 6:00 p.m. and Winter: 8:00 a.m. to 5:00 p.m.

A quick note on the Junior Ranger Programs. If you have younger kids, you likely know about this program. Almost every national and state park offers its own version of the Junior Ranger Program. The program allows children to explore and learn more about the park they are visiting. Each child receives an activity book that asks questions about the animals, plants, geography and history of the park. The booklets do take some time to fill out and parents can work with the younger ones to help. Upon completion, kids get a badge or patch and sometimes a park pin. The Junior Ranger Program is a great way to engage your family in the national parks, conservation and ecology. Depending on the ranger who reviews the completed activity book, the receiving of the official park junior ranger badge can be quite ceremonial with the entire visitor center applauding as the child receives public accolades for his/her accomplishment on becoming a Junior Ranger.

Zion Human History Museum

The Zion Human History Museum opens one to two hours later than the visitors center and requires taking a short trip on the shuttle. The museum itself is nicely laid out albeit fairly broad and basic in its offerings. The best part of the museum is its grand view located on the backside of the building. The museum was built with the view of the Court of the Patriarchs in mind—three immense and stately monoliths named after the biblical figures Abraham, Isaac, and Jacob. Whether the museum is open or closed, the trip is worth the journey for the view alone.

Tooling Around on the Shuttle

If you read this and find yourself not really wanting to hike a whole lot, take the shuttle and enjoy the view. The shuttle is a wonderful way to explore the park at your leisure. Shuttles are abundant, so it's easy to get off at the various stops, take in the view, explore a bit and then catch the next shuttle. The shuttles are designed to offer clear views of the canyon. The shuttles can get crowded, especially on a summer morning when everyone is trying to head to his/her chosen trailhead while the air temperatures are cooler.

Zion Lodge

The Zion Lodge was built in 1924 and is designated as a Historic Place by the U.S. National Register. There is a calm and rustic feel to the lodge and its surrounding two acres. The lobby is not as grand as some of the other lodges designed by architect Gilbert Stanley Underwood (see the history section for more on Gilbert);

Zion Lodge

however, the overall feel of the lobby with its wooden chairs and chessboard tables is one of peace and majesty. The lodge does have a nice café to grab a bite to eat or well-deserved ice cream or smoothie. There is a fair amount of outdoor seating next to the café as well as public restrooms. There is also a ranger desk to the right inside the lobby if you have questions and a gift store should you find yourself in need of a shot glass that says Zion NP on it.

The Triple H

Everest and Bryce with Mom at the grocery store..

[Everest]: Hey mom, can I ask you a question?

[Mom]: Sure.

[Everest]: Vegan is a healthy diet, right?

[Mom]: Sure, I guess.

[Everest]: And you want us to be healthy, correct?

[Mom]: Of course.

[Everest]: Okay, awesome!! Bryce! Grab some Dr. Pepper, Mountain Dew, Pringles and anything else in the snack aisle that doesn't contain meat or dairy. We are rewriting the books on veganism!

[Bryce]: "On it!"

[Mom]: "Sigh."

Whenever it came to asking my friends to go on a hike with me, most went once. Getting them to go a second time was a tall order. You see, as a kid I sucked at baseball, football, basketball—pretty much any sport that involved a ball, but there was one thing at which I excelled. That one thing was hiking. My friends nicknamed me "Billy Goat Henze" and referred to the hikes I took them on as "Triple Hs," which stood for "Henze Hike from Hell." A typical scenario went like this and usually started several miles into a trail.

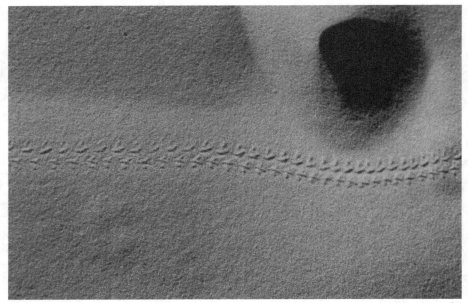

Insect tracks

"Hey, let's check out this trail!" I'd say.

"What trail? There is no trail where you are pointing."

"There's a deer track right there we can follow. See it?"

"Nope, I only see vast amounts of dense shrubbery."

I would divert off the main trail and take us on what was for me a wonderful bushwhacking adventure. I felt like a pioneer frontiersman, invigorated, forging new ground to reach a destination or some grand view that would be worth whatever suffering we would have to endure in order to get there. I was delighted to be able to take my friend on this journey with me as we climbed a steep and long hill to some praiseworthy destination. My comrade, my wonderful buddy! We would surely become closer friends as a result, having shared this painful but highly rewarding journey together.

While I passionately forged ahead at a steady pace, my friend just glared at me, knowing that he was in the middle of a horrific trip that after near heatstroke and a possible sprained ankle would lead him to a rock. A big freaking rock. A rock you could easily Google and see from a hundred different angles. It wouldn't look any cooler in real life, despite the enthusiastic ramblings of the madman who was carrying the food and water and was the only person who knew how to get him back. He was forced to follow me. As he climbed up the hot dusty line I called a trail, he plotted my death, if only to keep his mind off the burning pain in his legs.

Back during the prime of the Triple Hs, only the hikes marked "strenuous" were worthy. On a trip to Zion National Park, there was one such hike, a hike that not only was strenuous, but also whose trail was forged into the sides of the cliff walls of Zion itself. The trail climbed from the shores of the Virgin River to the very top of the massive sandstone walls of the park. The last leg of the hike involved climbing the back of a knife edged ridge that went steeply down on either side. Chains were installed to hold onto. Footholds were cut into the rock. The trail was pure adventure and not for those who were afraid of heights. If you had it in you to make it to the top, your reward was a view from the heavens. You would be standing on a mesa that jutted out into the valley of Zion, right in the middle of the valley, offering a full 360-degree view of magnificent and unparalleled beauty. The spot was so breathtaking it was called Angels Landing, reserved only for Heaven's most virtuous and hallowed in spirit. Anyone who has been to the top of Angels Landing knows they were on sacred ground.

It was twenty years ago almost to the day that I did that hike. Back then I was hiking with a buddy from England who had just finished a 30-day stint of tramping in New Zealand. He was a great hiking companion. We challenged ourselves to a speed climb to see how fast we could ascend to the top of Angels Landing. We made good time —great time. Today I wanted to challenge myself to beat that record. Sure, I was 20 years older and mainly sat in front of a computer all day, but I still had the passion, the fire to outperform my younger self. I was wiser, more confident. The fact we pulled into Zion during a heat wave didn't deter me; it emboldened me. Bring it. The harder the better. My wife, of course, thought I was nuts, even more so than normal. Then there was Everest. He wanted to go with me.

"What do you mean, you want to come along"? I said to Ev.

"I don't know, you've been talking about this hike for so long. I think it would be fun."

How could I explain this to him? We had done our family hike to the Emerald Pools earlier that morning, which meant the only time left for Angels Landing was during the heat of the afternoon. It would be unbearably hot. For a lack of gloves, I brought socks to put over my hands for the chains. A ranger had warned me that they were getting too hot to touch with bare hands.

"But it's 106, son! It's going to be a grueling hot hike. Straight up pretty much. I don't know..."

"Dad, come on! I want to do a hike with you. I think I'm ready for a Triple H."

I wanted to say no because I knew what this meant, there would be no ascending Angels Landing today. Everest would poop out half way up, and like a stubborn burro would turn on me until I agreed to turn back. Plus, how long would it be before I made it back out to Zion? This was likely my last chance at ever climbing Angels Landing again.

My son stood his ground. "I'll carry my own water, Dad. Please, I'm bored here. I don't want to sit in the RV with Bryce all afternoon. Please!" I looked at my young boy and realized I couldn't say no.

On the ride up the canyon, Everest read me the following passage from the park brochure:

"Caution: The route to Angels Landing involves travel along a steep, narrow ridge with support chains anchored intermittently along the route. Footing can be slippery even when the rock is dry. Unevenly surfaced steps are cut into the rock with major cliff drop-offs adjacent. Keep off when it is wet, icy or thunderstorms are in the area. Plan to be off before dark. Younger children should skip this trail; older children must be closely supervised."

"Are you worried, son?"

"Nope! This should be fun. Hey, can I see your hat?" I warily handed him the hat that had been on every hike I had taken for the last 30 years. It was a Peruvian wool hat and while unconventional, kept me cool in the heat of the sun and warm on colder hikes.

He took it and smelled it. "Wow!" he said looking up at me. "It smells like adventure! Can I wear it?"

I shook my head and smiled. "Sorry, this hat's been with me around the world and over many years." I took it back and smelled it. It did smell like adventure.

As we pulled up to the Grotto shuttle stop for Angels Landing, I saw a couple lying on their backs on picnic tables. They looked completely spent in every way and didn't move an inch as the bus pulled up. We were the only two that got off the shuttle at the Angels Landing trailhead. It was 3 pm and now an oppressive 107 degrees. I was beginning to have doubts that this was a good idea.

One of the prone hikers moved his head a bit. "How was the hike?" I asked.

"Good... good." Long pause. "Intense," said the man.

The woman opened one eye and glared at me. Her fevered stare said everything. She had to see who the really stupid person was who was stupid enough to go on a stupid hike in the middle of a heat wave.

"Bring water," she mumbled.

We made good pace, my son and I, traveling along the banks of the Virgin River. It was hot; no doubt about it, but the tall walls of Zion provided good shade in the late afternoon. The smell of cool waters flowing in the near distance invigorated me. My son was keeping up and I was glad to have him with me.

As we left the river, the trail steepened a bit and went from dirt to pavement. I quickened my step, and Ev followed immediately behind me. Up ahead was the first real challenge, a series of long switchbacks that went straight up the canyon's cliff face. These switchbacks were carved into the rock face itself. They were built in 1926 as a symbol of both the conquest and harmony of man's interactions with nature. The solid sandstone has held firm in support of this effort for almost ninety years, bearing the weight of man's inconvenience to its natural face gracefully and without much fuss.

As we literally walked up the canyon's wall, a sense of throbbing came over me. I had been drinking enough water, but my head would not be appeased no matter how much I quaffed. The pulse of my blood came to a high volume within my temple, and the air seemed to get unnaturally thinner as we climbed upward. The heat felt like a repressive weight upon me. I put myself into four-wheel drive mode, which is slower but ever so steady. All thoughts were put to keeping one foot moving in front of the other one, a repetitious and controlled meter up the steep incline. I thought the pavement would make the hike a cakewalk and at first condemned it for not being a true dirt trail. I now blessed the trailblazers who built this damned thing for making the trail a little bit easier. They were wise. We were going straight up a cliff face and needed every bit of help we could get.

"Do you mind if I lead, Dad?" Everest said cheerfully. "It's amazing how quickly you obtain elevation, right? Look at that view!" I stopped my slumped over sad oxen posture and turned around. I noticed through my heavy breaths that Ev was barely out of breath at all.

"You all right, Dad?"

"Yeah, yeah. Let's keep going. You lead but don't get too far ahead of me. Keep me in sight."

The switchbacks were a seemingly relentless hell. The trail never stopped chasing me upwards, never getting nearer, never getting farther, grinning in the heat of that hot afternoon sun like some dingo chasing a kangaroo. My son, however, was glowing, smiling, almost springy in his step. I was losing him. He would soon find me collapsed from the heat. He would be forced to stuff me into a crevice in the rocks for safety while he went to get help.

We reached a reprieve, an upper canyon within the main Zion canyon. The air was cooler and even better, this portion of the trip was flat. We sat and gathered ourselves, drank water, ate a granola bar. The combined effect rejuvenated me, filled me with renewal. The majority of Angels Landing was the West Rim Trail. Only the final half mile was the steep pitch with chained handrails to the top. I was almost there, I thought, one more final pitch, less than a half a mile, easy peasy. We can do this.

Then we got to Walter's Wiggles. I'd forgotten about that part. Walter's Wiggles are best viewed by taking your head and looking straight up, where you'll see a steep series of switchbacks, each climbing as sharply as the next. There are 21 "wiggles" in all, and before you can make it to the final ascent of Angels Landing, you must pass through the Wiggles of Walter.

"Wow, Dad! Check these out! Isn't it amazing that they built this up the side of the rock face?"

I looked at Everest like a beaten donkey being asked to carry the load of another recently deceased donkey.

"Oh, shit," I mumbled. "I forgot about these."

"Did you just curse, Dad?"

"Yeah. Ah no, no, come on! Let's do this!" The flat part had invigorated me enough to lie a little. I really didn't want to do this at all. The heat, these steep switchbacks. Shit.

"Hey dad, you want to do a speed climb like you told me you did the last time? Come on. Let's see how fast we can get up this part!"

"No speed climbing, too hot. We don't want to get heat stroke." The kid was obviously nuts.

"Oh, yeah, okay dad. I can stay with you, that's fine." Ev sounded defeated. He kept up with my glacial rapidity for about two Wiggles before we mutually agreed it was best if he went ahead. Within thirty seconds, he was out of range of sight and sound.

Alone, my pace upwards slowed to that of an intravenous drip feed. I figured I would soon pass out prone and stiffened on the side of the trail, feet in the air like road kill. Somebody would tie a "Get Well Soon" balloon to my boot and give word to the rangers when they got back down, perhaps cover me with leaves. That sounded like a fine plan; at least then I wouldn't have to continue walking. I

looked up. The top of those infernal switchbacks continued to look the same distance away. I was convinced they were building a new Wiggle for every one I completed. Somebody needed to stop this Walter guy.

I could see people below gaining on me and, out of delirious pride, I stopped and took pictures of the rocks as they passed. Of course they caught up to me in the least photographic section of the entire hike, but I stood there and clicked away as if these rocks were the most interesting things I had ever seen. "I could have easily beaten them," I thought. "Of course I wanted to take pictures of gravel."

At about Wiggle 16 Everest came running back down the hill.

"Dad! Oh my god! That was amazing! Can you give me the GoPro camera? I want to go back up."

"Go back up? Where? To the saddle?" I tried to not seem completely out of breath.

"No! I went to the top dad! The view was AMAZING! I love this! I told them I would run back down and get the GoPro."

"Them? Wait, what? How did you get to the top? I told you to stay at the saddle at the top of this…never-ending Wiggles thing. And who is 'them'?"

"Oh! I met a bunch of boys my age at the rest thingy. They belong to a club or something. We got to talking and we even waited around for you a bit and finally the scout leader asked if you would mind if he took me up."

"And you said yes…"

"Dad, he's taking the second group up in five minutes. Can I please take the camera and go with him? Please Dad!"

While I myself had given up hope of ever finding my second wind, my son stood in front of me with an overwhelming sense of boundless energy. He couldn't wait to run back up and join his new friends. I pursed my lips and said, "Son. Give me your hat."

"What?" Ev didn't understand.

"Just give me your hat, Everest."

Puzzled, he handed his baseball cap to me.

I removed my wool sombrero and put it on him. "Here, take it. It looks better on you anyway."

"Wow. Thanks, Dad!" He took the hat off, smelled it and then put it back on.

I cinched up the drawstring. "Don't lose it, okay?"

"No way! Thanks again, Dad. Can I have the GoPro too?"

"Oh yeah, sorry! Here, go. Take it. Do what the lead guy says and be careful. It's still dangerous up there".

"Sure! Will do, Dad." Ev started bolting back up the Wiggles as if they were level. One switchback up, he stopped and looked down at me.

"Hey, Dad! Thanks again for the hat!" he shouted.

I gave an ear-to-ear grin. "No problem son! You earned it."

"Oh and Dad, what did you say your time was that one time you did this?"

"70 minutes from the shuttle to the top." I shouted.

"Did it in 60."

"In this heat! That's just freakish."

"Sorry, Dad! See you at the top!"

At the top with my son, I never felt older or prouder. We were two people drenched in copious amounts of sweat, sitting on the top of one of the most transcendent and spectacular views in North America. We watched the slow migration of shadow against tremendous rock.

We witnessed light play of a thousand hues, dance inside subtlety, delight and strike deep inside. As grimy as he was, I put my arm around my son. I had finally found a friend who got this as much as I did.

My son took a drink of water. "So. Freakish, huh?"

"Yeah, that's right. It's 107 degrees outside. You were practically levitating up the trail. And that smile, you are actually enjoying this heat!"

"You realize it's your DNA, right?"

I paused, then said, "True enough, I started insisting on DNA testing after little Fatima was born."

"The brother with the afro that came before me?"

"That's him."

"How is little Fatima these days?"

"I'm not sure. We lost contact with him after we sold him. He paid for this trip, though."

Everest looked at me and started laughing. He gave me a solid hug and then raised his water bottle to Zion Canyon. "To Fatima!" he shouted.

"To Fatima!" I exclaimed. "Wherever you are!"

Bryce Canyon National Park

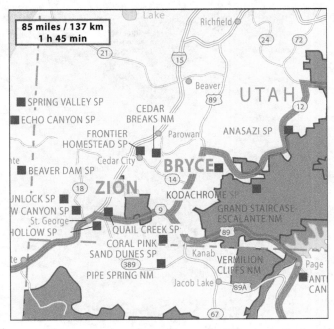

"*The desert takes our dreams away from us, and they don't always return.... Those who don't return become a part of the clouds, a part of the animals that hide in the ravines and of the water that comes from the earth. They become part of everything ... They become the Soul of the World.*"

—Paulo Coelho, *The Alchemist*

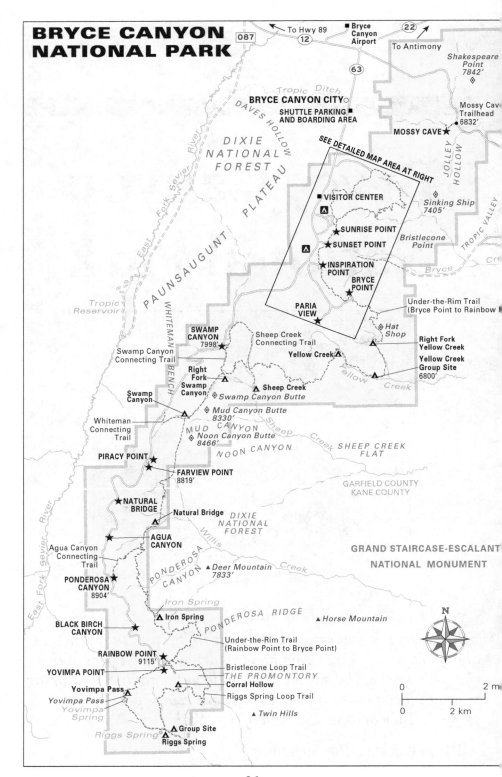

BRYCE CANYON NATIONAL PARK

To Hwy 89
Bryce Canyon Airport
To Antimony

087

12

22

63

Shakespeare Point 7842'

Tropic Ditch

BRYCE CANYON CITY

SHUTTLE PARKING AND BOARDING AREA

Mossy Cave Trailhead 6832'

DAVES HOLLOW

MOSSY CAVE ★

DIXIE NATIONAL FOREST

East Fork Sevier River

SEE DETAILED MAP AREA AT RIGHT

■ **VISITOR CENTER**

Sinking Ship 7405'

JOLLEY HOLLOW

★ **SUNRISE POINT**

★ **SUNSET POINT**

Bristlecone Point

★ **INSPIRATION POINT**

BRYCE POINT

TROPIC VALLEY

Bryce

Cre

PAUNSAUGUNT PLATEAU

Tropic Reservoir

★ **PARIA VIEW**

Under-the-Rim Trail (Bryce Point to Rainbow)

◇ Hat Shop

WHITEMAN BENCH

SWAMP CANYON 7998' ★

Sheep Creek Connecting Trail

Right Fork Yellow Creek

Swamp Canyon Connecting Trail

Right Fork Swamp Canyon

Yellow Creek

Yellow Creek Group Site 6800'

Swamp Canyon

▲ **Sheep Creek**

◇ *Swamp Canyon Butte*

Yellow Creek

Whiteman Connecting Trail

◇ *Mud Canyon Butte 8330'*

MUD CANYON

Sheep Creek

PIRACY POINT ★

◇ *Noon Canyon Butte 8466'*

NOON CANYON

SHEEP CREEK FLAT

★ **FARVIEW POINT** 8819'

GARFIELD COUNTY
KANE COUNTY

★ **NATURAL BRIDGE**

Natural Bridge

DIXIE NATIONAL FOREST

Willis

Agua Canyon Connecting Trail

★ **AGUA CANYON**

GRAND STAIRCASE-ESCALANTE

PONDEROSA CANYON

▲ *Deer Mountain 7833'*

NATIONAL MONUMENT

Creek

PONDEROSA CANYON 8904' ★

Iron Spring

PONDEROSA RIDGE

▲ *Horse Mountain*

BLACK BIRCH CANYON ★

▲ Iron Spring

East Fork Sevier River

Under-the-Rim Trail (Rainbow Point to Bryce Point)

RAINBOW POINT 9115' ★

Bristlecone Loop Trail

THE PROMONTORY

YOVIMPA POINT ★

Corral Hollow

Yovimpa Pass ▲

Riggs Spring Loop Trail

Yovimpa Pass

Yovimpa Spring

▲ *Twin Hills*

N

0   2 m

0   2 km

▲ **Group Site**

Riggs Spring

Riggs Spring

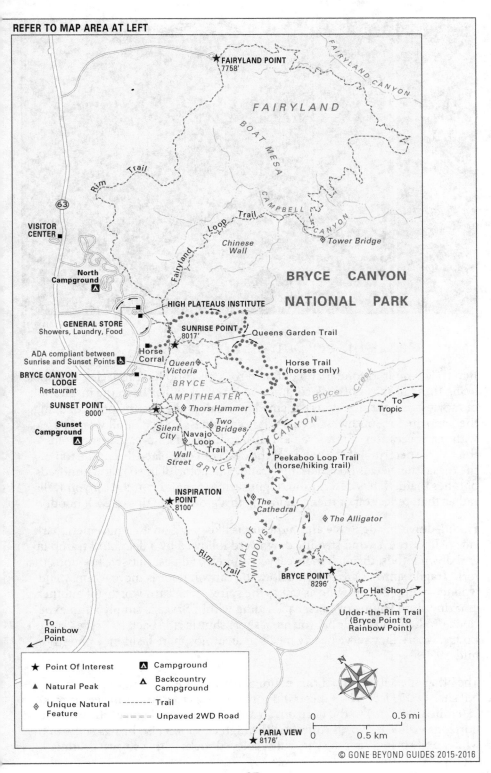

FAIRLAND POINT
7758'

FAIRYLAND

BOAT MESA

FAIRLAND CANYON

CAMPBELL CANYON

63

VISITOR
CENTER

Rim   Trail

Loop   Trail

Chinese
Wall

Tower Bridge

BRYCE   CANYON

North
Campground

Fairyland

NATIONAL   PARK

HIGH PLATEAUS INSTITUTE

GENERAL STORE
Showers, Laundry, Food

SUNRISE POINT
8017'

Queens Garden Trail

ADA compliant between
Sunrise and Sunset Points

Horse
Corral

Queen
Victoria

Horse Trail
(horses only)

BRYCE CANYON
LODGE
Restaurant

BRYCE
AMPITHEATER

Bryce   Creek

To
Tropic

SUNSET POINT
8000'

Thors Hammer

Two
Bridges

CANYON

Sunset
Campground

Silent
City

Navajo
Loop
Trail

Wall
Street

BRYCE

Peekaboo Loop Trail
(horse/hiking trail)

INSPIRATION
POINT
8100'

The
Cathedral

The Alligator

WALL   OF   WINDOWS

Rim   Trail

BRYCE POINT
8296'

To Hat Shop

To
Rainbow
Point

Under-the-Rim Trail
(Bryce Point to
Rainbow Point)

★ Point Of Interest

▲ Natural Peak

◇ Unique Natural
   Feature

△ Campground

△ Backcountry
   Campground

------ Trail

==== Unpaved 2WD Road

N

0   0.5 mi

0   0.5 km

PARIA VIEW
8176'

© GONE BEYOND GUIDES 2015-2016

Bryce Canyon

What Makes Bryce Canyon Special

Bryce Canyon is a wonderland of fluted rock and hoodoo pinnacles, hoodoos being thin tall spires of rock common in this park. It has been the inspiration of movies, desert rides, desert-themed musicals and art to the point of being the template for Southwest scenery. It is grandness and color all wrapped within a succession of massive natural amphitheaters. Bryce Canyon holds the entire spectrum of the colors of the desert in one place. From the top of the mesa, the view is breathtaking, grand, and colorful in so many hundreds of tones that it defies description. Light seems to emit from the canyon walls rather than reflect off of them, radiating to a glow at the tips of each hoodoo.

Hiking down inside Bryce amphitheater is like going on an amusement park ride. All journeys wind steadily downward followed by a delightful tramp up and down knolls, through man-carved tunnels and past massive hoodoos that form fragile spires. Once down below, the canyon floor is more whimsy and wonder with pines growing as tall as the spires, each turn worthy of another amazing shot. Hiking or horseback riding within Bryce is simply a fun experience. When you are done, you are a short shuttle ride back to Bryce Canyon Lodge, where they serve hearty meals in an atmosphere fashioned after the mid-1920s.

The other special quality of this national park is its elevation. Bryce Canyon NP sits at 9000 feet (2743 meters). From the mesa tops, one can see clear out 150 miles (241 km) to the horizon, an amazing view and one of the farthest horizons visible in North America. The high elevation also brings snow in the winter and spring, capping the fruity-colored rocks with a sugary coating.

In the summer, Bryce Canyon NP is typically cooler than the neighboring parks and acts as a wonderful reprieve from the heat of the lower Utah deserts. The water tastes wonderful and is always cold. You can listen to pine needles sing in the wind, and while you may find yourself catching a breath due to the elevation, rest assured each one is delightfully crisp and clean. At night, the sky is one of the darkest places in the contiguous United States. The Milky Way is clearly visible and all the stars seem closer and brighter. For this reason, Bryce is a favorite of astronomers looking for a better glimpse of the heavens. Whether touring overlooks via the shuttle bus, hiking into the hoodoos themselves or stepping out into the vastness of a starry night, Bryce will help reset the traveler and affirm that the decision to tour the Grand Circle was a great one.

Staying in Bryce

Bryce Canyon Lodge and two RV friendly campgrounds are located within the park, plus there is more lodging and camping just outside its boundaries. North Campground has the most RV sites and is closest to the visitor center. Sunset has fewer sites but is closer to many of the hiking trails. Finally, there is Ruby's Inn, which is only a half-mile (0.8 km) from the park and provides an abundance of amenities, including creature comforts such as pizza. RVing inside the park is $15 a night though there are no hookups. Ruby's offers full hookups but is considerably more. For those whose idea of camping is trekking to the ice machine, Ruby's also offers lodging. See below for details.

Staying Inside the Park

Bryce Canyon Lodge

The Bryce Canyon Lodge is the only original lodge designed by Architect Stanley Gilbert Underwood that remains standing within the Grand Circle. To be fair, many of the lodges have been rebuilt with Underwood's design and intentions in mind. That said, Bryce Canyon Lodge is an original. Located inside the park, the Bryce Canyon Lodge is everything you would imagine it to be. It is filled with character and nearly 100 years of history. Simple yet artistic, non-demanding yet graceful, a great example of the Arts and Craft period of architecture done only as Underwood could have done it.

The lodge contains rooms, suites and cabins, 114 in all. The cabins are one of the better bets for a family, containing two queen beds and a little more privacy. The cabins come with a full bath and semi-private porch plus a heater. Many of the lodge rooms come with two queen beds plus have a refrigerator, the one thing the cabins do not have. None of the rooms have a TV or air-conditioning. Both the cabins and the rooms fill up pretty quickly, so definitely plan ahead to get a reservation. The other thing to note is the lodge is not open year round, closing in winter and reopening in early spring. For reservations, go to http://www.brycecanyonforever.com/lodging/.

Panorama of Bryce Canyon

North Campground

North Campground is right inside the entrance to the park (as well as its exit, there is only one-way in and out of Bryce Canyon NP). It sits across from the visitor center and is within walking distance of both the center and the shuttle. There are 99 sites, 52 of which are designated for RVs, found in Loops A and B. Of these, 13 sites can be reserved during the summer months in Loop A, but they go very quickly, so count yourself either lucky or a very good planner if you get one. To reserve, call (877) 444-6777 or click www.recreation.gov. All sites for both campgrunds are $30 for RV's and $20 for tents.

There is a central dump station but it isn't always open, especially early in the season and in the winter. There is also potable water available and a slop sink near the flush toilets. Beyond that, there are no hookups for water or electricity, though each site does come with a picnic table and fire ring.

The sites are all within a tidy, fresh smelling pine forest. Nearby is a walking trail to the visitor center. The campgrounds are not guaranteed to be open during the winter months due to snow. Laundry and showers can be had at nearby Ruby's Inn.

Sunset Campground

Like North Campground, the campsites at Sunset Campground are nestled among the pines and are fairly well laid out. Sunset is about 1.5 miles (2.41 km) farther down from the visitor center and is closer to some of the more popular hiking trails. There are 100 sites total, 48 of them designed for RVs, all in Loop A. While there are 20 tent sites that can be reserved, all RV sites at this campground are first come first served. Sunset Campground is at a similar elevation as North and may be closed due to snow. A dump station is available during the summer months for a $5 use fee.

If you are wondering which campground is better, they both have tradeoffs. Sunset is closer to the general store, laundry and showers as well as closer to the canyon itself and all of its trails. North is probably slightly better suited for families with small children who like to take in a deeper exploration of the visitor center and gift shop. That said, these are small tradeoffs.

Staying Outside the Park

The selection of places to sleep and eat are less than at Zion NP, but there are still plenty to be found. For a complete list of motels and lodges, go here: http://www.brycecanyoncountry.com/. For most folks, Ruby's is the place and is detailed below.

Ruby's Inn, RV Park and Campground

300 South Main Street, Bryce Canyon City, UT 84764, Phone: (435) 834-5301

Ruby's Best Western is pretty basic, but otherwise fits the bill for cleanliness and good value. What really makes Ruby's stand out are the folks that run it. The staff are super friendly and have done a great job at making this a fun place to stay, especially for families. Small rooms come with two queen beds with larger suites also available. There are small touches that fill out the experience, such as cribs, rollaway beds and adjoining rooms. Ruby's is a great hotel.

If you are looking for more of an upscale approach to RVing and need full hookups, Ruby's is your best bet. It is so close to Bryce Canyon NP that the shuttle stops there as part of its regular route. Ruby's does a great job of being able to accommodate just about any need, including larger RVs and folks who are looking for optional hookups (water, electrical and wastewater). Nearby is a fairly decent selection of restaurants, including a steak house and a pizza place. Hot showers, laundry, cable, a heated swimming pool and clean restrooms round out the offering.

All this RV luxury does come at a price. Prices start at around $40 per night and go up depending on amenities selected and the number of people in your party. Ruby's also has cabins, an inn and even a set of tipis for the adventurous at heart. While you may think this could be a full-blown cheesy tourist trap, Ruby's staff really does a fantastic job of creating a fun experience. For many, it is a highlight of their trip within the Grand Circle.

Bryce Canyon Geology

When looking at Bryce Canyon from a geologic point of view, the first problem to overcome is its name. Bryce Canyon is not a canyon; it's the edge of a mesa. The various campgrounds, visitor center and overlooks are located at the top of the Paunsaugunt Plateau (pronounced "PAWN-suh-gant"). At the plateau's rim, water runoff has eroded away the edge of the Paunsaugunt creating the fins and hoodoos that make up Bryce Canyon.

The Paunsaugunt Plateau is the earliest member of the Grand Staircase, an enormous dissection of rock layers starting from the Grand Canyon to Bryce Canyon. The Grand Canyon holds the oldest layers while Bryce Canyon is made up of the youngest layers. The Paunsaugunt Plateau is cut by the East Fork Sevier River to the west.

While both Zion and Bryce Canyon were formed by water erosion, Zion was carved primarily by the Virgin River, whereas Bryce Canyon was carved by rainfall and snowmelt eroding away at the edge of a plateau. Much of the hoodoos and fins you see before you were formed 60 million years ago. Water runs off the rim finding the path of least resistance, which is typically the softest portion of the plateau's edge. These paths become gullies for the water runoff, which enlarge over time from the scouring of softer rock by any debris as it flows downhill. Gullies slowly widen to become canyons and, at the same time, continue to eat away the rim's western edge.

The Grand Staircase

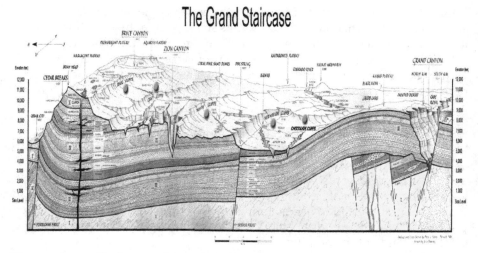

The canyon walls that are formed are not frozen in time but are themselves subjects of erosion. The park has about 200 days each year that temperature is below freezing. As you know, water expands when it freezes. This simple law of nature does an amazing amount of the carving of Bryce Canyon. Water fills the vertical cracks within the canyon walls and then freezes overnight. The pressures on the rock are enough to peel off layers, which over time create the hoodoos and narrow the canyon walls to fins. In the wintertime, it is actually possible to hear the walls crack under the might of water.

As mentioned, the erosion of the plateau's rim continues every day, pushing the creation of gullies, fins and hoodoos in a westward direction. The plateau including Bryce Canyon is eroding at a fairly rapid rate of 2–4 feet (0.6–1.3 m) every 100 years, primarily due to the softness of the rock layer itself. What this means is the canyon's creation will continue westward and one day erode into the campgrounds, lodge and visitor center. Eventually, Bryce Canyon will erode all the way to the East Fork Sevier River itself. When this happens, the river will become the dominant erosional factor, which will likely wash away the hoodoos and fins. Not to worry, though, you still have plenty of time to enjoy the scenery. The estimated time for Bryce to meet with the Sevier River is a very long 3 million years from now. Still, it is interesting to note that what you look down upon from the overlooks is not at all a constant. Each day brings change to Bryce Canyon.

Bryce Canyon History

Early Inhabitants

There is a fair amount of evidence to suggest that the Ancestral Puebloan Indians hunted in Bryce Canyon and lived in the nearby vicinity 2000 years ago. The Fremont Indians and then the Paiute Indians were the next sets of inhabitants.

Bryce Cabin circa 1881

The Paiutes tell of the real reason for the existence of Bryce Canyon. There was an ancient people known as the To-when-an-ung-wa. They were a greedy selfish lot who did not care about sharing their environment. They ate all the food and drank all the water, leaving little for the animals that lived with them. The animals took their complaints to Coyote, who is a powerful trickster god. They explained the rude behavior of the To-when-an-ung-wa, and Coyote agreed he would do something about it.

Coyote invited the entire tribe of the To-when-an-ung-wa to a huge feast, a feast that had all manner of food and drink and lasted all day. The To-when-an-ung-wa were very excited for such a feast and came to the location Coyote specified. They dressed in their best outfits and painted their faces and bodies with the colorful red, orange and yellow war paints for the occasion. Before they could take one bite, however, Coyote cast a spell on each of them, turning them to rock. The people of the To-when-an-ung-wa can be seen climbing on top of each other to get to the top of the plateau.

Some of the Paiutes could identify the past personages of the hoodoos they saw and named off many of them to Wesley Powell when he came through the area. They felt the place was haunted and indeed, even the current definition of hoodoo means both a rock formation and a spell cast on others. Perhap the cracking of the rocks at night are the sounds of the To-when-an-ung-wa trying in desperation to free themselves from the spell that binds them to the edge of the Paunsaugunt Plateau.

Mormon Life and Park Creation

Bryce Canyon was not a preferred spot for Mormon settlement and was left alone during the initial years. By 1875, Ebenezer Bryce saw the area both as land suitable for raising cattle and as a climate more suitable for his wife's fragile health. He moved down from Salt Lake City with a handful of other families to form a life in the valley near the current town of Cannonville, Utah. He built a seven-mile (11.2 km) irrigation ditch from the Paria River to provide water for his livestock and crops.

The amazing scenery near his settlement was soon referred to as Bryce's Canyon. Ebenezer once remarked the area was "a hell of a place to lose a cow." Looking for lost cattle was for the most part the only way Ebenezer Bryce could explore his canyon as most of his days were spent scratching out a life in this remote area.

Douglas Fir in Navajo Trail

There was a small amount of surveying in the canyon, but for the most part, Bryce Canyon was virtually unknown to most of America. While other major destinations of scenic wonder had nearby towns and railroad access, Bryce had only a roughly hewn wagon road to the rim of the Paunsaugunt Plateau. This changed in 1915 when J. W. Humphrey became the Forest Supervisor for the Sevier National Forest. Upon visiting Bryce Canyon, Humphrey knew he had to promote it to others. He built the first trail and the first real road to the rim, and he organized the distribution of the first promotion through articles in the Union Pacific Railroad publication.

By 1919, the unique qualities of Bryce Canyon enabled Utah State to enact legislation for its preservation. The canyon was then established as a National Monument in June 1923 by President Warren G. Harding and finally became Bryce Canyon National Park in 1927. At the time, Bryce Canyon received 24,000 visitors. Today it receives more than 1.5 million visitors each year and has become an icon of the west.

Wall Street Section of Navajo Trail

Things to Do in Bryce Canyon

There is plenty of enjoyment to be had simply taking the shuttle to each of the overlooks within the park and looking out at the different amphitheaters of colored rock. On a clear day, it is possible to see more than 150 miles (241 km) to the horizon, and the views beneath you are as spectacular as they are unique. If you do get a chance, however, hiking down into Bryce Canyon is well worth it.

Keep in mind that all hikes down are steep, so if you don't like hills, stick to the rim trail. Getting down into the amphitheaters gives an up close and personal view of the numerous hoodoos, fins, and colors of Bryce Canyon and really enriches the visit to this spectacular national park. Many of the hikes, such as Queen's Garden, are fairly easy; however, the longer hikes like Peekaboo and Fairyland Loop give more solitude and a deeper immersion into the landscape.

Bryce Point in Winter

If you do go hiking, bring plenty of water. Bring 1 quart/liter per person, per 2-3 hours of hiking. It's also good to bring additional layers in the cooler months as it does get chilly. Sunscreen and a nice brimmed hat are a must as well.

Queen's Garden Trail

Easy – (1.8 mi / 2.9 km), round trip, allow 2 hours

Queen's Garden is 0.9 miles (1.4 km) down and the same distance back up. The trail is the least strenuous in terms of steepness compared to the other trails that head into the canyon, but it is by no means a flat trail. Picking up the Queen's Garden trail from Sunrise Point, hike down and wind your way through tunnels to the hoodoo called Queen Victoria and the surrounding rock formations that make up her garden. You can follow the trail back to the top, though many folks opt to combine this trail with the Navajo Trail to create a loop.

Rim Trail

Easy – (0.9 mi / 1.5 km), one way, allow 1 hour

The Rim Trail from Sunrise Point to Sunset Point is flat and offers a leisurely way to take in the park. Pick up the trail from either point and follow the well-marked path. The Rim Trail does continue south from Sunset Point for a total of 5.5 miles (9.2km) one-way, but the trail from here has a lot of ups and downs and is considered strenuous.

Navajo Trail

Moderate – (1.3 mi / 2.2 km), round trip, allow 1.5 hours

While the NPS designates the Navajo Trail as moderate and Queen's Trail as easy, they are both similar in that you go down and come back up. That said, it may be a tad easier to go up Queen's Trail than up Navajo Trail. Navajo contains an incredible slot canyon that holds at its bottom singular stands of old growth Douglas fir. These massive trees grow as tall and mighty as the hoodoos they stand next to, and the combination of green might against brightly colored rock is a photographer's dream. The Navajo Trail is picked up from Sunset Point and, as stated earlier, is often combined with Queen's Trail to make a loop. Both of these trails are quite popular and receive a fair amount of traffic.

Sunrise Point and Sunset Point

During the day both Sunrise Point and Sunset Point are popular destinations and, like all of the shuttle stops with vistas, their views are amazing. Many people tend to flock to Sunset Point at sunset and Sunrise Point at sunrise; however, there is no real advantage to doing this. Given that Bryce Canyon is carved out the eastern edge of the plateau, the sun will set behind you and rise in front of you as you gaze out. If you are going during the popular summer months, try going to Sunset Point for the sunrise and Sunrise Point for the sunset. You will enjoy the same amazing view but with fewer people.

If you are looking to photograph, the lighting tends to be warmer and richer in the fall and spring and sharper and more direct in the summer. Winter also allows for great photography with the combination of rock color and contrasting white of the snow. Winter and summer rains also moisten the rock, bringing out a richer color.

Rush Hour

Peekaboo Trail

Strenuous – (5.5 mi / 8.8 km), round trip, allow 3 – 4 hours

Peekaboo is one of the best trails in Bryce Canyon. The loop is picked up from either Bryce Point or Sunset via the Navajo Trail. The trail gives the hiker a sense of remoteness and a personal experience as you walk up and down gullies and past goblins, fins and rows of hoodoos. Every bend rewards the hiker with a different view of often-unimaginable rock shapes.

In addition, you will find yourself a ways from the rim, in the heart of the amphitheater, which gives a better sense of grandness of Bryce Canyon. The loop can be done on its own or combined with Navajo or Queen's Garden Trails. Peekaboo is not terribly crowded, though it does get a fair amount of horse traffic.

Fairyland Loop

Strenuous – (8 mi /12.9 km), round trip, allow 5 hours

Fairyland Loop is similar to Peekaboo but as it is a little longer, offers even more to the hiker. There is plenty to see on the trail, including China Wall, an impressively long wall of rock. You can also see a double arch with unique monolithic sentinels called Tower Bridge. Fairyland Loop is the least crowded trail of the popular trails at Bryce Canyon and is well worth it if you want to do a longer hike. Pick up the trail at Fairyland Point. The trail uses the Rim Trail to create a full loop.

Hat Shop Trail

Moderate – (4.0 mi /6.4 km), round trip, allow 2 - 3 hours

From Bryce Point, descend via the Under the Rim Trail for 2 miles to a set of thin spired hoodoos with delicately balanced capstones defying gravity. The hike is a down and up, there and back hike. There are ample other Bryce Canyon type features along the way to the final destination.

Swamp Canyon

Moderate – (4.3 mi / 7.2 km), round trip, allow 2 - 3 hours

Swamp Canyon Trail starts at about the mid-point in the park, further south of the main amphitheaters. This loop trail offers a mixture of denser forest and the famous hoodoos. Unlike the endless stream of hikers coming down Navajo Trail, Swamp Canyon is definitely more intimate and may be a better option on crowded days.

Tower Bridge

Moderate – (3.0 mi / 4.8 km), round trip, allow 2 – 3 hours

See Fairyland Loop for additional details. The trail starts at Sunrise Point and follows Fairlyland Loop partially down until a juncture to a short spur trail to view Tower Bridge. Tower Bridge is a formation of two colorful hoodoos connected by a fragile layer of rock mid-way down the "towers". There is another natural bridge that can be seen in the same view. Head back up the same way you came down or continue onwards on the longer Fairyland Loop.

Bryce Canyon Lodge

Bryce Canyon Lodge is certainly worthy of a visit. The lodge was built from local materials in 1924 and was designed by architect Gilbert Stanley Underwood. This is the only original Grand Circle lodge left that Underwood designed. The ones at Zion NP and the North Rim of the Grand Canyon were destroyed by fire and rebuilt. The lodge serves hearty meals throughout the day and the staff is very courteous. Eating in the open dining hall with its wooden beams and high ceilings is really a unique experience. Much of the lodge is done in an Arts and Craft style, which tried to combine soulful humility with elegance and grandeur. On cooler days, there is often a hearty fire and it is easy to imagine what life might have been like in the heyday of the 1920s.

Bryce Canyon Lodge

Where's Bryce?

Why you should never name your kids after famous places ..

[Everest]: You love my brother more than me.

[Me]: What! Why do you say that?

[Everest]: You got him a bumper sticker that says Bryce National Park.

[Me]: You realize that it's a three-week trek just to get to the base of Everest and that it's a full day's plane ride to fly over there and that they don't have a gift shop at the base camp and that what you are asking for likely doesn't even exist, right?

[Everest]: Still.

I felt the RV rumble enough to wake me from my dead slumber. Opening one eye, I noticed the slide-out of our RV was mysteriously pulling itself back in. This getting my other eye's attention, I looked up to discover that Bryce, in only his tighty whiteys, was stretched with one skinny leg on the bunk ladder and the other on the kitchen counter. His head was scraping the ceiling. He had figured out how to gain access to the normally inaccessible RV control panel and was operating the slide-out, but why I thought? Before I could give it too much thought, my attention was diverted to the sound of a plastic water bottle being mangled under the moving dining room table. The bottle pleaded to be released from its torment before being crushed fully into silence.

With all sounds stopped, I closed my eyes again. No harm, I thought. I'm sure that water bottle won't destroy any chance of getting our deposit back. Besides, what could I do now at six in the morning? From the sound of things, that bottle wasn't going anywhere. So I again let myself fall into the dreamlands of slumber, but right before I dropped completely, I sensed a presence and reopened an eye. It was Bryce, now inches away, looking at me in casual observation. I wondered how long he had been standing there and how it was I hadn't heard him get down

Bryce's First View of Bryce Canyon

from his acrobatic perch. I then began to wonder if I should be concerned about this ninja-like quality down the road when he was older and could get into more trouble.

With drowsy eye contact made, my youngest decided it was okay to engage in conversation. "So, Dad, you know how you said we could leave early for Bryce?"

I sat up on one elbow and blinked a bunch of times to get a little more focus. "Well, yeah, we did talk about heading out early to make sure we get a campsite. We don't have a reservation at Bryce Canyon."

"Well, umm, I have everything packed up," Bryce said. "We can leave now if you want."

"What do you mean 'everything'?"

"Well, I kinda snuck out, you know, and packed up all the chairs. Then I got water and made sure the fire was fully out. Oh and I unplugged the electrical outlet and plugged it back into the RV and locked up all the storage cabinets and then I pulled in the RV thing."

"Wow!" I said nodding in affirmation. He was obviously proud and I was amazed how quickly he had figured everything out. "Yeah, I heard you pulling it in!"

"Yeah, Dad! It was kind of hard to get to the switch so I kinda, you know, had to stretch across the bed to the counter and well, then I could hit the pull-in switch. At first it didn't work and then I remembered you had to start the engine, so I kinda did that first. Then I got the slide-out pulled in."

I just then realized the RV engine was running and leapt out of bed. I ducked under the stairs to the driver's seat and turned it off. Bryce was beaming with pride over his accomplishments; I had to find a positive way to handle this.

I got down to his height and looked him in the eye. "Bryce, that's awesome you did all that, but next time, don't ever start the RV without my permission okay?"

"Yeah, sure. Sorry, Dad, I just, you know, wanted to get everything ready for you. So can we go, you know to Bryce Cannon? I kinda want to see it."

Bryce was excited to see his namesake and yes, he does, despite being nine years old and having been corrected countless times, pronounces "canyon" as "cannon."

I was on board. Why not? Let's get a move on to our next national park, I thought! Ang rolled over in bed and groaned on seeing my enthusiasm. I did a quick survey of Bryce's handiwork and then sped off at the crack of dawn to the Zion Tunnel.

To get to Bryce you need to go through the Zion Tunnel. To get through the Zion Tunnel in an RV, you need to buy a permit and have the park ranger help you get through the tunnel. This is for one simple reason; the tunnel was built before big fat RVs. The tunnel is very narrow.

As we drove up to this burrow of rock, I learned the hard way that it is always helpful to read the directions with regards to tunnels that may be obstacles to your passage. I had failed to pay attention to the operating hours on the tunnel permit, which meant that we had woken up far earlier than we needed to. We got to the tunnel in record time only to wait for it to open. It was not a terribly long wait, a mere two hours, but two hours my family reminded me were hours they could have slept in had I simply read the permit. I made coffee and eggs as penance.

When the tunnel finally opened and we were allowed to go through it, I set off with much enthusiasm. We were all anxious to get to Bryce. What I failed to figure out is how to engage the headlamps prior to setting out. As your RV slips into a cave-like darkness, you immediately realize this is crucial knowledge to have to avoid crashing into the tunnel. There were no cars in front of me, but as there was a line of cars behind me, I didn't want to be the guy that held up the entire caravan. I scrambled to maintain speed while frantically trying to figure out where the lights were. Just before we lost the remaining slivers of sun, I managed to find the lever that flashes the high beams. This prevented the crashing into the tunnel part, except now I had to steer with one hand and hold the lever with the other all while driving through a tunnel that seems about a quarter inch higher than the RV itself. It was all very dignified and a defining moment for this authoritative figure on how to operate an RV.

"Honk the horn!" Bryce said. I ignored him. With one hand on the light switch and the other on the steering wheel, both hands were occupied.

"Honk the horn, Dad!" Everest commanded.

I'm thinking, "Come on kids, I only have two hands here and the slightest deviation will scrape off the roof. Let's not honk the horn."

Everyone, including my wife now chanted in a choPrused mantra, "Honk-the-horn! Honk-the-horn! Honk-the-horn!"

With pressures mounting, I managed to find a way to honk the horn by quickly letting go of the steering wheel. I honked it a few times all the while without my wife ever knowing how close we came to careening through one of the gallery windows to our fiery deaths as I lost control of the RV. It would have been spec-

tacular. People would have pulled over and looked down on us. We would have exploded when we hit the bottom, and I'm pretty sure Bryce would have jumped out at the last minute, barely clenching to the edge of the cliff. He's good like that.

As we drove the 84 miles to Bryce Canyon National Park, our son Bryce read out loud the 14-page collection of facts he had pulled from the Internet. We asked both kids to help us choose what to do in the various National Parks and sites along the way. Everest did zero research while Bryce spent several days copying and pasting a volume of work all around one subject: Bryce Canyon. He then printed it out and performed mandatory book readings, usually in captive audience situations. We were certainly well informed going into this park.

After about two hours or, as I timed it, four readings, we pulled into Bryce Canyon and found a few campsites available. Finding a good campsite is a bit like finding good parking. If parking is tough, you can take the first one you see way out in the boonies, but you don't know if there is a better one unless you drive around more. Of course, in looking for the better spot, you are giving up the one you just found. Picking an RV spot is the same thing, only you are finding a place to park your home for the night. After looping around the campground several times, we found a level one suitable to everyone's liking and immediately set off to see the views.

We walked to the shuttle stop and waited. I listened to this couple discuss the shuttle route, which went in one continuous circle to Bryce Point and back. It seemed easy enough. On discovering we had about ten minutes to wait, Ang took the boys in to get Junior Ranger activity books.

When she came back she asked, "How long did you say we were in Bryce again?"

"Just today."

"We need to stay longer," she said.

"Why is that?"

"The Junior Ranger activity book requires seeing a ranger program. At the minimum we need to get to Inspiration Point for the next one at 11:30am."

I looked at the clock. It was 10:50.

"Let's see if we can make it. If not we can figure something out."

"We need to make this ranger talk. I want Bryce to get his junior ranger pin. This is his park after all."

"Okay okay. Look, there's the shuttle now." We got on the shuttle. Bryce looked around and immediately became stoic and quiet. All around him his name was plastered in large letters throughout the bus. Back at the visitor center it was on pamphlets, T-shirts, letter openers and refrigerator magnets. Plus he had heard what his mom said. This was his park. He filled out the Junior Ranger activity book as if it held lost treasure. He only looked up when someone used the word Bryce in a sentence.

Our first stop was Bryce Point, and we all walked to our first viewing of the canyon. Bryce folded his hands on the rail and looked deep into the colored hoodoos and spires below. It was a thoughtful repose as if he was looking at a puzzle, a question without an answer. I've never seen my son look at something so deeply.

We lost some time at the first stop, but it was well worth it. It was "Bryce's Point," after all; this was the spot he requested to go to first. The next stop was Inspiration Point where the ranger's talk would be held.

With now just 15 minutes to get to the talk, the shuttle seemed to slow through time. My wife kept twisting my wrist to see what time it was on my watch. Three minutes to talk time. Angela does not like to be late to anything and while technically we could have taken our time in an enjoyable manner and strolled up for the last five minutes of the talk, she would have none of that. We had to be there on time.

"When is this blasted shuttle going to get to the next stop?" she asked. I had been married long enough to know not to answer rhetorical questions as they only encouraged additional questions of an unanswerable nature.

"We're going to miss it. We are going to miss the talk," she said, looking ahead of the bus for anything that would indicate Inspiration Point was close.

"I'm sure we will catch most of it, if not all of it," I said calmly. She was only being Type A out of love for her son.

"What if they run out of seating and we miss the whole thing?"

"We won't miss it dear, don't worry." I saw a sign. "Look, we're here."

As the shuttle pulled to the stop, everyone stood up in preparation to disembark. Ang helped lobby the kids for a quick exit. She clapped her hands to rally their attention and said, "Okay kids, get your water bottles back in your packs. Let's get ready to go. We don't want to miss the ranger talk."

The kids gathered their stuff as the bus pulled up. We all got off the shuttle in a manner of hurried patience as we melded with the crowd around us. Everyone seemed to be getting off the shuttle at this stop. I watched the kids get off and

then ran to catch up with Ang, who was speed walking to the edge of the canyon.

"Come on! We are going to miss it!" she said loudly to the people in front of her. No time to turn around for this woman. She was going to make this talk.

"Okay, okay! Kids, come on." I motioned for Ev to take the lead in front of me. "Come on, Ev."

"Sure, Dad", and then with a slight pause Everest added, "Dad, where's Bryce?" I turned around to see the shuttle bus driving away and then turned my attention to the crowd, quickly surveying it. Bryce was not with us. Then as the shuttle was pulling out of reach I saw him, on the bus.

"Ang! We left Bryce on the bus!"

"No we didn't, he got off with me."

"He's not here, dear. He must have gotten back on the bus."

Ang stopped dead in her tracks so fast everyone behind her had to quickly adjust to avoid running into her. "What?!" she exclaimed.

"He's not here." I tried to sound calming, as if that would help.

"Eric! BB! Oh my God! BB's lost! We need to find him!"

"I'll go see when the next shuttle's coming! See if you can find someone." I ran over to a kiosk that showed the shuttle times. Another shuttle would come in less than 10 minutes.

Ang saw the ranger who was going to give the geology talk. She stopped him in his tracks and said in a panicked flurry of words, "Excuse me! You have to help me please! We've lost Bryce! We've lost our Bryce!"

The ranger looked at her confused and took a step back. "I'm sorry, ma'am. You've lost Bryce?"

"Yes! Where's Bryce? Where's Bryce! We've lost Bryce!" she said in a frantic Southern undertone.

The ranger maintained composure. "Not to worry, ma'am, lots of people get disoriented up here. Bryce is right over there." The ranger pointed to Bryce Canyon. "I'm pretty sure it's not lost."

Ang looked briefly at where he pointed and then turned right back to the ranger. "What! No! You don't understand! Listen! Bryce is gone!"

"Ma'am, I ah..." the ranger looked confused and now a little concerned at my wife's odd behavior. A couple of tourists gathered to help calm Angela down by repeatedly pointing to the rim of Bryce Canyon and saying, "Bryce is right there! Bryce is right there!"

"I'm not looking for the stupid canyon, I'm looking for Bryce! My Bryce!" she exclaimed.

Everest quickly stepped in. "My brother's name is Bryce and he got back on the shuttle," he said, trying to help.

"Please! He's only nine years old!" she cried.

"Oh! You have a son named Bryce!"

"That's what I've been saying! Bryce David! He's lost on the shuttle!"

By this time a small crowd had gathered around my wife to either help or try to make sense of the lost crazy woman. I ran back from the kiosk with a plan to get on the next shuttle and have Ang stay put with Ev. If Bryce got off, I would find him. If he stayed on the shuttle, it would eventually return to Inspiration Point.

This proved unnecessary thanks to the ranger's walkie-talkie. Once the ranger understood that we were indeed looking for our son Bryce, he called the shuttle drivers. After a short back and forth between the drivers and the ranger, there was a sigh of relief. They found him.

I returned as the ranger said into his walkie-talkie, "Put him at Table 3."

"Table 3?" I asked.

"You'll find him at Bryce Lodge. Take the next shuttle and get off at the lodge and find the hostess. Her name is Phyllis. Don't worry, we have a system.   You aren't the first parents to lose your child in Bryce Canyon, but I have to say you are the first to lose one named after Bryce Canyon."

My wife was profoundly grateful. "Thank you! Thank you so much. I'm so glad you found him! I'm sorry I got so excited. Bryce is a Celtic name, you know."

"I'm just glad we found him ma'am. Sorry for not understanding you at first," he chuckled. We were still a little too shaken up to laugh at that point, though it was the topic well into the evening of how we lost Bryce in Bryce and how only Bryce could pull that off.

We found our B Bear at Bryce Canyon Lodge enjoying a hot fudge sundae. He was nonplussed at the situation. "Hey, Mom" he said calmly, giving a short wave.

"We normally just give them a scoop of ice cream," the hostess said. She was a kind maternal woman. "But he was so cute; I gave him a full hot fudge sundae. I hope you don't mind. I couldn't help but spoil him a little. Unless a child is closer to the visitor center, they drop him off here at the lodge. He said he forgot his junior ranger book and that he was named after the park and didn't want to not miss getting his junior ranger badge. You had quite an adventure today, didn't you Bryce?" She patted him on the head.

Bryce took another bite of hot fudge. "Ummmm. I guess so. I'm sorry, Mom! I just wanted to get my badge!"

"BB! We were worried sick about you!" Ang exclaimed, hugging him and then petting his hair.

"Sorry Bro Bro, were you scared?" Everest asked.

"No, not really. They just asked if there was a Bryce Henze on the bus and I said yes and they put me here and gave me ice cream. I figure it's because I'm, well, you know, we're in Bryce Cannon and I'm named Bryce, just like the cannon." He then pointed at the hostess. "She told me I was lost and should be happy that they found me, but come on, guys! I would have just taken the shuttle in a circle back to where you were. It's not like I'm 4!"

Ang chuckled and hugged her little man. "Bryce, what am I going to do with you? You are going to be the death of me."

"Me too!" Everest stated. "I was freaking out!" He let out a big sigh and piled onto mom's hug.

I joined in on the group hug. I was so glad we had found our little guy.

"B Bear," I thought. "Our skinny little bundle of chaos, what are we going to do with you indeed."

Capitol Reef
National Park

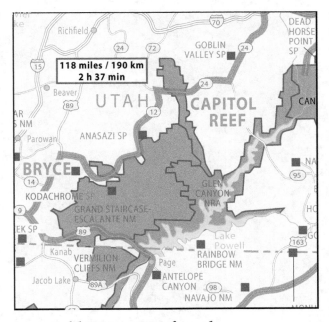

"*To see a world in a grain of sand,*

And a heaven in a wild flower,

Hold infinity in the palm of your hand,

And eternity in an hour."

—William Blake, *Auguries of Innocence*

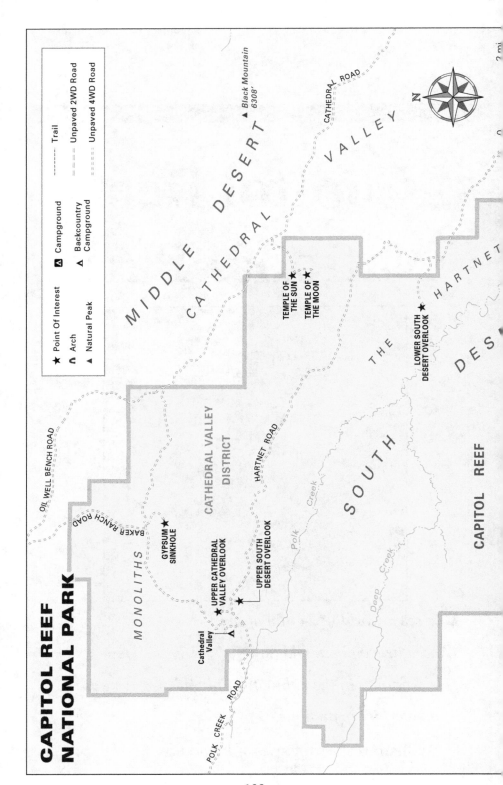

CAPITOL REEF NATIONAL PARK

Legend:
- ★ Point Of Interest
- ⌂ Campground
- ⋂ Arch
- ▲ Backcountry Campground
- ▲ Natural Peak
- ------ Trail
- ==== Unpaved 2WD Road
- ===== Unpaved 4WD Road

MIDDLE DESERT

CATHEDRAL VALLEY

▲ Black Mountain 6308'

CATHEDRAL ROAD

★ TEMPLE OF THE SUN
★ TEMPLE OF THE MOON

HARTNET

★ LOWER SOUTH DESERT OVERLOOK

DES

OIL WELL BENCH ROAD

BAKER RANCH ROAD

MONOLITHS

★ GYPSUM SINKHOLE

CATHEDRAL VALLEY DISTRICT

HARTNET ROAD

★ UPPER CATHEDRAL VALLEY OVERLOOK

UPPER SOUTH DESERT OVERLOOK

▲ Cathedral Valley

THE SOUTH

Polk Creek

Deep Creek

CAPITOL REEF

POLK CREEK ROAD

N

2 mi

108

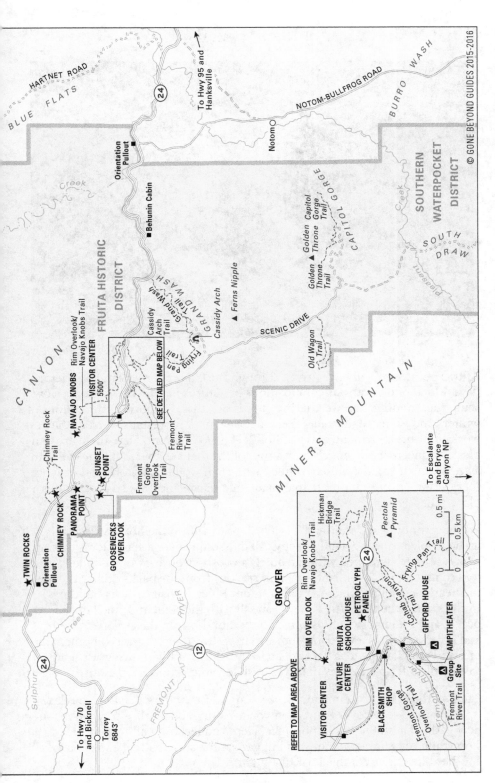

© GONE BEYOND GUIDES 2015-2016

HARTNET ROAD

BLUE FLATS

24

To Hwy 95 and Hanksville →

NOTOM-BULLFROG ROAD

BURRO WASH

Notom

SOUTHERN WATERPOCKET DISTRICT

Creek

SOUTH DRAW

Creek

Orientation Pullout

Behunin Cabin

FRUITA HISTORIC DISTRICT

CAPITOL GORGE

Golden Throne ▲

Golden Capitol Throne Gorge Trail

Golden Throne Trail

▲ Ferns Nipple

Pleasant

GRAND WASH

Grand Wash Trail

Cassidy Arch Trail

Cassidy Arch

SCENIC DRIVE

Old Wagon Trail

C A N Y O N

Rim Overlook/ Navajo Knobs Trail

NAVAJO KNOBS ★

VISITOR CENTER 5500'

SEE DETAILED MAP BELOW

Frying Pan Trail

Fremont River Trail

M I N E R S   M O U N T A I N

To Escalante and Bryce Canyon NP →

SUNSET POINT ★

Fremont Gorge Overlook Trail

PANORAMA POINT ★

Chimney Rock Trail

CHIMNEY ROCK ★

Orientation Pullout

GOOSENECKS OVERLOOK

★ TWIN ROCKS

REFER TO MAP AREA ABOVE

Hickman Bridge Trail

Rim Overlook/ Navajo Knobs Trail

24

▲ Pectols Pyramid

RIM OVERLOOK ★

FRUITA SCHOOLHOUSE ★

PETROGLYPH PANEL ★

Frying Pan Trail

Cohab Canyon Trail

GIFFORD HOUSE

0.5 mi

0.5 km

0

0

GROVER

NATURE CENTER

VISITOR CENTER

BLACKSMITH SHOP

Fremont Gorge Overlook Trail

△ AMPITHEATER

△ Group Site

Fremont River Trail

Creek

RIVER

12

FREMONT

24

To Hwy 70 and Bicknell ↓

Torrey 6843'

Sulphur Creek

109

What Makes Capitol Reef Special

Pendleton Barn in Fruita

At this point, you will have driven through the Colorado Plateau for several days. Much of it is various compositions of nature's handiwork in stone; slow sculpting, sanding, and weathering of red rock that was born from millions of winters and as many summers. Each national park represents some of the best works for our enjoyment, and Capitol Reef is no different. Here there are temples of stone, magnificent cliffs and monoliths that are able to fill the eye with awe. As much as Capitol Reef is filled with such wonders of rock and canyon, there is something a bit more manmade that makes the park so special. It is a place called Fruita.

Fruita (pronounced "fruit-ahh") is a lush oasis within the hot dry desert. It is green, cool, and wonderfully sleepy. All day somewhere a sprinkler is casting sprays of water wrapped within a quiet "swoosh-swoosh-swoosh" lullaby. Visitors can pick their own fruit (when in season) from the park's orchards, view the nearby rambling waters of the Fremont River or visit historic buildings. In the spring, the tidy little valley is awash with the sight and smell of cherry, peach, apple and apricot blossoms. The rest of the year, the air smells fresh and green, which is a welcome reprieve from the desert. They sell homemade pies and your campsite is flat and surrounded by freshly mown grass. Large tree trunks lift up a canopy of leaves to shade you. Fruita is a paradise.

After all the hiking in Zion and Bryce, Capitol Reef offers a chance to relax. It is a place to rediscover the reason you took time off work, a place to reconnect with what in life has importance. Here you feel okay allowing time to stop while you simply do nothing but gaze at the surrounding cliffs and take another bite of pie. All this for $10 a night.

Staying in Capitol Reef

While Zion has a plethora of lodging and Bryce has a fair assortment, the weary traveler realizes that the variety has narrowed by the time you get to Capitol Reef NP. For those travelling by RV or tent, it can be said that you have chosen wisely as Fruita is one of the nicest campgrounds in Utah. For those looking for a motel, there are several and they do the job nicely, but they are a good 10 miles outside the park in Torrey, UT.

Also unlike Zion and Bryce, Capitol Reef doesn't have a lodge. Putting this all together in a good light, the lack of lodging is part of what makes Capitol Reef special. It is one of the over looked national parks, but is indeed as great a national park as any that garner the title. For this reason it is a hidden gem amongst the Grand Circle and I hasten to even write about it, lest I spill the secret out and the area becomes laden with all manner of hotels and inns. Capitol Reef contains areas that you can have all to yourself at times and those that stay a night or two within it are indeed the lucky few. This too is one of the main reasons why this book pushes the RV mode of travelling, it gives the family vacationer increased choice and consistency in the more remote areas along the Grand Circle journey.

Staying Inside the Park

Fruita

As mentioned, the campsites of Fruita are the best option available. Fruita is nestled in a small canyon near the Fremont River. The entire area is encapsulated by massive red rock cliffs that are spectacular in the late afternoon light. There are 71 sites, all available on a first come,

Fruita Orchards

first served basis. There are three loops that all offer great sites. Loops A and B are open year round, loop C and the group site closes from late fall to early spring. The campground is within a short walk of the Gifford house and the orchards. Across from the barn is a colony of marmots living in the nearby hills. Please watch from a distance so as not to disturb their community.

Fruita was listed in Sunset Magazine's 2013 Camping Guide as one of the best places in the nation to camp. While the official thumbs up are welcome in some ways, it means the word is out on this campground. Plan to arrive early; typically the place fills up by 10am in spring and fall.

There is a campground host and a self-service kiosk for the easy payment of $20. The campground also has two dumping stations, which is included in the camping fee. Generator hours are strictly enforced. You can only run your generator for two hours in the morning and two hours in the evening (8-10 am and 6-8 pm). The limited generator hours does add to the overall peace and harmony of the place, but it makes it hard to charge electronic devices.

Staying Outside the Park

All of the hotels outside the park are in or near Torrey, UT, a very small town about 10 miles from the park's entrance. All of the hotels in this area are nice clean establishments and offer a decent place to sleep for the night with great local hospitality. Many are open seasonally, so check before you go. The best site for all lodging information is Torrey's town website itself: http://www. torreyutah.gov/. A few notable standouts are listed below:

Capitol Reef Resort

2600 E Highway 24, Torrey, UT 84775, Phone: (435) 425-3761

Closest and one of the nicer places to stay in the area. Rooms are clean and the views are expansive. There is a large swimming pool and restaurant onsite. What makes this place incredible is the ability to sip a cup of morning coffee while taking in the incredible red rock views.

Austin's Chuckwagon Lodge and General Store

12 West Main St., Torrey, UT 84775, Phone: (435) 425-3335

Austin's Chuckwagon Lodge has all the ingredients for a perfect family vacation destination. Lodge amenities include a heated swimming pool, bakery, deli, free Wi-Fi, and a great staff. It is in the center of Torrey, UT which is a fun small town to check out in its own right. The owners have recently built a few cabins as well. All rooms, including the cabins, are affordable.

Wonderland RV Park, Torrey, Utah

44 Utah 12, Torrey, UT 84775 Phone: (435) 425-3665

If you find yourself out of luck at Fruita or craving more amenities, the Wonderland RV Park in Torrey, Utah is a good alternative. This park accommodates large RVs, has great Internet and free cable and is reasonably priced with sites starting at $35 per night. There are only 35 sites with full hookups and while hot showers and clean restrooms are available, there is only one set of each. Long lines for both the showers and bathrooms have been observed.

Capitol Reef Geology

It's interesting to write about Capitol Reef National Park from a geologic standpoint because this national park was created primarily to protect a very special form of geology. In fact, it's the largest form of this type of geology in North America. What is this amazing geological feature you ask? Why, it's a monocline! I know, fascinating right?! Okay, if you are like 99 percent of the population and saying to yourself, "What the heck is a monocline?" keep reading.

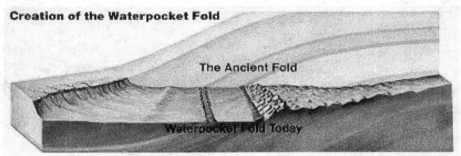

Cross Section of Waterpocket Fold

To best describe a monocline, look no further than Capitol Reef's very own Ripple Rock Nature Center. Designed for kids, they have a big layered piece of colored foam to help folks understand the definition of a monocline. If you simply set the foam down on a table, you can visualize layer after layer of sediment placed one on top of each other over the eons. If you push one end of the foam off the table, it bends. That bend is described as a monocline when it happens on a geologic scale.

There are other types of "clines" which are equally easy to explain. If you took the foam and bent it upward into a hill shape, you would have an anticline. If you bent it the other way to look like the letter "U," you would have a syncline. You are quickly becoming an expert in geology; you now know all the major clines!

Let's get back to Capitol Reef. Capitol Reef National Park protects a monocline called the Waterpocket Fold. If you think the foam version that you created in your head was cool, imagine it being comprised of a whopping 7,000 feet worth of different sedimentary deposits. These strata were then eroded along the bend exposing each of the layers. Going back to the foam example, it is as if a big chunk of the foam was removed, revealing all of the different layers at the surface. The oldest strata exposed are on the western side of the monocline with the youngest on the eastern side. The Waterpocket Fold is exposed north to south stretching for 100 miles (160 km).

Waterpocket Fold Looking South From the Strike Valley Overlook

The Waterpocket Fold is one of many monoclines that developed during the creation of the Rocky Mountains. As one tectonic plate pushed under the other, the Rocky Mountains rose as a result. While the brunt of the action was at the point of impact between the two plates, there were also gentle upward folds of rock layers that occurred downstream from the major action, folding the rock layers like waves.

The Waterpocket Fold was then eroded over time to expose the angled rock strata that you see today at Capitol Reef NP. These massive layers of rock, thrust up at acute angles, presented a huge challenge to pioneers who were driving westward. The Waterpocket Fold, with its length of 100 miles (160 km) was a barrier that could take days to get around. They saw this great land barrier as similar to the oceanic reefs around which some of the settlers had sailed previously. To the pioneers, the Waterpocket Fold was a land reef and thus the meaning of the second part of the park's name. By the way, the first part of Capitol Reef's name is also geologic in nature. The Navajo Sandstone layers at the tops of Capitol Reef NP have eroded away into soft white domes, resembling the United States Capitol.

While the Waterpocket Fold is the major geologic feature and is completely encompassed by Capitol Reef National Park, each individual layer is fascinating in its own right. For the geologic enthusiast, the best place to start understanding these layers is the Capitol Reef Visitor Center. The rangers hold a wealth of information and are happy to share what they know. For the casual observer, the biggest thing to keep in mind is that the oldest rock layers are on the western side of the park and the youngest on the east. If you are coming from Bryce and heading to Canyonlands, keep this in mind as you drive in and out of the park. The oldest rock layers in Capitol Reef date back some 270 million years. By the time you leave the park, the layers are merely 80 million years old.

Capitol Reef History

Native Inhabitants

The earliest recorded evidence of habitation in Utah dates back 12,000 years. These were among the first North Americans, traveling over land bridges of ice created during the last Ice Age. Evidence is hard to find, but research suggests a people who lived in caves and natural rock shelters. They hunted mammoth and smaller game with sharpened chert arrowheads. There is no evidence that these early people lived in the Capitol Reef area, but there is enough to piece together the plausibility that they at least migrated through the Waterpocket Fold.

As the climate changed, so did the ecosystem. The native inhabitants changed with their environment and are characterized as people known as the Desert Archaic Indians. Living some 8,000 to 1,600 years ago, there is more evidence on these peoples that allow archaeologists to piece together their life. They were fairly nomadic, following the migration patterns of the animals they hunted. They had extensive knowledge of the plant life around them and from this wove baskets and clothing. They relied on plants for food, harvesting and grinding nuts and seeds into a flour.

They hunted game with throwing spears called atlatls. An atlatl is pretty ingenious. It comes in two parts and is similar in principle to a modern day tennis ball throwing stick for dogs. There is the dart, or spear, which has a sharpened point. The other piece

Atlatl

is the atlatl which is a straight handle-like stick. One end has a buttress for the spear to rest against. The other end is where the hunter holds the device. A hunter holds the atlatl and the spear in one hand and casts the spear in a similar motion you would use to throw a ball or stick. The lever-like action of the atlatl creates a fast-moving extension of the throwing arm. This extra length increases the force of the dart and the distance it can travel.

Evidence suggests that the native inhabitants began to incorporate farming into their lifestyle around 2,000 years ago. These inhabitants are referred to as the Fremont culture, named after the nearby Fremont River.

The Fremont culture expanded on their ancestral knowledge. They continued to hunt and live off of gathered plants and to follow the migrations of animals and seasonal patterns. There is evidence they used rock shelters as before. They also began to build their own shelters by digging pit houses, which are areas dug into the ground and then covered with brush. There is evidence that they lived within a social structure consisting of several families. Living by the Fremont River, they grew squash varieties, beans and corn to augment their diets.

There are four traits that distinguish the Fremont from other native cultures. They utilized willow, yucca and other natural fibers to create a unique style of basketry referred to as one-rod-and-bundle. This style of construction wraps fibers around willow or other naturally bendable rods in the form of a circle. They created moccasins from the hock of a deer or mountain sheep leg. Other tribes also made moccasins but in a very different method, using woven yucca. The third trait can be seen in their petroglyphs, examples of which can be seen right off of Utah Highway 24. The panels represent figures in trapezoidal shapes, which are unique to the Fremont. Lastly, their gray coil pottery is constructed in a fashion similar to that of other cultures but with unique patterns.

Petroglyph in Capitol Gorge

Evidence of the Fremont culture ceases to exist around CE 1300. There is no one archaeological study that has managed to explain why the Fremont ended their lifeway. It will likely continue to remain a mystery to both researchers and casual observers for generations to come.

Explorers, Surveyors and Pioneers

The historic period of early exploration of the Southwest was an exciting time. There were formal expeditions to find routes for man and rail. There were other less formal expeditions carried out by true frontiersman who took several years to cross from the East Coast to the west, hunting and trapping along the way, always a rifle in hand. They found a warm protected valley during the winter and built their only shelter for the season to protect them from the cold. While the tales of these informal expeditions are captured only in journals, they tell of a country that was truly grand and untamed, pure.

Of the formal expeditions, there are two of note. One was led by a couple of Franciscan Priests sent to find a route from Santa Fe to the second California Mission San Carlos Borromeo de Carmelo in 1770. Francisco Atanasio

Domínguez and Silvestre Vélez de Escalante set out with a handful of men in 1776, and while they neither went through the Waterpocket Fold per se nor made it to Carmel, California, they did cross through what is now Utah. Their detailed records added greatly to the relatively scant knowledge of Utah, which comprised the last territories to be charted in the lower 48 states.

Explorer John C. Fremont set out in the winter of 1853 to find a passable winter route for the railroad. This was Fremont's fifth expedition within the western territories and the second attempt at finding a decent railway route to California from Saint Louis, and he was well prepared for the challenge. However, the Waterpocket Fold with its repeated impassability of rock and a particularly harsh winter made the journey difficult to the point that they lost one of their men and were forced to eat their horses. They did get out of the Capitol Reef area and were befriended by the inhabitants of a small Mormon settlement in nearby Parowan.

Capitol Gorge Road

The Church of the Latter-day Saints in Salt Lake City sent pioneers to settle the Capitol Reef area. They established several settlements, including that of Junction, which was later renamed Fruita. Major Wesley Powell and several geologists and geographers also mapped out the area during this same period in the 1870s. These settlements did well along the Fremont River, including those of Loa, Bicknell, Torrey and Fremont. By 1880, Nels Johnson moved into Junction and leveraged the nearby river to plant apples, plums, pears, peaches, walnuts and almond trees. The settlement was renamed Fruita at the turn of the century and was nicknamed The Eden of Wayne County.

In 1892, a wagon trail was cleared by a group of pioneers led by Elijah Cutler Behunin, finally allowing passage through the Waterpocket Fold. The Fruita Schoolhouse was completed in 1896 from land donated by Behunin. His twelve-year-old daughter Nettie became the school's first teacher. The land was farmed successfully. No more than ten families worked and lived in the settlement at any given time. Life was good, work was hard and the area remained remote, fostering a tight community. The 1920s and the onset of the automobile brought Fruita a little closer to the rest of the world, but by 1941, the Fruita Schoolhouse closed and students were consolidated to Torrey schools.

The Gifford house was built by Dewey Gifford, one of the last settlers to farm in Fruita. He and his wife Nell built the two-story house and raised

117

four children. Dewey later ran a small motel for visitors when the area was known as the Capitol Reef National Monument. They were the last settlers to leave Fruita, moving to nearby Torrey in 1969.

Creation of Capitol Reef National Park

In 1921, Ephraim Portman Pectol and his brother-in-law, Joseph S. Hickman, lived in nearby Torrey, Utah, and began to promote Capitol Reef in periodicals and newspapers. They created a local promotion booster, collected $150 to hire a photographer and called their club the Wayne Wonderland Club. Pectol was a Mormon Bishop at the time, but in 1928, he was elected to the Utah State legislature. He continued to attract interest to the area by going straight to President Roosevelt, asking for the creation of the Wayne Wonderland National Monument. President Roosevelt was convinced and on August 2, 1937 set aside 37,711 acres (15,261 ha) for the creation of the Capitol Reef National Monument.

The park was put under the control of Zion National Park. In 1943, Charles Kelly was appointed "custodian without pay" of Capitol Reef National Monument. Charles was passionate about the area, studying the area's history and archaeology. He finally became the park's first superintendent in 1950 at the age of 62. In the 1950s, the U.S. Atomic Energy Commission successfully lobbied to open up the area in and around Capitol Reef to uranium mining, which deeply troubled Kelly. This was a time of national security taking the front row given the demands of the Cold War. To the fortune of the park, there was not enough mineable uranium in Capitol Reef, and by the 1960s, the park's future was brightened by Mission 66.

The National Park Service was seeing demand increase at all of their parks and created Mission 66 to help meet this demand. The Fruita campground was built along with a new visitor center and staff housing to accommodate the increase in park personnel. This along with a paved road through the Fremont River canyon saw the park's visitation climb to nearly 150,000 in 1967. Along the way, the NPS began purchasing private land parcels at Fruita and Pleasant Creek.

In 1970, two bills were introduced into Congress to protect the entirety of the Waterpocket Fold by creation of a National Park. On December 18, 1971, President Nixon signed the act to establish 254,000 acres to be set aside as Capitol Reef National Park.

Today, the awe of Capitol Reef is in the fact that it has been relatively left alone since the Franciscan priests ventured through Utah in 1776. Much of its wonder must be discovered on foot. Much of its treasure comes only by getting out of one's car and, even then, the amount of land that is protected is enough for a lifetime of adventure. Yet even if you never stray from the campground, the presence of "Eden" is undeniable. There is a soft, enduring timelessness about Capitol Reef. Its future in the chronicles of history is represented by its visitors and what they do or, more importantly, don't do.

Things to Do in Capitol Reef

Capitol Reef NP is a vacation unto itself. It is a completely reasonable diversion to park the RV at Fruita as your day camp, rent a four-wheel drive in Torrey or don a backpack and explore. There is only one paved road that crosses the park and no more than two unpaved roads. Much of Capitol Reef NP can only be discovered on foot or four-wheel drive, and this is what makes it so special. You will be trekking on land that has been little touched by man or beast.

If you go this route of rugged adventure, first off, awesome choice! You will be rewarded with a great adventure. Secondly, leave this book in your RV. This book will be focusing on shorter hikes, drives and smaller adventures that are possible with a motorhome. There are great books online and at the visitor center to help plan a bolder trip within Capitol Reef NP.

Because you can't eat the pie tin

Gifford House (Pie Shop)

The Gifford House is listed here first because it contains one very important thing: fresh pies for sale. This is not to diminish the self-guided historical tour of the Gifford Home, but let's get our bearings straight. You are on vacation. You have been traveling together for several days at this point, roughing it to some extent and burning off a lot of calories exploring Zion and Bryce canyons NPs. Its likely hot outside, at least one of your family snores too much and while that RV shower does get the job done, it is hardly resort pressure.

Plus, let's not forget one simple fact. You are out in the middle of nowhere, literally.

Yet here, in the middle of the desert, is pie. Not only pie, which in and of itself is flaky and wonderful yet not too sweet, but ice cream as well, in multiple flavors. The point here is that there has never been a time in your life since your childhood when the stars have aligned to quite this extent that you can sit down and eat a big piece of pie with ice cream without feeling one weensy iota of guilt. It's one of those more straightforward "you deserve it" decisions.

The pies are made locally in Torrey, Utah. The offering varies, but typically you can choose from apple, cherry, berry, peach, blueberry, and strawberry rhubarb. Each comes in its own individual-sized tin. There are covered picnic tables and even recycle bins specifically made for the pie tins. The gift shop also has locally made salsas, breads, scones, jams and other assorted goodies.

The Gifford House itself has been well restored to represent the mid 20s and earlier and, as stated, has many historical artifacts and a self-guided tour. The Gifford House is within walking distance from the Fruita campground. If you head toward the Fremont River, there is a quick back entrance trail to the home.

Scenic Drive

(8.2 mi / 13.2 km), one way, allow 1 – 2 hours

There is an entrance fee of $5 per vehicle, which is covered if you have the Annual Pass. The drive provides a nice view into the initial heartlands of Capitol Reef. It is paved for the 8.2 miles and is thus accessible for an RV. Keep in mind that this is not a loop, but there is an obvious turnaround at the end of the paved road. Also, RV's over 27 feet are not recommended on any of the spur roads of Scenic Drive.

Capitol Reef Scenic Drive

Scenic Drive contains a full day's worth of activities, including spurs into Capitol Gorge and Grand Wash Roads. Both are dirt roads and may not be suitable for an RV. The best way to experience the Scenic Drive is to pick up a Guide to the Scenic Drive available at the visitor center and online through the National Park Service. With the guide you can discover old uranium mines, ancient sand dunes that now look like Swiss cheese, coastal tidal flat fossils and even some Mormon graffiti.

Capitol Gorge Road

Easy – (5 mi / 8.0 km), round trip, allow 2 - 3 hours

Until 1962, this was the only road that passed through the Waterpocket Fold. The road passes through a high cliff-walled gorge that presents pleasant shadows in the late afternoon. For those up for a short hike, continue to the Pioneer Register, which contains the names of early Mormon pioneers etched into the side of the canyon. Across the wall where the pioneers "signed in," one can find petroglyphs as well. RV's over 27 feet not recommended.

Golden Throne Trail

Strenuous – (4.0 mi / 6.4 km), round trip, allow 2 - 3 hours

Golden Throne trail is a short but steep trail that winds through the backcountry of the Waterpocket Fold. It takes the viewer to the base of a large monolith known as the Golden Throne. This up-then-down hike gets the hiker up in elevation quickly, climbing 800 feet and following a series of well-marked switchbacks. This is a great hike to climb up into the higher realms of the backcountry in short order and still leave time to take in the amazing views.

Golden Throne

Goosenecks Overlook

4 mi / 6.4 km drive from Fruita Campground

Goosenecks Overlook is an easy drive and subsequent walk from the camp-ground and gives nice views of the goose-necks of Sulphur Creek. Goosenecks are rel-atively rare geologic formations. They are formed when the un-derlying rock is thrust upward where a creek is running. With the creek running over soft sandstone, it is allowed to cut deeper into the rock, imprinting the ini-tial meanderings of the creek or river into a deep impression as a gooseneck.

Goosenecks Overlook

Cohab Canyon Trail

Moderate– (1.7 mi / 2.7 km), one way, allow 90 minutes

When Federal law officials were looking for polygamists in the late 1800's, the men folk of Fruita would hide all but one wife in nearby Cohab (short for co-habitation) Canyon. It's not hard to imagine that the phrase, "all those other beds are for guests", was a common one when the law came around.

Hickman Bridge

Of course this is pure legend and would have many a park ranger rolling their eyes when asked about the provenance of the canyon's name, but it does make for an interesting story. The trail itself, being close to Fruita campground, is one of the most popular hikes in the park. The hike climbs 22 switchbacks for 400 feet elevation gain to give some great views of Fruita and the Fremont River.

After completing the switchbacks, the trail become flat to the mouth of Cohab Canyon. Inside the canyon, one is surrounded by Wingate Sandstone. In many places you can see "tafoni" formations, which look like Swiss Cheese like holes in the rock walls. Tafoni are formed when the calcium carbonate holding the sand together into sandstone dissolves, leaving a sponge like system of holes.

Inside Cohab Canyon are several side canyons worth exploring, locally referred to as the "Wives". In the main canyon, look for the Cohab Arch and some solitary hoodoos. If you want to add a little more to the hike, take the spur trail from the Cohab Arch to the Fruita Overlooks. This side trip is well worth taking, providing some excellent views of the Fremont River Canyon and Walker Peak. There are two overlooks, named North and South respectively. The spur trails add an additional 1.2 miles and an hour to the hike.

Back on the main trail, continue heading up Cohab Canyon. Along the way, the trail passes Frying Pan Trail and onwards to Highway 24 a little more than a half mile further on. This final leg gives some great views of the Fremont River Canyon and Capitol Dome off in the distance. Hikers can opt to get picked up from here, head on to Hickman Bridge or turn around and head back.

Hickman Bridge

Strenuous – (1.8 mi / 2.9 km), round trip, allow 1 hour

Hickman Bridge is a wonderful example of a natural bridge The bridge has a span of 133 feet (45 m). The trail climbs steeply then levels out moderately until the arch is reached.

Rim Overlook / Navajo Knobs Trail

Strenuous – (4.6 mi / 7.4 km), round trip for Rim Overlook, (9.4 mi / 15.2 km), round trip for Navajo Knobs)

The Rim Overlook starts from the Hickman Bridge trail. The full hike is strenuous due to elevation gains. The Rim Overlook is 4.5 miles (7.2 km) round trip, climbs 1,110 feet and gives great views of Fruita and the surrounding valley. The Navajo Knobs trail extends from the Rim Overlook trail. The Knobs are a collection of Navajo sandstone hills that are uniquely formed. The trail leads to one of the smaller knobs, though it is possible for a skilled scrambler to scale the other formations as well. The Navajo Knobs give 360-degree views as the reward for climbing an additional 500 feet over 2.5 miles (4.0 km).

Cathedral Valley

The Cathedral Valley Loop is listed here because it is such a striking gesture of landscape as to demand inclusion. For the RVer, it is out of bounds, needing a high clearance vehicle to pursue. However, if you are so lucky as to have such a vehicle in your tool kit, the Cathedral Valley offers a great day's escape into the wilds of Utah red rock.

Upper Cathedral Valley

This is an area of majestic views and very few people. It is a place to be alone, to lose oneself, to be swallowed by the inspired views and towers of rock with names like Temple of the Sun and Moon.

Most visitors take the 59-mile (95 km) loop starting at the River Ford to Hartnet Road. River Ford is 11.8 miles or 19.0 km east of the visitor center on Highway 24. From Hartnet Road connect with Cathedral Road (aka Caineville Wash Road), which winds back to Highway 24.

Both roads are suitable for most SUVs and trucks. There is a river crossing at River Ford. The ford is typically about a foot deep, with a rocky hard-packed bottom, and is passable nearly year round. Please note that Cathedral Valley is prone to flooding from Monsoons and heavy rain events. Monsoons can change driving conditions on roadways very quickly. If the ford appears to be flooded, do not attempt to cross. Also, this ford is on private land, so stick to the designated easement across and camp once you are back inside the park.

Distances from the River Ford in Cathedral Valley:

- 9 miles (14.5 km) Bentonite Hills
- 14 miles (22.5 km) Lower South Desert Overlook Spur Road
- 27 miles (43.5 km) Upper South Desert Overlook Spur Road
- 27.5 miles (44.3 km) Junction of the Hartnet/Polk Creek/Cathedral (also known as the Caineville Wash) roads
- 28 miles (45.1 km) Cathedral Campground
- 30 miles (48.3 km) Upper Cathedral Valley
- 33 miles (53.1 km) Junction of Caineville Wash and Baker Ranch roads
- 33.1 miles (53.3 km)Gypsum Sinkhole Spur Road
- 42.5 miles (68.4 km) Lower Cathedral Valley Spur Road (Temples of the Sun & Moon, Glass Mountain)
- 59 miles (95 km) Hwy 24 at Caineville Wash Road

The Speed Queen

On seeing a Star Wars mug at the gas station ..

[Bryce]: Dad, how does Darth Vader go the bathroom?

[Everest]: Yeah, wouldn't his cape touch the ground? That doesn't sound sanitary.

[Angela]: Oh boy. I guess it was only a matter of time before we went here.

[Bryce]: Hey Ev, What did Obi Wan Kenobi say to Darth Vader when he saw him in the restroom?

[Everest]: Ummm. I don't know.

[Bryce]: He said, "That's no moon, it's a space station!" (All of us laugh)

[Bryce]: Do you think Darth talks to the Stormtroopers at the urinal?

[Me]: Of course he does, sports mainly. Perhaps the latest on the Death Star construction.

[Everest]: Speaking of which, forget Darth Vader! How do Stormtroopers pee?

Pondering silence fills the motor home.

Near the Middle of Nowhere

Given this was a vacation, my wife went to great measures to not have to do any laundry for the entire trip by packing about a month's worth of everything for our 10-day RV journey. She had brought along a large Nike duffle bag that said "Just Do It" in big letters for any used clothing that might be too dirty to reuse. The problem with this theory is "used clothing" to our sons was a term given to anything worn for more than four minutes. As a result, the duffle bag grew quickly. It started out as a discretely hidden thing in the closet on day 1 of the trip and then found its way to hanging on the bathroom door by day 3. By day 5, it had become the size of our youngest child and lay like a fat overstuffed worm on the floor.

As we were pulling into a small Utah town, Everest stepped over the "Just Do It" bag and asked, "Hey Dad, can I ask you a question? Is it possible for laundry to become sentient?"

Ang gave a confused, "What"?

"You know, become a living thing. I think the duffle bag might just become aware of itself and maybe kill us in our sleep or something."

"Yeah Mom", Bryce chimed in, "I think I saw it move last night. It said, 'Wash me. I'm really starting to smell.'"

"Zombie laundry!!" Everest cried. "It would be cool if clothing itself could be zombified and forced you to do zombie-like things."

"Yeah, like you put on a zombie T-shirt and it makes you eat other people's brains."

"Or maybe your own brain!"

"What if you put on zombie pants? Then you know..." Everest asked.

"Oh God!" Bryce laughed. "Your pants would eat your, you know (in whispered voice), your wiener!" Bryce went into a small fit of uncontrollable laughter that usually accompanies anything that involves the nether regions.

"Bryce!" Ang said sternly.

"Sorry Mom! It's just so funny, you put the pants on and then they eat your..."

I swooped in, "Yes, we know B Bear, no testicular-related comments, please."

Everest, "LOLS."

Ang let them all in on the agenda for the day as we too had smelled the rankness of the duffel bag. "We are going to do laundry at the next town, boys. I didn't want to have to do this, but I'm tired of smelling dirty laundry."

"Oh come on!" Everest protested. "Really? We have plenty of clothes!"

"Mom! I thought we were going to Goblin Valley today?" Bryce asked, dejected.

"And we will, we just need to run a few loads through. It won't take long. If we all work together, we should get in and get out pretty fast."

Everest shook his head. "Face palm. We will be there all day in some stupid town in Utah."

I interjected. "Guys, we will be going to Goblin Valley and then on to Canyonlands. We do need to stop and take care of this errand first. It will not take all day."

Everest interjected in his all-knowing teenage voice. "Let me get this straight. We are going to wash a week's worth of laundry, then tour Goblin Valley, then explore the largest National Park in Utah. Got it. You parents really have a lot to learn about time management, don't you?"

(Note to new parents: If you are sarcastic in any way, do not use your sarcasm in front of your children. They will learn it, master it and use it against you once they hit double digits. It's too late for us. You have been warned.)

"Ev, we are just going to get to Canyonlands today. We won't be exploring it too much until tomorrow."

Just as Everest was going to throw in more of his irrefutable logic, Bryce interrupted.

"Hey guys, I think I've seen something that will scar me for life. There was this guy in underwear standing on his doorstep."

"BB, you are probably hallucinating," Everest stated.

"Well, he was wearing Superman underwear, but no shirt. He was standing on his porch."

I agreed. "No, I saw a weird looking dude, too, but I didn't see the details."

Bryce said, "You mean the guy with the slingshot?"

"Oh man really?" Ev said now, looking backwards. "OMG, Bryce you're right!"

I looked across at Ang and mouthed "What??" We chuckled at the randomness but as we entered the town, it became evident that Mr. Superman Slingshot was only the beginning. The town had one main street with pre fab houses and bordered up businesses on either side. We passed the Hong Kong Restaurant, the only thing open as far as we could see. There had been other businesses—a café, a hardware store, even a dance studio, but the owners had packed up and taken everything except for the signs.

We drove past an empty children's park laid out in cement surrounded by a chain link fence. It looked like a prison. There were no trees, no grass, nothing that would even remotely entice a kid to want to use the park. Rusted swings and one slide were bolted down. Weeds grew within the cracks in the cement.

"Did that used to be a parking lot, you think?" my wife asked.

We both looked concerned. It was surreal to think people called this place home, that this was where kids went to play.

"I'm not even sure it's being used as a park," I said dryly. This is when I noticed the wind moving the swings wildly. The wind was tremendous, relentless and willful. It was strong enough to keep people off the streets, which were deserted save for one poor fellow getting battered and tugged by the large gusts. The wind tore at the roofs, ate at the paint of homes, stripped trees down to just a handful of leaves. It blew dust continuously down the street and as much as it blew it out of town, more dust came in.

We parked the RV within walking distance of the Speed Queen Fluff and Fold. Everest opened the trailer door and pushed 'Just Do It' down the steps like a dead body. Little beads of sand stung my calves like needles as I picked up the duffle bag. I felt like I was being stripped clean by the wind and sand. Inside the Speed Queen, there was a middle-aged woman standing over a massive pile of laundry. She was drinking a beer and was dressed in under-sized spandex pants that wrapped her to just within splitting tolerance. I tried not to look. The front door continually pushed in on itself from that devil wind and its howl overtook the hum of the machines. The place smelled of fabric softeners, warm clothes and cigarettes. It was too late to turn back. We pressed on.

"Honey, we need some quarters. I don't have enough," Ang said to Everest. "Sweetheart, get your dad and go get some quarters for us."

"Dad, we need..."

"I heard, thanks. Come on, son. There's a little convenience store down the street. We can head there."

We stepped out into the wind, leaning into it as we walked up the street to the corner store. The wind was amazing in its strength. Both of us squinted to keep the grit out of our eyes. I could feel it sandblasting the flesh off my legs and everything else in the town. It seemed to take about a half a day to go the two blocks to the store.

The relentless energy-depleting squall went silent after getting inside the store. We were greeted by cool air conditioning and the faint sounds of soft Christian rock in the background. The woman at the counter looked directly at us, as she had the whole time, but said nothing. I nodded in her direction, but after not getting any deviation from her original stare, went about my business. Everest headed straight to the soda area and picked out an assortment of drinks for everyone. I grabbed a bag a chips and cookies. I looked around and realized this was not just the town's convenience store, it was their only store. There was a small produce section with a couple of tomatoes and heads of wilted lettuce. They had eggs and wrapped ground hamburger, one of everything you needed to survive. There was a whole section devoted to nail polish that seemed much larger than it should have been for a store of that size.

We plopped down the various items we had accumulated on our journey and handed them to the clerk. She was about 27, but with a smoked-since-birth look that brought her in closer to 43. She was bone thin, with short dry brown hair shaped in a simple bowl cut. Her nails looked impeccable, blue with little star flecks on them.

"Is this it?" she asked. She spoke as if she was smacking gum. One side of her mouth seemed to do all the talking, while the other side was just along for the ride.

"Yep, thanks", I said hesitantly, but then lightened up on remembering the need for quarters. "I think that will do'er! Oh, I also need some quarters for the Laundromat. Can you spare any?"

"I figured that's why you came in. I saw you guys coming in from the old Laundromat and figured, 'Yep, they'll want some quarters.' I have about $10 worth, that's it. Will that do?"

I nodded. "Oh, yeah, that should be plenty. We are just doing some laundry." Her weird half-faced-gum-smacking-without-gum way of talking was throwing me off my game.

"Where are you guys from?"

"California."

"You going to Capitol Reef?"

"Ah no. We came from Capitol, going to Canyonlands."

"Most people do it that way. For some reason I thought you might be different."

"It is sure windy here," I said, trying to change the subject.

"Yep, it's windy here every day. Every day. Just like this…windy. Always the wind. You don't even need to shower in this town, just stand outside in that wind and have it sandblast the dirt off ya. It will even sandblast your clothes clean too." She looked out the window and just stared for a moment. Outside the wind was sucking the soul out of a heavyset woman trying to get across the street.

"Is it really like this every day?" Everest said, gullibly stunned.

The clerk relaxed a little. "Every day, son. They say the pioneer settlers that first came out this way were horrified by the wind. It took over their wagons and they couldn't push on. The wagon master told his group that they would stay put right here until that wind died. They waited day after day, but the wind, it never did stop, not once. It kept blowin' strong just like it's blowin' right now. Eventually, they had to build more permanent shelters to wait out that wind and it turned into this town.

That wind out there, it never died, so they never left. They say this is the windiest town ever known." She laughed a little, probably at the look on our faces. Her tongue was sickly black and her teeth were badly stained. I tried to not look disgusted, though Ev didn't do such a good job.

"You know, I have to ask. As we drove in, there wasn't much around. A lot of the buildings look boarded up. Did something happen?"

"No, it's always like this. Folks try at something and then it dies and others take over the building and try something else and that dies too. This store and the Laundromat. Oh and the Chinese restaurant and gas station. You've been at the two longest running businesses in town. I guess everybody needs groceries and to clean their clothes at some point."

I couldn't disagree on that one. I wondered about what people did for employment. This town was in the middle of nowhere. There were no services to speak of, no hotels or jeep rental places, nothing. I asked, "I don't really see much in the way of an industry or a mine or anything around here. So what do folks do around here for work?"

The cashier stopped packing our groceries and stood still as if she had been waiting her whole life to tell me what this town did. She looked at me with an expression of lost acceptance, with a look that betrayed she had given up hope so deeply that the whole notion of even asking what they did for work was hilarious. There was a slight tragedy to the smile she displayed. From this very expression I was to understand that there was no work now or ever in this town. This town existed against all manner of reason and the only collective thing the people of this community did, did often and did well, was the one thing she was about to cry out. She looked me in the eye and said, "What do we do for work? We pray!" and then cackled openly, showing that odd black tongue of hers and those stained teeth.

I was reeling from the answer and began to wonder at the wisdom of stopping here. This was quite possibly the genesis community of every small town horror film ever created. I assumed that in short order a monster of a man with greasy arms and a shotgun would come out the back and we would never be heard from again. As I stood within the vision of our doom she asked, "Will there be anything else?" and handed the quarters to Everest.

After stepping back out into the exfoliating relentlessness, Ev leaned in close to me. "Dad! OMG!"

"I know son. That was surreal!"

"What is up with this town, Dad?"

"I don't know, they're just poor, son."

Back at the Laundromat, Angela was busy sorting and prepping. "What took you so long? Come on, I'm ready to rock and roll here. I've got four machines loaded up waiting for quarters."

"My, I see why they call this place the Speed Queen," I said.

"You got it, sweetheart. You think I want to be here?"

We combined the wash cycles with snacking, taking over a small corner of the Laundromat. The chairs were hard with thin metal legs capped with plastic. There was nowhere to set anything, but it didn't matter. We had food.

The dry cycle was a different beast altogether. We gathered like a tribe around the dryers and watched them spin around and around. No one spoke at first, zoned out, becoming one with the dryers, watching the red LED minutes tick down slowly before us. One dryer seemed to be ticking down faster than the others.

Bryce had a revelation during his dryer meditations. "Mom, what do you think would happen if they put a Wendy's inside a McDonald's?"

"Oh, B Bear that would be awesome! It would be like combining square hamburgers with the best French fries in the world," Ev said.

"I don't know about the best," I said.

"Dad, when McDonald's French fries first come out, they are sooo good. But you are right, after five minutes they start to taste like salty cardboard."

Bryce asked, "What if Ronald Macdonald and Wendy herself got together, you know, like got married?"

I inserted, "I guess that could happen. I wonder what kind of children would they have?"

Ev piled on, "They are both redheads! Bryce that's brilliant. They would have all these little red headed clown children running around with pony tails and big red noses."

"You could call the place McWendy's!" Bryce joked.

"That's kind of gross if you really think about it". Ang said.

I eyed the bag of cookies and changed the subject. "How about these Keebler Elf cookies? I mean, what's up with the whole process of some magical elves making cookies for the masses inside some tree that's outside the jurisdiction of the health department?"

"You know, you're right, Dad. I think I found a little elf hat in one of those cookies we had."

"Or a little elf Band-Aid maybe."

"Boys!" Ang scolded mildly.

Bryce took the subject to its logical conclusion. "Oh, or worse dad. What if one of the Keebler elves fell into the vat of cookie dough! Oh god!"

"Lols."

I said, "You know guys, I read a story about a couple that died hours apart from each other after 71 years of marriage. It's a heartwarming story. Your great grandpa Charlie and his wife Ruby did the same thing. He had a heart attack and she went into the hospital that same day. He had a second heart attack two days later and she died that night. Almost 60 years of marriage."

"Eric, come on, do we have to talk about this stuff?" Ang never liked the topic of death.

"How did she die, Dad?" Bryce asked.

Everest interrupted, "Mom, it's not bad, it's good. They used the power of love. I think it's kind of cool. They used the power of love to die."

"So she died by love?" Bryce asked again.

"Kind of B Bear. She just loved him so much she didn't want to be without him. So when he died, she went with him."

"Mom, do you want to do that when dad dies?"

"Wait a minute, how do you guys know I'm going first?" I asked.

Ang answered wryly, "I don't mind going first, and I kind of want a few years of peace in heaven."

"I agree with mom. She needs to rest in peace."

I agreed. "You know, you're right, I wouldn't mind a few years to myself. I'm due."

Ang slapped me on the arm and belted out my name in exclamation.

I rethought my answer. "Actually, I think maybe I should die first. You always did say you'd come back to haunt me."

"Oh, yes dear, I will. Trust me."

"I'm not sure I can handle that. You'll be backseat driving everything I do, except then you'll have access to my every move. I can see it now. 'Turn left', 'Are you really going to eat that? You had enough sweets today.' 'You better not say that out loud!', 'You can do better than that old bag. She's just after your money!'"

"Are you done?"

"Look, I will haunt you, but only because I love you," Ang smiles. "You're clueless without me."

"I'm clueless with you too, but perhaps you're right."

The dryer's beeped almost in unison. The clothes were extracted from their tumbling adventures, folded modestly and assigned for portage back to the RV with their respective owners. The blasts of hot wind continued to wail as we loaded the clothes into their drawers. They shook the motor home like they meant it. The wind moaned against the buildings, causing trees to whip themselves without control, and pushed us in unwelcome fiery gusts until we were well out of town.

"I think that was the weirdest town I've ever been in," Everest said.

Ang turned around as if taking inventory that everyone was safe. "Well, I'll tell you all one thing. I'm definitely bringing more clothes if we ever do this again."

Canyonlands National Park

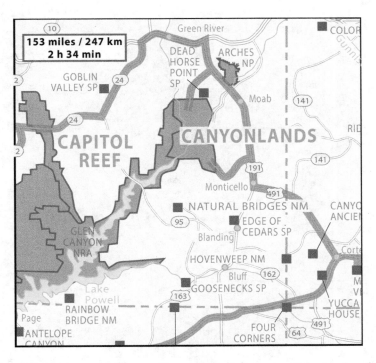

"*Nothing human is of long duration. Men and their deeds are obliterated, the race itself fades; but Nature goes calmly on with her projects.*"

—John C. Van Dyke, *The Desert*

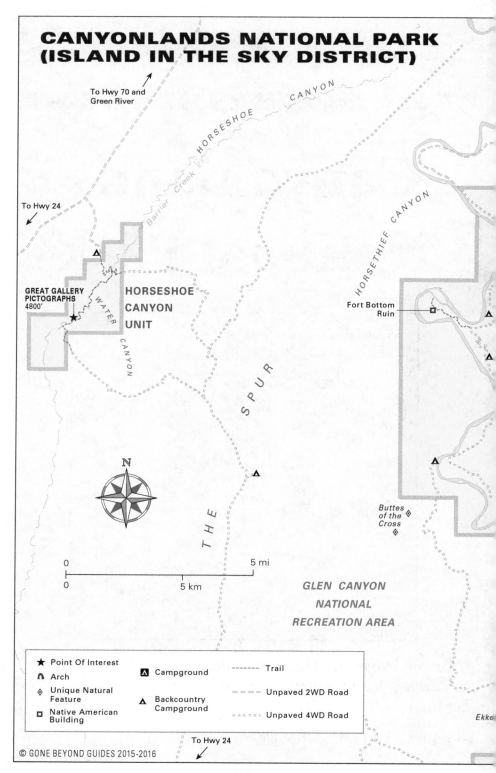

CANYONLANDS NATIONAL PARK (ISLAND IN THE SKY DISTRICT)

To Hwy 70 and
Green River

CANYON

HORSESHOE

Barrier Creek

To Hwy 24

HORSETHIEF CANYON

GREAT GALLERY
PICTOGRAPHS
4800'

WATER

HORSESHOE
CANYON
UNIT

CANYON

Fort Bottom
Ruin

S P U R

N

Buttes
of the
Cross

T H E

0   5 mi
0   5 km

GLEN CANYON
NATIONAL
RECREATION AREA

★ Point Of Interest
∩ Arch
◈ Unique Natural
   Feature
▫ Native American
   Building

◮ Campground

▲ Backcountry
   Campground

------ Trail

= = = Unpaved 2WD Road

= = = Unpaved 4WD Road

Ekke

© GONE BEYOND GUIDES 2015-2016

To Hwy 24

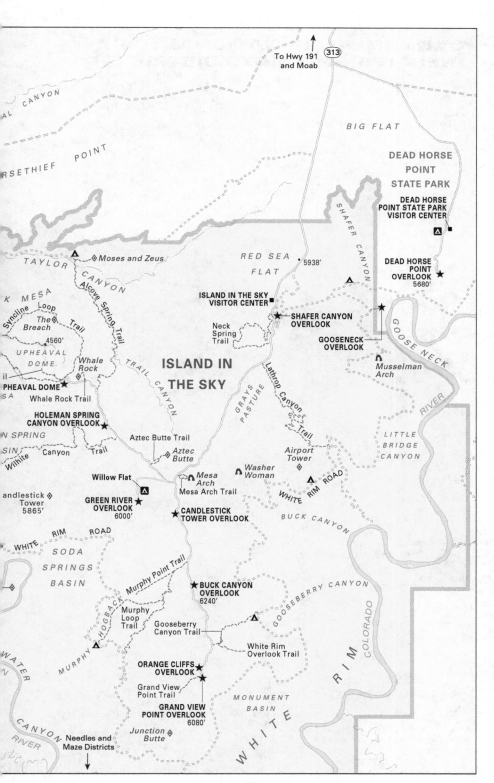

To Hwy 191
and Moab
313

BIG FLAT

DEAD HORSE
POINT
STATE PARK

DEAD HORSE
POINT STATE PARK
VISITOR CENTER

DEAD HORSE
POINT
OVERLOOK
5680'

CANYON

RSETHIEF   POINT

TAYLOR   CANYON

Moses and Zeus

Alcove Spring Trail

RED SEA
FLAT   5938'

ISLAND IN THE SKY
VISITOR CENTER

SHAFER CANYON
OVERLOOK

SHAFER CANYON

K MESA

Syncline   Loop
The
Breach   Trail

4560'

UPHEAVAL
DOME

il

PHEAVAL DOME

SA

Whale Rock Trail

Whale
Rock

Neck
Spring
Trail

GOOSENECK
OVERLOOK

ISLAND IN
THE SKY

TRAIL   CANYON

Musselman
Arch

GOOSE NECK

RIVER

LITTLE
BRIDGE
CANYON

HOLEMAN SPRING
CANYON OVERLOOK

N SPRING

SIN

Wilhite   Canyon   Trail

Aztec Butte Trail

Aztec
Butte

GRAYS
PASTURE

Lathrop Canyon Trail

Washer
Woman

Airport
Tower

WHITE RIM ROAD

Willow Flat

andlestick
Tower
5865'

GREEN RIVER
OVERLOOK
6000'

Mesa
Arch
Mesa Arch Trail

BUCK CANYON

CANDLESTICK
TOWER OVERLOOK

WHITE   RIM   ROAD

SODA

SPRINGS

BASIN

Murphy Point Trail

BUCK CANYON
OVERLOOK
6240'

GOOSEBERRY CANYON

COLORADO

MURPHY HOGBACK

Murphy
Loop
Trail

Gooseberry
Canyon Trail

White Rim
Overlook Trail

WHITE

RIM

WATER

ORANGE CLIFFS
OVERLOOK

Grand View
Point Trail

GRAND VIEW
POINT OVERLOOK
6080'

MONUMENT
BASIN

CANYON   RIVER

Needles and
Maze Districts

Junction
Butte

137

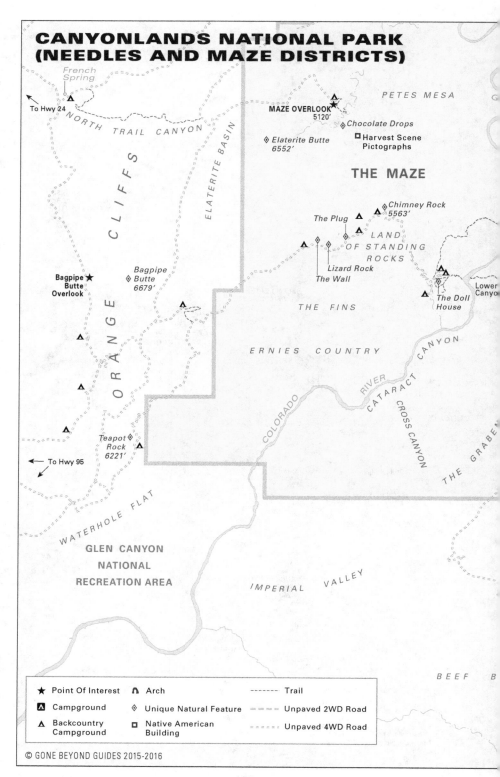

CANYONLANDS NATIONAL PARK (NEEDLES AND MAZE DISTRICTS)

French Spring

To Hwy 24

NORTH TRAIL CANYON

ORANGE CLIFFS

ELATERITE BASIN

PETES MESA

MAZE OVERLOOK
5120'

◈ Chocolate Drops

◈ Elaterite Butte
6552'

◻ Harvest Scene
Pictographs

THE MAZE

◈ Chimney Rock
5563'

The Plug

LAND
OF STANDING
ROCKS

Lizard Rock

The Wall

Bagpipe ★
Butte
Overlook

◈ Bagpipe
Butte
6679'

▲ The Doll
House

Lower
Canyo

THE FINS

ERNIES COUNTRY

COLORADO RIVER

CATARACT CANYON

CROSS CANYON

THE GRABE

◈ Teapot
Rock
6221'

← To Hwy 95

WATERHOLE FLAT

GLEN CANYON
NATIONAL
RECREATION AREA

IMPERIAL VALLEY

BEEF B

★ Point Of Interest	⌒ Arch	------- Trail
◮ Campground	◈ Unique Natural Feature	≡≡≡≡ Unpaved 2WD Road
▲ Backcountry Campground	◻ Native American Building	≡≡≡≡ Unpaved 4WD Road

© GONE BEYOND GUIDES 2015-2016

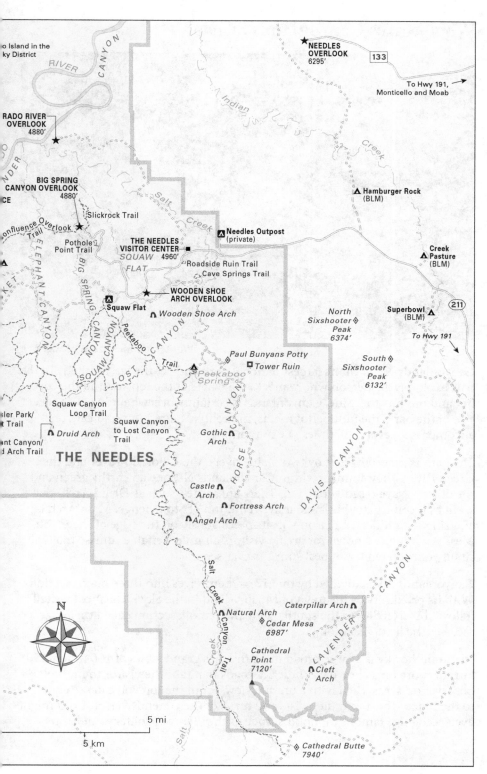

Island in the
ky District

RIVER

CANYON

★ NEEDLES
OVERLOOK
6295'

133

To Hwy 191,
Monticello and Moab

Indian

RADO RIVER
OVERLOOK
4880'
★

DER

Creek

BIG SPRING
CANYON OVERLOOK
4880'
CE

▲ Hamburger Rock
(BLM)

Salt

Slickrock Trail

Creek

onfluence Overlook

Pothole
Point Trail

⊞ Needles Outpost
(private)

Creek
▲ Pasture
(BLM)

THE NEEDLES
VISITOR CENTER ■ 4960'
SQUAW
FLAT

BIG

SPRING

Confluence Overlook
Trail

ELEPHANT CANYON

Roadside Ruin Trail
Cave Springs Trail

Superbowl ◈
(BLM)

211

▲

KET

★ WOODEN SHOE
ARCH OVERLOOK

North
Sixshooter ◈
Peak
6374'

To Hwy 191

▲ Squaw Flat

∩ Wooden Shoe Arch

CANYON

SQUAW CANYON

Peekaboo

South
Sixshooter ◈
Peak
6132'

LOST CANYON

Trail

Paul Bunyans Potty

ler Park/
t Trail

Squaw Canyon
Loop Trail

∩ Druid Arch

Squaw Canyon
to Lost Canyon
Trail

▲ Peekaboo
Spring

□ Tower Ruin

HORSE CANYON

Gothic ∩
Arch

DAVIS CANYON

nt Canyon/
d Arch Trail

THE NEEDLES

Castle ∩
Arch

∩ Fortress Arch

∩ Angel Arch

CANYON

Salt

Caterpillar Arch ∩

N

∩ Natural Arch

Creek

◈ Cedar Mesa
6987'

LAVENDER CANYON

Cathedral
Point
7120'

∩ Cleft
Arch

Canyon Trail

5 mi

5 km

Salt

◈ Cathedral Butte
7940'

What Makes Canyonlands Special

Washer Woman from Mesa Arch

Canyonlands NP is Utah's largest national park and yet the least visited. To the true explorer, the person who wants to see what's at the top, around the corner and on the other side, Canyonlands is certainly overwhelming. The sheer size of the park, the number of mesas, monoliths, buttes, fins and canyons encompasses several lifetimes of exploration.

The park is carved in part by two major rivers, the Colorado River and the Green River. They connect within Canyonlands NP, one an earthy green and the other a Navajo sandstone red. There are arches, such as Druid Arch, that seem as if some giant built a massive rendition of Stonehenge. Mesa Arch is amazing for a different reason—it sits precariously on the edge of sheer cliff. Mesa Arch is also known for giving visitors an unforgettable sunrise that will sit on your top ten list of best sunrises ever seen.

Canyonlands NP is divided by the rivers themselves into three major sections. With its proximity to the town of Moab, Island in the Sky is the most visited, followed by Needles to the south, while the remote section called the Maze receives the least visitation.

Island in the Sky is a large broad mesa that has grand views of 100 miles (160 km) or more on a clear day. There are roads that take the visitor to multiple observation areas, each with a unique view. From the top you can see across to the Maze, down into the twists and turns of the Green River, and you might even recognize famous monoliths, such as the 305-foot solitary sandstone pillar called Standing Rock. To really explore Island in the Sky, you may want to consider renting a jeep or a jeep guided tour. This will allow you to get down off the mesa and into some of the canyons you look down on from the overlooks. There are a several hikes on the mesa as well as others that require dropping into the canyons below.

The Needles District is less crowded and has exceptional hiking opportunities that are easily accessible. This section of the park is vastly different from the Island in the Sky District in that the visitor is immediately in the canyons, allowing close and personal views of the various pinnacles. Needles is named after the many monoliths banded in red and white Cedar Mesa sandstone. The monoliths go by funny names like Paul Bunyan's Potty and Caterpillar Arch. Druid Arch is one of the gems of this section and is one of the most popular longer hikes in Needles.

The Maze District is the third and least visited district in Canyonlands NP, receiving only 3 percent of its total visitors. This is with good reason as it is one of the most remote places in the nation. Visitors to this rugged area must have a high degree of self-sufficiency and overall desert skills. Typical visits to this region are 3–7 days simply because of the preparation and planning that goes into such a trip. The Maze holds remarkable journeys, vast silence, tests of ones abilities and purity within adventure. For most visitors, these journeys will have to remain dreams, something pragmatically unattainable. This remote location, out of reach yet only just, helps add to the siren call of Canyonlands NP.

There is a fourth element to the park, the rivers themselves. Before joining together, the Green and Colorado Rivers independently carve deeply into the sandstone layers, creating quiet channels of water with sheer walls of rock on either side. Once the Green River merges with the Colorado, the combined power of these waters creates a 46-mile (74 km) stretch of rapids through Cataract Canyon. From high above at the confluence overlook, you can hear the roar of the rapids. Down in the river visitors can experience some of the wildest rapids in North America, with some stretches as intense as anything you'll find in the Grand Canyon.

There is nothing quite like Canyonlands. Whether you simply look out at the vast southwestern vistas from the top of the Island in the Sky, hike to Druid Arch, spend a week in the Maze or shoot down either of the park's two rivers, you will have a life memory. There is, as Edward Abbey once said, nothing else like it in the world.

Staying in Canyonlands

For those that are looking for a hotel near Canyonlands NP, look no further than Moab, Utah. Moab offers a decent selection of lodging to meet all needs and wants and is a pleasant if not understatedly hip town. This is a good thing, as lodge offerings within the park are non-existent and the number of campsites are slim. Canyonlands NP is the largest national park in Utah so expect some driving to and from your hotel, especially if you are visiting the Needles District.

The official campgrounds in both Island in the Sky and Needles districts are small, offering just 12 and 26 tent and RV campsites respectively. Additionally, both campgrounds only offer sites on a first come first served basis. Whether it is peak season or not, camping within the park itself is a matter of luck and arriving early.

While it may seem curious that the largest national park in Utah offers the smallest number of campgrounds, the reason for this is sound. The natural state of Canyonlands NP is a desert. Water is scarce. While it is possible to build a lodge with rooms, food and showers or even a large campground, it would require a tremendous amount of water to support the infrastructure. The small footprint of campsites helps to maintain the natural ecology of the parks. All water for use at the visitor center is trucked in. This helps keep water scarce for plants and animals alike, which is the natural order of things for Canyonlands NP.

In planning where you will be staying for this part of the trip, it's useful to plan with both Canyonlands and Arches NPs in mind. Both are relatively close to each other. This affords the visitor a strategy for either finding a central campground near both parks and staying in that one spot or moving around to various campgrounds based on proximity to the park you are visiting. There are a number of campgrounds that are close to Island in the Sky, Arches and Moab.

For our trip to Canyonlands, we tried our luck at finding a campsite within Island in the Sky but struck out and stayed at Horsethief Campground just outside the park. For Arches, we chose a location just off Highway 128, which put us close to both Moab and Arches. By this point in the trip, we were blistered and achy from so much hiking and yearned for a little civilization. Moab does a decent job of catering to the tourist and our centrally located campground strategy helped us continue our exploration of the parks while enjoying a bit of Moab hospitality.

Island in the Sky District

Willow Flats Campground

Twelve sites are available on a first come, first served basis. Each site contains a picnic table and fire grate. Vault toilets are provided but no water. The maximum length for an RV is 28 feet. Fee is $15 per night. Groups of up to 10 people and 2 vehicles are allowed. You can inquire at the entrance booth on availability; however, the most up-to-date information is at the visitor center. The campground is worth waking up early for as it is within walking distance to the Green River Overlook. Views here at sunset often dress the red rock canyon walls and mesa tops in a warm glow as the Green River snakes its way silently in the distance.

Horsethief Campground

Horsethief Campground is located 9.5 miles (15.3 km) from the Island in the Sky visitor center on Highway 313. There are 56 sites that typically never fill up completely, even during the peak seasons. There are many sites that accommodate large RVs. Campsites are offered on a first come, first served basis and have a picnic table and fire grate. Vault toilets are provided, but there is no running water. The campground has a few trails for hiking right outside its boundaries and provides incredible stargazing opportunities. There is a campground host; cost is $15 per night.

Dead Horse Point State Park – Kayenta Campground

Staying at Dead Horse Point State Park will cost more, but it does come with certain advantages. First of all, you can reserve the site through Reserve America. In addition, each site has a fully paved driveway or pull-through, tent pad, electrical outlets and covered picnic area at every site. Add in the fact that you are now inside one of the most photographed state parks in Utah, there is a lot going for this campground.

Entrance fees for the state park itself are $10 plus $28 per night for the campsite. The campgrounds are clean and well designed with privacy in mind. There is water and a dump station on premises.

BLM Campgrounds on Highway 128

There are several campgrounds along the Colorado River just north of Moab on Highway 128. All of these are first come, first served and each has the same basic amenities, including a picnic table and fire pit. None have water and provides only the basic vault toilet, but they all have a campground host on duty. These campgrounds are the farthest from Island in the Sky but are centrally located if you are looking for one site for the duration of your stay within Canyonlands and Arches NPs. The other great feature of these campgrounds is the Colorado River. Each campground offers a different scenic view of the river as it quietly rolls by.

There aren't any dump stations at these BLM campgrounds, though there is a dumping station at the Farm & City Feed Store located at 850 S Main St. in Moab. It will be on your right-hand side on the south side of town. The place is super nice, charges $5 for dumping and carries a limited supply of RV parts.

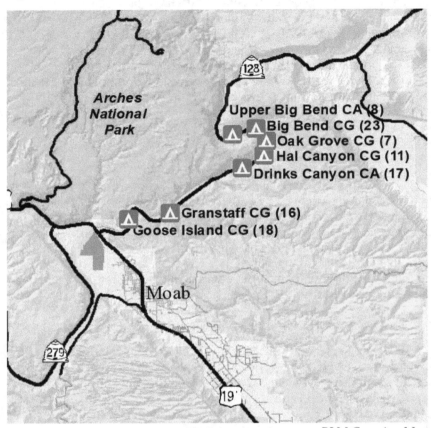

BLM Camping Map

Goose Island

This is the closest of the Highway 128 BLM campgrounds, located just 1.4 miles (2.3 km) from Highway 191. There are 19 sites available at $15 per night. The campground is against a high red rock wall and gets good shade in the afternoon. While many of the sites are close to the river, the high banks of the river's edge make cooling off a challenge.

Granstaff, Drinks Canyon, Hal Canyon, Oak Grove and Upper Big Bend

All of these campgrounds are designated for tent camping only and are offered on a first come, first served basis at $15 per night. Like all of the campgrounds in this area, you are setting up and sleeping next

144

to the Colorado River. This whole section of campgrounds is situated in a wide valley of red rock carved by the river. All of them have suitable flat campsites and while you are next to a highway, traffic is practically non-existent after sunset. The biggest differentiation between these sites are availability and distance from the parks you are visiting. Granstaff is one of the more popular sites since it is the closest tent only campground to both Arches and Canyonlands. Granstaff is also a great starting point for the Porcupine Rim Trail, a popular mountain biking trail.

Big Bend

Big Bend is 7.4 miles (11.9 km) from Highway 191 and can accommodate large RVs. There are 23 campsites and good afternoon shade similar to Goose Island. While Big Bend is 6 miles (9.7 km) farther out, there are several advantages to this campground. It contains a sandy beach and river walkway as well as more expansive views than Goose Island. It is also close to the popular Negro Bill trailhead, which is a pleasant 2-mile (3.2 km) hike along a year-round stream to a 243-foot-span natural arch named Morning Glory Bridge.

Lodging in Moab

There is a lot of choice when it comes to lodging (and eating) in Moab, Utah. The town offers a very nice respite from the sandstone and grit of a long day's outing. The best resource for finding all manner of Moab lodging, look no further than www.discovermoab.com. Here you will find all hotels, inns and resorts, plus vacation rentals and guest houses. Below are some notables:

3 Dogs and a Moose Cottages

171 & 173 W. Center St., Moab, Utah 84532, Phone: (435) 260-1692, http://www.3dogsandamoosecottages.com

This establishment contains but four cottages on its property and only two are large enough for families. That said, this is a very cool and unique property. The cottages are within a short walking distance from downtown Moab, the landscaping is full of color and the cottages themselves are nothing short of amazing. If you are looking for a "home away from home" and want to give the hotel scene a break, this place is worth looking into.

Red Cliff's Lodge

Mile Marker 14 Hwy 128, Moab, Utah, Phone: (866) 812-2002, www.redcliffslodge.com

This lodge is a bit of a drive from either national park, but it makes up for itself by the amenities it carries. It's a big property, with a wine tasting bar, swimming pool, horseback riding, restaurant and gift shop. This is in addition to the 110 rooms, suites and cabins. One of the best parts of Red Cliff's is the Moab Museum of Film and Western Heritage. This free attraction holds memorabilia from every movie made in the area including some made at the lodge itself. This museum is a fantastic way to spend an hour or two with the kids and holds over 100 years of history.

Private Campgrounds in Moab

There are several private campgrounds in and around Moab itself. These offer full hookups and have the obvious advantage of being in town, so you are closer to restaurants and other common amenities. There are many private RV campgrounds to choose from in Moab, and not all are listed here.

Moab Valley RV Park

1773 N Hwy 191, Moab, Utah 84532, Phone: (435) 259-4469

Located right at Highway 128, this RV park has 69 sites that accommodate RVs up to 60 feet. This park is close to both Canyonlands and Arches NP. Amenities include full hookup; a large, clean swimming pool, a hot tub and free Wi-Fi. Price per night varies by site type and whether you are staying a weekday, weekend or holiday. Prices begin at $39 per night and go as high as $55 per night for two people. Each person over six is an additional $5 per night.

Moab Rim RV Park

1900 South Hwy 191, Moab, Utah 84532 Phone: (888) 599-6622

Located just as you enter Moab. 28 sites for RVs up to 60 feet. Full hookup pull-through sites for $39 plus tax for two people, includes cable TV and Wi-Fi plus 50A and 30A power. There are also power-only sites for $34 plus tax for two people. Stay a week and get the 7th night for free.

Okay RV Park

3310 Spanish Valley Drive, Moab, Utah 84532, Phone: (435) 259-1400

Nice and clean just outside of south Moab. 73 sites accommodating RVs up to 80 feet, ranging from $39 to $45 a night. Kids stay free from June to August for RV sites. Free Wi-Fi. Subtle rustic southwest charm.

Needles District

There is one small campground inside the Canyonlands Needles District plus a few others outside the park. Closest lodging is in Monticello.

Squaw Flat Campground

There are 26 sites available accommodating RV lengths up to 28 feet. These sites have water, vault toilets, fire grates, picnic tables and tent pads. Cost is $15 per night and is available on a first come, first served basis.

Needles Outpost

Needles Outpost has six campsites for $20. The sites are pretty basic, but the campground is just outside of the NP. There is a store and gas station supplying basic camping and food supplies. The prices are representative of a place literally in the middle of nowhere.

The management is brimming with character, especially one woman who gets mentioned a lot in online reviews as being rude. If you think about it, there are really only two ways to play being out in the desert and running a store, gas station, café and campground all by yourself. You are either the most radiantly enlightened person in the world or the most cantankerous. Looks like she is the latter.

During my visits, I've never met this infamous woman and have had good service. They even offered to take me around Canyonlands by plane for only the price of the gas (that was years ago; the airport has since closed). If you do meet the cantankerous woman, I highly recommend opening with either a lot of patience or the stupidest question you can possibly think of and see how things go from there.

Hamburger Rock Campground

Hamburger Rock Campground is certainly off the beaten track, but as there are few options in the Needles District, it is worth pointing out. There are some caveats to this campground. There are eight campsites total, and they are officially designed for tent camping. It is possible to drive a smaller RV into many of the sites, but you will need to navigate a 2-wheel drive unpaved road for 2.2 miles (3.5 km). The sites have fire grates, picnic tables and pit toilets, but no water. Fee is $6 per night. The adventure of taking your RV on a dirt road for a chance of finding a site large enough to park it aside, Hamburger Rock campground is one of the most enjoyable in the area. It has great views, it's quiet, it's close to Canyonlands, and it has a minor twist of adventure thrown in to keep the trip interesting.

The Maze District

As stated earlier, this section is remote. There is no food, water, gas, lodging, or other amenities other than the Hans Flat Ranger Station, which sells maps and books. To give a hint at how remote the Maze District is,

The Maze District

147

it's about 3-6 hours of driving in a high clearance 4-wheel drive vehicle just to get to the outer Maze District boundary from the ranger station. Getting to Hans Flat Ranger Station itself is a 2.5-hour (46 mile / 74 km) drive on a 2-wheel drive dirt road from Green River, Utah. In other words, it takes a good portion of a full day just to get to the Maze from the nearest town. That's one remote national park!

Canyonlands Geology

Describing the geology of a place as big as Canyonlands can be a daunting task. There is no place quite like it anywhere in the world. Describing the geologic rationale behind all those canyons, fins, grabens, pinnacles, monoliths, goblins, arches, upheaval domes, needles and horsts is a book in itself if you want to satisfy a geologist.

Fortunately, this book is for the average traveler and there is a much simpler big picture expla-nation, one that sums up Can-yonlands geology nicely and leaves plenty of time to take in the view, which, let's face it, is the reason you came. This section will try to summarize the 10,000-foot view of the geological story behind Can-yonlands NP and then highlight

Lost in the Wonder of Canyonlands

some of the most unique geological artifacts that are worth pointing out.

The Big Picture

If you have been reading the geology of each section in this guide, you have by now noticed a theme. All of these parks sit on the Colorado Plateau. This plateau comprises some two dozen layers of rock strata that were deposited beginning some 300 million years ago. Canyonlands itself displays eleven dominant layers (Paradox through Navajo Sandstone). On top of these eleven are another twelve that were more recently deposited.

Then, all these layers were lifted upward slowly enough to allow the rivers, winds, ices and general erosion to cut into them. Here's the magical part, which is true in general for the Colorado Plateau but especially true for Canyonlands NP: These enormous masses of rock, all eleven thick layers of strata, were lifted straight up for the most part. There is a slight tilt to the strata here and there, but nothing compared to the twisted chaos of what happened to the rock layers of, say, Death Valley National Park.

This is huge geologically. Events this perfect don't typically happen, especially given the time involved. All of these layers of rock strata were allowed to deposit slowly over hundreds of millions of years, one on top of another, like a cake. Then, as these massive layers were lifted up from underneath, they were done so without upsetting these cake layers. They all remained flat, level and essentially perfect. They became a canvas for the patient artists of nature to carve them into the majestic yet impossibly delicate towers and rock faces you see today.

Given this perspective, geologically speaking Canyonlands NP is a work of art. There are no volcanic mountains born out of an immense chaos of fire, no earthquakes to topple the sculptures you see before you, no lava to bury them, no immense pressures to pit one rock stratum against another. What you see is the gentle patience of water, the etchings of wind, and the chisels of ice, combined with, by our standards, an unimaginable amount of time on layers of rock that have stood in place for millions of years.

And what water there was and still is. Today there are two major rivers that flow through Canyonlands NP, and it is in large part their handiwork that shaped much of what you gaze out upon. Flash floods today can completely wipe a landscape clean. They can move boulders the size of VW Bugs and transport tons of sediment from upstream to down. Back during the Pleistocene Era, the effect of water was magnified. There were several ice ages during this time and as the earth warmed and glaciers melted, water was a tremendous force, keeping up very well with the continual uplift from underneath. During the Pleistocene Era, water roughed out what you see. Then, as the climate changed, lesser amounts of water put their final touches on the land, creating chimneys, fins, and arches that defy belief. Look out before you. Canyonlands is stunning, a truly extraordinary place.

Unique Geological Notables

Grabens

Grabens are a very cool feature that are not unique to Canyonlands NP but are certainly plentiful in the Needles District and deserve mention mainly for the magic act of how they are formed. Rock layers actually disappeared!

First off, what is a graben? The word graben is German for ditch or trench. Geologically, it's used to explain any linear down thrust in rock strata. Imagine a layer of rock where a section has been removed underneath it, leaving a valley.

Grabens in Canyonlands are extensive on the east side of Colorado River's Cataract Canyon running for about 15.5 miles (25 km). There are literally row after row of collapsed valleys that run roughly parallel to the Cataract Canyon of the Colorado River.

While grabens can be formed by faulting, the grabens of the Needles District did not experience any faulting because—as you now know—this is stable land. How these grabens formed is a puzzler. We start with knowing that a large portion of one of the rock layers disappeared in certain sections and the rock layers on top simply sank down through the mighty force of gravity.

Aerial View of Grabens in Needles District

So how does a large sedimentary layer underneath a bunch of other rock layers simply disappear? And why did all of these disappearing rock layers vanish in parallel lines to the Colorado River itself? The hint is the river itself along with a very interesting 300-million-year-old layer called the Paradox Formation.

Here's the secret of the Paradox Formation. It is the result of a shallow sea that deposited a large amount of salt along with other sediments. This layer was then buried by millions of years of sediment, which became rock layers themselves. The salts lay trapped until about 10 million years ago when the Colorado Plateau rose up and the Colorado River was allowed to cut all the way back down and into the Paradox Formation.

Another subtle but huge factor at play in the grabens of the Needles District is the Rocky Mountains, which tilted the Needles District slightly westward. This tilt allowed for gravity to act as a component in the grabens' formation.

We now have all the puzzle pieces to figure out how a rock layer can just disappear. We have the Paradox Formation that was primarily a large salt deposit. We know that lots of pressure was then applied to this layer, which in turn was cut into by the Colorado River, creating less pressure on the Paradox formation in that section. Also throw in that slight tilt of the Paradox Formation by the uplift of the Rocky Mountains 350 miles (563 km) away. Finally, let's add the final piece of the graben puzzle. Under immense pressure, salt flows plastically, like a slow-moving liquid.

Now we can piece together why grabens are formed near the Colorado River. The salt was under this enormous pressure from the layers above and for years it couldn't go anywhere. It was under so much pressure it started acting like a very thick liquid. Then the Colorado River cut into the layer and the salt was allowed to escape at a glacial pace into the Colorado River, being pushed by gravity and the pressure of all that rock above it. As the salt left, a void was created and the ground above then sunk down into this trench-like void, creating grabens.

The grabens of the Needles District are young geologically, beginning about 55,000 years ago and continuing today. They are thought to move very slowly, dropping nearly undetectably toward the Colorado River, about an inch per year.

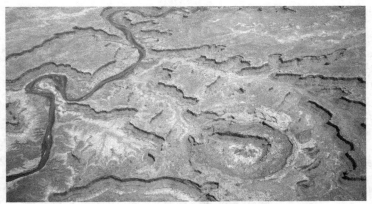

Upheaval Dome with Green River for Scale

Upheaval Dome

While grabens are a complex but solvable puzzle, Upheaval Dome is an enigma that has yet to be solved. Located in the Island in the Sky District, Upheaval Dome looks like a 3-mile (5 km) circular meteor crater. The rock layers are completely deformed, which is a big contrast to the layers outside the dome, which are characteristically stable. The center of the structure contains rock layers that have been pushed up into a true dome. Some of the layers are pushed up such that they are nearly vertical and they are pushed up on all sides, forming a circle. The area surrounding the dome has been pushed downwards, again in a complete, very large and very natural circle.

Upheaval Dome is estimated to be 60–170 million years old. It's easy to look at the dome and imagine a massive meteor blow to the rock strata, which caused the rocks to rebounded back up under the intense heat and pressure to form this true geologic dome. No one has found any pieces of a meteorite, however, so the thought is that it has long since eroded away, leaving only its impact.

While this is the obvious theory, it isn't the only one, leaving Upheaval Dome as one of the more hotly debated topics among geologists. The other prevailing theory is that of a salt dome. Again, we need to bring in the Paradox Formation, the 300-million-year-old rock layer that is mainly comprised of salt. Remember it was then buried by the sediment above it and, under the immense pressure, the salts began to liquefy. The theory is that since the salt is less dense than the rock layers above it, it started to flow plastically upward as a big salt bubble. This bubble rose through weaker layers until it heaved the overlying strata, creating a dome. The sandstone continued to erode, the salt dissolved and there you have it, the resulting Upheaval Dome before you. This is called the Salt Dome Theory. There are smaller confirmed salt domes in in the world, but not within the Paradox Formation. If this theory is correct, the Upheaval Dome would be the most deeply eroded salt structure on the planet.

Needles

The needles in the Needles District are, in themselves, interesting from a geologic standpoint. The Needles are comprised of a layer of rock called Cedar Mesa Sandstone. This sandstone layer is cut like a checkerboard, with parallel lines running from both north to south

Needles District

and another set of lines running from east to west. From the air, the sandstone truly looks like a checkerboard of red rock.

The two sets of parallel lines are created from very different geological functions. The east to west fractures are caused by the uplift of the rock strata itself. The north to south fractures are caused once again by the Paradox Formation, which runs thousands of feet underneath the Cedar Mesa Sandstone. The Paradox Formation, which has a large amount of salt in it, is slowly flowing toward the Colorado River, taking the surface layers with it. These north south formations are similar to the graben but on much smaller scale.

This criss-cross pattern is then slowly eroded at the rock joints by water and ice erosion, creating the beautiful spires that make up the Needles District. If you are able to hike among the Needles, think about how the land must have looked as a vast stretch of sand dunes 200 million years ago, how these dunes hardened into sandstone and have been slowly eroding, resulting in what you see before you. This view is but a snapshot in time. The Needles, like everything, are in constant flux.

Canyonlands History

Ancestral People

Evidence indicates that the Paleo-Indians hunted in Canyonlands as far back as 10,000 years ago. They hunted large game such as the mammoth and mastodon. From 8000 BCE to 250 BCE, the lifeway of these people developed as they became more accustomed to the land. Now living in the area, they utilized stone tools and the atlatl. This period, known as the Desert Archaic Period, is represented well in art pictographs and petroglyphs. Some of the best examples of these can be found in Horseshoe Canyon, which contains twenty life-size anthropomorphic images, some seven feet tall.

The Ancestral Puebloans and the Fremont cultures inhabited the area next starting in CE 250. They are distinguished by the introduction of farming techniques. Distributions of this lifeway were centered on the few areas that had water and a proper area for farming. Salt Creek Canyon in the Needles District had a large group of ancestral Puebloans, as evidenced by storage structures and granaries. This area was believed to have been populated around CE 1200. Within a hundred years, the group abandoned this lifeway and moved south to Arizona and New Mexico for reasons that are not entirely known.

Explorers and River Mappers

During the 1770s, the Spanish were interested in finding a route from Santa Fe, New Mexico, to their newly created missions in Monterey, California. The Spanish parties led by Escalante and Dominguez went around the difficult terrain rather than try to find a way through Canyonlands. French and American trappers looking for otter pelts did enter Canyonlands and are considered the first Europeans to have gone through the region. In 1838, a trapper named Denis Julien carved himself into history by etching his name throughout Canyonlands, along the banks of the Colorado River and even in Arches NP.

By 1859, southeast Utah was finally mapped accurately through an expedition led by Captain John N. Macomb. Macomb was sent by the U.S. Army to explore and map the Colorado Plateau with the goal of finding a wagon route from New Mexico to Utah.

In 1869, John Wesley Powell took on a bold expedition to map the Colorado River, Green River and its tributaries. Powell was a former Army major in the Civil War and had fought in the Battle of Shiloh, where he lost most of his right arm. After the Army, he became a professor of geology at Illinois Wesleyan University as well as curator of collections at the Museum of the Illinois State Natural History Society. He left a permanent position at the museum for the adventures of exploring the American West.

Powell set out with nine men, four boats and enough food for ten months. They started from the Green River in Wyoming on May 24, 1869 and finished on August 30, nearly three months later. His journey took him to the confluence of the Green and Colorado Rivers and on into the Grand Canyon and beyond to the mouth of the Virgin River.

Before his expedition, very little was known of the rivers in this area. His journey was groundbreaking on a number of accounts. He became the first European to navigate the Colorado through the Grand Canyon and was the first to give thorough accounts of the Green and Colorado rivers.

For nineteenth century America, Powell's descriptions of navigating hair-raising rapids, native encounters and dangers became instant legend. Of the ten men who started the journey, only six finished the 930-mile (1500 km) journey. Many of the features of the Colorado River, including Glen Canyon, were named by Powell and his men. Powell repeated the trip in 1871.

First Settlements and Ranching

By 1883, Mormon settlements formed near Canyonlands, including the town of Moab. The first pleasure run through Cataract Canyon wasn't done until 1907, nearly forty years after Powell's first expedition. In 1911, the first motion pictures of the canyons were filmed by Emery and Ellsworth Kolb.

The Mormon settlements took up cattle ranching primarily, and through 1975 much of Canyonlands was used for ranching. All three districts had areas that were decent for both cattle and sheep grazing. Many of the early ranchers named many of the park's features. On a mesa west of the Maze there lies a refuge called Robbers Roost, which was a hideout for cattle rustlers and outlaws, including Robert Leroy Parker, aka Butch Cassidy.

Mining Paves the Way

Up until the 1950s, Canyonlands was widely inaccessible. There were few roads, and most exploration of the area was done either on foot or by horseback. Then came the Cold War between Russia and the United States, two superpowers with drastically different opinions regarding economy and politics. The Atomic Energy Commission (AEC) was created in 1946 with a primary goal of stockpiling nuclear weapons for national defense and, ironically, to promote world peace. The AEC offered monetary incentives to anyone who had an interest in discovering and delivering uranium ore. They gave out instruction brochures explaining everything from how to prospect for uranium to how to use a Geiger counter.

The United States urgently needed uranium for national interests and put out an entire marketing campaign, including bonuses along with inflated prices, for ore. Prospectors headed into Canyonlands feeling they could earn good money mining "radioactive gold" while fulfilling a duty to their country in the interests of national security.

During this period nearly 1000 miles (1600 km) of road were built through the efforts of the AEC. Many were built through the hard hand labor of the prospectors themselves. In the end, the promise of plentiful supplies of uranium in Canyonlands didn't pan out. The prospectors left, but the roads, including White Rim Road, remained. As quickly as the miners left, casual travelers began to use these same roads to explore Canyonlands. The roads had opened up the area to the industry of tourism.

Even before the uranium mining craze, Bates Wilson had an eye on Canyonlands as a National Park. Wilson was the superintendent of the then-Arches National Monument and had tried unsuccessfully at getting Congressional attention for Canyonlands. He paused during the mining phase and fully expected it would be the end of this amazing area. With a sigh of relief that uranium was not all that plentiful, he was ready to take up the cause again. His early jeep tours with government officials would not be entirely in vain. They drew some early attention and awareness to the area.

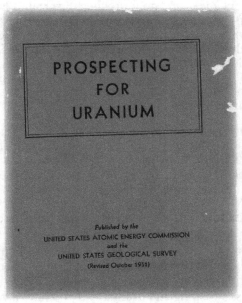

PROSPECTING
FOR
URANIUM

Published by the
UNITED STATES ATOMIC ENERGY COMMISSION
and the
UNITED STATES GEOLOGICAL SURVEY
(Revised October 1951)

What could possibly go wrong?

In 1961, Secretary of the Interior Stewart Udall traveled by plane to the Grand Canyon. On the way, he requested the plane fly over Canyonlands and ended up circling the confluence of the Green and Colorado Rivers several times. Udall contacted Bates Wilson, and in July 1961, the two went on a much-publicized trip around the area. Wilson was keen on creating a park within the Needles District. Secretary Udall thought on more grand terms and suggested an area of one million acres. By 1962, the Canyonlands park bill was introduced, though it was trimmed back to a quarter of the initial one-million-acre plan of Udall. After some debate and posturing by locals who had pre-existing claims on the land, President Lyndon B. Johnson signed Canyonlands National Park into existence on September 12, 1964. The park was expanded on November 12, 1971, to 337,598 acres, adding the Maze and Horseshoe Canyon to the park's boundaries.

Things to Do in Canyonlands

If you a working stiff like most of us, a vacation of the entire Grand Circle doesn't leave much time in any one park. Since Canyonlands NP is so big and much of it remote, it is hard to take in the entire park within a limited amount of time. Some folks decide to spend a few extra days in one park, and Canyonlands is certainly a candidate for being that park. Even if you don't have too much time to spend in Canyonlands, there is good news—there are tons of great single-day adventures that are both big and bold.

If you are up for a bit of adventure, this is a great park to plan out a big thing. Rent a jeep and go four wheeling around Island in the Sky; get off the mesa and get deeper into the park. Hire a rafting guide and glide down the gentler portions of either the Colorado or Green Rivers. If you are in need of more adrenaline-pumping action, brave Colorado's Cataract Canyon, some of the most respected sets of rapids the river offers. Try canyoneering, mountain biking or rock climbing. This is wild, untamed country. With a little planning you can build a day that will sit with you as possibly one of the most adventurous things you've ever done.

Of course, clinging to the edge of a cliff in a rented four-wheel drive with your spouse at the wheel may not be your cup of tea. Perhaps shooting down a mile-long stretch of unforgiving rapids falls closer to your "never in a million years" list of activities. Don't worry. For the rest of us Canyonlands still provides plenty for the casual visitor.

The Island in the Sky District has a plenitude of scenic overlooks, short hikes to amazing mesas and moderate jaunts for those who want to check out Upheaval Dome. For the most part, Island in the Sky by car is all about the views. On a clear day you can look out some 100 miles (160 km) in any direction. The views are dramatically different from those of the Grand Canyon, but no less sweeping and dramatic. If you have a very limited amount of time in Canyonlands, go to Island in the Sky and look out at the twisting rock canyons carved by the two most legendary rivers of the southwest.

If hiking is more your speed, Needles offers a more accessible view of Canyonlands. There are many hiking trails that loop within each other, offering many variations and lengths of hikes from which to choose. For a longer hike, Needles contains Druid Arch, which is a unique and massive double arch that, while naturally formed, hints at being built by some large giant.

The Maze is out for anyone who doesn't have a week or two of time, with one exception—Horseshoe Canyon. Horseshoe Canyon has arguably one of the most significant displays of rock art in North America. Horseshoe Canyon is detached from the rest of the park and reachable for most cars on a maintained unpaved road via Green River, Utah. The canyon includes the Great Gallery, a panel of rock with twenty life-size anthropomorphic figures painted some 2000 years ago. Take a look at the full description below for more detail. It is truly a remarkable site that is well worth a day trip in itself.

Hiking – Island in the Sky District

Mesa Arch

Easy – (0.5 mi / 0.8 km), round trip, allow 30 minutes

Mesa Arch is easy to find, easy to hike and has incredible views. The trail ends at Mesa Arch, which spans 50 feet and sits right on the edge of a 500-foot cliff wall. Other arches, including the well-known Washer Woman Arch, are visible. This hike is great for sunrise shots and is popular with photographers due to the ability to capture the light, views and arch all in one shot.

Mesa Arch at Sunrise

Upheaval Dome

Easy – (2 mi / 3.2 km), to second overlook, allow 1 hour

Upheaval Dome as a geological feature is explained in some detail in the Canyonlands Geology section of this book. As a hike, it allows the visitor to get out and into the slickrock of the park without much fuss. It is only about a mile (1.6 km) to the first overlook roundtrip. It is well worth the extra effort to the second overlook, which will take you deeper into the red rocks. Be sure to follow the markers that have been laid out, as in some portions the trail is simply walking on slick rock with the markers as guides.

Upheaval Dome

Whale Rock Trail

Moderate – (1 mi / 1.6 km), to overlook, allow 1 hour

Whale Rock Trail gives an alternative view of Upheaval Dome. There is a short climb up a large rock that indeed does look like a whale. The trail ends with a nice "big picture" view of Upheaval Dome.

Aztec Butte Trail

Moderate to Strenuous – (2 mi / 3.2 km), round trip, all 1.5 hours

This is a very rewarding and unique trail as it offers a lot of variety in a small package. The visitor will enjoy hiking through level, undisturbed grasslands toward the distant dome-shaped butte rising above. There is a short, steep climb to the rim of the butte where one can see ruins of Pueblo granaries. The trail loops around the top of Aztec Butte, providing inspiring views of Taylor Canyon.

Along the Aztec Butte Trail

Syncline Loop

Strenuous – (8.3 mi / 13.3 km), round trip, start at Upheaval Dome Trailhead

For a longer hike, take this loop that circles the entirety of Upheaval Dome. There is a spur trail that leads to the center of the crater as well. Allow another 3 miles (4.8 km) for the spur trail. Another spur trail along the loop (7 miles/11.2 km) leads to the Green River. The elevation change is about 1,300 feet. Note that this is a very rugged and strenuous trail and includes a mixture of boulder fields, steep switchbacks and plenty of slickrock. This is a fine example of a challenging hike that puts you inside one of the more remote sections of Canyonlands.

Warning: nearly all rescues in Canyonlands NP come from this trail. Route finding can be very difficult and there are many false spur trails. Also, given the various ups and downs on this loop, the actual elevation change is closer to 2900 feet. **This trail is for experienced hikers only.**

Hiking – Needles District

There are a lot of hikes in the Needles District and the ones listed below are by no means exhaustive. With Needles, hikers can immerse themselves directly within the park within a short distance from the trailhead. Each trail provides great adventures and views. Some of the most rewarding and easily accessible hikes are listed here.

Druid Arch / Elephant Canyon
Strenuous – (11 mi / 18 km), round trip, allow 5 - 6 hours

This is arguably one of the best hikes in Needles, with incredible views along the entire trail ending at Druid Arch. A quick glance at a park map will show that there are many routes from which to choose. This description starts at the Chesler Park access trail and follows up Elephant Canyon. The entire route is well marked and while the trail is long and it is not otherwise terribly strenuous except for the end. Once on the canyon floor you'll find it contains some sand and loose gravel, which makes hiking slower. This continues to the end of the canyon, where the last pitch is a steep climb of a quarter mile (0.4 km) involving a little scrambling up slick rock and even climbing a ladder.

Druid Arch itself is well worth the hike. The views along Elephant Canyon are spectacular and the arch is one of the more unique-looking arches, with much angularity and several keyhole windows within a fin-like blade of rock. The one thing any picture doesn't do is portray the enormity of the structure, which is humbling.

Druid Arch

Confluence Overlook

Moderate – (10 mi / 16.5 km), round trip, allow 5 - 6 hours

This hike for the most part covers a fair amount of open country, leaving the hiker time to take in the surroundings. Pick up the trail at the Big Spring Canyon Overlook and follow the well-marked path along the same geologic faults that helped create the needle formations. The trail ends at an overlook where one can see and hear the confluence of the Green and Colorado rivers. Depending on the weather and the resulting color of the rivers, it is possible to see the relatively green waters of the Green River mix into the Navajo Red waters of the Colorado. The water's powerful journey is heard echoing throughout the canyon, sometimes as a distant rumble, occasionally louder as the wind changes directions.

Confluence of Green and Colorado Rivers

Peekaboo Trail

Strenuous – (10 mi / 16.5 km), round trip, allow 5 - 6 hours

Peekaboo is an excellent trail for seeing the Needles District. The trail is strenuous, and you will need to pay close attention to the rock cairns pointing the way. The route contains wonderful views of sandstone features, and it crosses both Squaw and Lost canyons. There are two ladders that must be climbed. The trail ends at the seasonal Peekaboo spring and primitive campground.

Roadside Ruin Trail

Easy – (0.3 mi / 0.5 km), round trip, allow 20 minutes

This easy hike gives a nice example of a Pueblo granary.

Slickrock

Moderate– (2.4 mi / 4.0 km), round trip, allow 90 minutes

Slickrock has a bit of everything that Needles offers. There are four viewpoints that give commanding views of Island in the Sky District to the north and different views into the canyons below. The trail passes by a fragile arch and travels on both slickrock and actual trail. Each viewpoint is different and some offer long views into the canyons cut by the Colorado River. The Needles can also be seen in the distance.

Squaw Canyon Loop

Strenuous– (7.5 mi / 12.0 km), round trip, allow 4 hours

There are some pretty steep patches and about 500 feet in elevation gain, but gives a really nice immersion into the Needles backcountry. The trail, as described here, starts in Squaw Canyon and travels to its head. From there, it's up and over into Big Spring Canyon for the return.

At the trailhead, walk within a large desert valley to a juncture. Staying left puts you into Squaw Canyon. The canyon itself starts out wide and inviting and then narrows as it heads inward. Stay on the trail to Squaw Canyon, avoiding the two junctures to the left to Lost Canyon. At a well-marked juncture the trail goes up and over some slick rock which may look challenging but is fairly easy to navigate when dry.

Take a moment at the ridge to enjoy the views and the canyon you just walked up and then come on down the other side into Big Spring Canyon. The trip down into the canyon has some steeper spots, but these are short. Note that while the slickrock offers firm holds when dry, it's a different story when wet or frozen, so use proper judgement here.

The trail ambles through Big Spring Canyon before climbing out and following closer to the Squaw Canyon side of the ridge back over and down again to the trailhead. Big Spring Canyon offers nice vegetation and great views of the Needles as you make the return.

Squaw Canyon to Lost Canyon

Strenuous– (8.7 mi / 14.0 km), round trip, allow 5 -6 hours

This trail is similar to the one described above for Squaw Canyon. The hike heads up Squaw Canyon and then diverts left to Lost Canyon, travelling up that canyon and then crossing over again up and back over into Squaw. So, Squaw Canyon up, ridge climb over, Long Canyon up (if doing the canyon clockwise), ridge climb over, Squaw Canyon down and out.

This trail is a bit longer and there is reliable water to be found. The trail also contains more than a few cairns that lead the way, requiring a sharp eye to maintain to the trail at times.

Cave Spring Trail

Easy – (0.6 mi / 1.0 km), round trip, allow 45 minutes

Start this trail from the Cave Spring parking lot. The trail ends at some pictographs and a cowboy line camp ruin from a bygone era. There are two wooden ladders that need to be climbed as part of the hike.

Pothole Point Trail

Easy – (0.6 mi / 1.0 km), round trip, allow 45 minutes

The Pothole Point Trail gives great views of Needles and a collection of shallow potholes that create little puddles after a rain. Most of the trail is slickrock.

Horseshoe Canyon

Horseshoe Canyon is one of the most significant examples of rock art in North America and is certainly the best example of Barrier Canyon Style rock art. It is also one of the most recognizable. The life sized anthropomorphic figures with their unique trapezoidal shapes sit as reproductions in both the Denver Natural History Museum and the Museum of Modern Art in New York.

The centerpiece of Horseshoe Canyon is the Great Gallery. Within it is a panel of rock measuring 200 feet long (61m) and 15 feet (4.6m) high. The panel contains 20 elongated floating limbless humanoid figures, all life-sized, with one measuring over seven feet (2.1m) tall. The figures seem to float as ghosts on the rock, having no feet and distinctive trapezoidal shoulders. A visit to the Great Gallery is certainly a high-water mark for any trip.

Horseshoe Canyon is a separate unit from the main section of Canyonlands NP. It is best accessed from the west near Goblin Valley State Park at Highway 24. This road is often accessible for two-wheel drive vehicles and is okay for smaller RVs. It is graded along the 30 miles (48 km). It is hard to give a full recommendation to take the RV on this road as it changes dramatically during storms. The guidance here is probably okay for smaller RVs, but use your own judgment. You can also take a 47-mile (75 km) dirt road from Green River, but it has similar caveats and is longer.

Once out to the Horseshoe Canyon unit, it is an additional 7-mile (11 km) round trip hike to the Great Gallery. Allow about four hours for the hike, leaving plenty of time, water and food for the strenuous climb back out of the canyon. During the spring and fall, guided walks are held by the park's rangers. Aligning with these guided tours is an excellent way to see the petroglyphs and pictographs. The rangers do an amazing job of tying in the interesting details of what you are seeing and bringing historical context to your trip.

Great Gallery Detail in Horseshoe Canyon

Go to www.discovermoab.com for a complete list of guided tours to Horseshoe Canyon and for rafting, jeep and horseback riding tours.

Note that the roads may be closed seasonally during monsoon season. Check with the ranger station before heading out.

NAVTECH Expeditions has a tour of Horseshoe Canyon from Moab. This is a full-day trip and is an easy way to see this amazing place.

NAVTEC Expeditions: 321 North Main Street, Moab, Utah, Phone: (435) 259-7983 or (800) 833-1278

River Rafting

Rafting the Colorado River with a competent tour company is a safe way to have a story you can tell well into your nursing home years. There is much adrenaline-pumping and exhilaration, many brief moments of unholy terror and, simply put, a tremendous amount of overwhelming adventure.
You are seeing Canyonlands up close and personal, sure, but what you are really doing is exploring some of the last untamed wilderness in the contiguous United States. Canyonlands is vast, and it is nearly impossible to see it all in a normal vacation window. If you need to focus your visit, white water rafting is certainly a top consideration.

You will benefit from a little planning. There are many tour companies, but many of them are simply affiliate travel agencies disguised as rafting companies. They will book whatever you want but without any guarantee or knowledge that the river is running in the manner you imagined. It pays to go with knowledgeable outfitters that can help you plan the trip that's right for you. This guidebook references only the highest recommended local rafting tour groups operating in Moab.

Another reason to put some planning muscle into a rafting trip is that they aren't cheap. Costs range from a couple hundred dollars per person for scenic overnighter trips to $1000-plus per person for the multiday whitewater rafting trip.

When to go is important. Between May–June and sometimes into July, Cataract Canyon is a popular destination. This is a 46-mile (74 km) section just after the confluence of the Green and Colorado rivers. The spring runoff creates intense whitewater. The canyon is obstructed by tremendous boulders that create up to Class V rapids (Class VI is considered un-runnable, so Class V are serious rapids). Some of the rapids are notorious enough to get their own names, including Satan's Gut, The Claw and "Little Niagara." Most of Cataract Canyon is Class III to IV.

From July to October Cataract Canyon is still a great adventure, but the lowered water levels come with lowered whitewater difficulties. Many visitors find themselves disappointed since most of the rafting sites show photos of the

Cataract Canyon Whitewater

exciting torrents of spring and not the tempered waters of summer. If you are looking for full immersion into true whitewater, go in the spring.

How long you go is important. Some tour guides offer 1-day trips, but they are long days and cut out much of the soul of a rafting trip. They get you there, you shoot some rapids, and then you come back. If you can help it, don't do a 1-day trip. The most popular durations are 2-3-day trips.

These will include more hiking side canyons, eating BBQ or some other hot meal with your fellow rafters, explorations into native ruins and a chance to sleep out under the stars with the Colorado by your side. Many tour groups offer even longer tours of up to six days. In general, the longer you can get out, the more you will see and experience.

Don't feel it has to be Cataract Canyon. There are many destinations offered by the same tour groups that do Cataract Canyon. Some of these are outside of Canyonlands and include travel as part of the package. Desolation Canyon is a great destination if you are looking for Class II–III rapids and perhaps more isolation. There are still rapids up to Class IV in Westwater Canyon during the summer and is the go-to spot for summer whitewater.

For first-timers or for a more relaxed scene, Fisher Towers (aka 'The Daily") provides some mild rapids and is appropriate for children of ages five and up. Fisher Towers is considered one of the most scenic parts of the Colorado in Utah.

Recommended Rafting Outfitters:

Adrift Adventures:
378 North Main Street, Moab, Utah, Phone: (435) 259-8594 or (800) 874-4483

NAVTEC Expeditions:
321 North Main Street, Moab, Utah, Phone: (435) 259-7983 or (800) 833-1278

Sheri Griffith River Expeditions:
2231 South Highway 191, Moab, Utah, Phone: (800) 332-2439

Tag-A-Long Expeditions:
435 North Main Street, Moab, Utah, Phone: (800) 453-3292

Explore by 4WD

Canyonlands NP is a rough and rugged realm. The term "road" is at times a loose and relative word and is best understood under the guidance of a 4-wheel drive high clearance vehicle. The 100 miles (160 km) of White Rim Road, for example, is considered moderately difficult under favorable weather conditions. There are some sections, such as Elephant Hill and the Silver Steps, which will certainly test one's 4WD skills. I've seen younger kids drive up

Shafer Canyon Overlook and Road

a slope as sort of a race and I've also seen fathers ask their families to get out during certain sections due to the very real feeling that your jeep will tip over.

The point here is if you are looking for real adventure, renting a jeep or other 4WD vehicle in Moab will certainly not disappoint. If you'd rather not do the driving but still want to see the backcountry by vehicle, you can hire someone to lead the way on your adventure. Either way, exploring Canyonlands NP by 4WD is again one of those life moments you will be talking about for, well, the rest of your life.

Six Shooters Peak in Needles District

For tours and guides, Adrift Adventures and NAVTEC Expeditions (listed in the rafting section) are both great outfitters. They offer a wide range of tours from single- to multiday trips.

Canyonlands Jeep Adventures
225 South Main Street, Moab, Utah Phone: (866) 892-5337

Enterprise Rent-A-Car
Moab Airport, N Highway 191, Moab, Utah Phone: (435) 259-8505

Cliffhanger Jeep Rental
40 West Center Street, Moab, Utah Phone: (435) 259-0889

Horseback Riding

Exploring the depths of the red rock canyons by horseback is a great alternative for those looking to connect with nature without a motorized vehicle.

The caveat of horseback riding is simple: if you haven't done it in a while or ever, be prepared for some sore muscles in unexpected places. The upside is well worth the effort, but it's good to set expectations.

Red Cliffs Lodge is a great detour and not just for horseback riding. Rides are half day, starting daily at 8:30 AM and available for children 8 and up. While you won't be riding within Canyonlands NP itself, the area around the lodge is not only spectacular, it also follows some of the same trails used in John Wayne movies.

The lodge also contains a very nice movie museum with trivia and memorabilia from nearly all of the movies shot in the Moab area. There is a restaurant and even a wine tasting room featuring Utah wines. It's possible to make a full and fairly relaxing day out of the lodge if you are looking for something a bit slower.

Red Cliffs Lodge

Mile Post 14 Hwy 128, Moab, Utah 84532 Phone: (866) 812-2002

Driving Around

Canyonlands NP is smack dab in the middle of a Grand Circle journey. Blistered, sunburned, sore and drained from the heat, the thought of doing nothing more than driving to an overlook and peering over the edge may seem to be the perfect thing to do. If this is your group, take heart; there are many overlooks in Canyonlands NP, each with stunning grand views that make up the definitive heart of the Southwest.

Most of the overlooks are naturally atop the Island in the Sky. These are listed in order of appearance as you enter the Island in the Sky District.

Shafer Canyon Overlook

Easy to miss as you come in, this overlook is more of a pull-out for an RV and is easily navigated as you make it back out of the park. What makes this view cool is the view of the 4WD Shafer Road, which somehow manages to twist and turn its way through tight loops down the canyon.

Green River Overlook

As you head into the park's Island in the Sky District, turn right toward Upheaval Dome and look for the spur road to Green River Overlook. There is ample parking with a short paved access trail to the edge of the mesa. The views on Green River Overlook are spectacular, and while it's hard to call any one of the overlooks here "the best," this is certainly a contender.

Holeman Spring Canyon Overlook

From Green River Overlook, turn left and continue toward Upheaval Dome. Again, this one is easy to miss as it is more of a pull-out and best viewed coming back from Upheaval Dome. The overlook has northern views of the park.

Buck Canyon Overlook

This overlook is a loop for easy driving and parking and overlooks the eastern side of the mesa, offering very different views from the other more westward facing turnouts.

Grand View Point Overlook

This is the end of the road and most southern overlook in the Island in the Sky District. The overlook offers some of the most dramatic views in the park commanding a broad swath to the west and south of the park. This is definitely worth the drive.

Green River Overlook

Wooden Shoe Overlook

Stay to the right just after passing the visitor center to catch this first of two formal overlooks in the Needles District. There isn't much pull-through parking for this area, which can make parking an RV a bit tricky on crowded days. The pullout gives a distant view of an arch formation that looks unmistakably like a wooden shoe. While the views themselves are certainly worth a stop, the shoe is fairly well out there. If you are going for a shot of the Wooden Shoe, bring your telephoto lens.

Big Spring Canyon Overlook

Once in Needles, follow the signs north to the end of the road at Big Spring Canyon Overlook. Easy parking for RVs. This is a great place to get out and take in the very different views compared to Island in the Sky. There are several tabletop pinnacles, which resemble tables of rock perched on a slimmer stand of rock.

Newspaper Rock

While not actually part of Canyonlands NP, it is right off the road en route to the Needles District. It is not only one of the most easily accessed petroglyph sites, it is one of the largest collections of rock art in North America and one of the best preserved. There are more than 650 petroglyph representations of humans, animals, abstract forms and other symbols. Some of the petroglyphs tell stories while others are seemingly random. The petroglyph panel is over 200 square feet in area and dates back some 1500 years ago to as recent as this century. Take Highway 211 toward the Needles District for 13 miles (21 km). The day use area has good parking and pit toilets.

To see a rainbow in the desert is to visualize the play of imagination

The Photographer's Wife

[Me]: Bryce, do you like cheeseburgers or just hamburgers?

[Mom]: He's always liked cheeseburgers.

[Me]: Oh, why Bryce, you have an entourage. You mom answers for you whenever I ask you a question.

[Bryce]: Well, I'm a busy man.

Ella's shot of the family

There was one evening that our family walked the short distance to the edge of Mesa Arch in Canyonlands. It's a trip most people do in the morning, capturing the sunrise as it lights up the distant canyons from the edge of the horizon. For us, though, we were content to visit it at dusk. There were only a couple of cars in the parking lot, and it seemed like a quiet way to end the day.

When we arrived at the arch, an Indian gentleman, looking a little spooked, was telling his wife to watch out. He didn't realize that the arch literally sits at the edge of a cliff and tried to walk through it before catching himself at the last moment. After telling his wife, he warned us as well.

"Do be careful, it is very deceptive," he said in a dirty British accent. I smiled and thanked him. The arch was deceptive. It is a bit of a siren, drawing your attention and sloping upwards at the end so you really can't see the nothingness that follows until it is upon you.

We allowed the kids to sit on their bellies and peer over the edge while I snapped pictures. An older woman was sitting straight as an arrow on a nearby rock. I was at first drawn to her simply because I hadn't even noticed her before, though we had been there about ten minutes with her sitting fairly close to us. She had simply managed to blend with the stillness of the rocks themselves. It was only when she moved that I noticed her.

She caught me looking at her and came over. "Would you like a family photo?" she asked.

"Oh, that would be wonderful!" my wife responded.

"My name is Ella," she replied and shook my hand and then my wife's as we introduced ourselves. She had a German accent with a round face centered by a small nose. Her eyes were a clear blue that seemed to pierce through whatever walls you had in place.

Ella took a couple of pictures of us, getting us to say cheese on her commands. She took shots with the arch in frame and then suggested we get some with the Washer Woman in the background.

"That is the Washer Woman there," she said to the boys. "She is called that because she looks like a woman washing clothes. She has been here since the first time I came here in the seventies. We have some good photos of the Washer Woman."

My wife hadn't noticed the Washer Woman arch, so she corralled the boys and me once again for "a few more photos." We put on our most perfect smiles at the assigned moment and Ella pushed the camera's "easy" button. Nothing happened. We fell back to our default faces for a moment, slouched a bit, then organized back to the perfect family pose. At Ella's warm command we put our most sincere smiles and straightest of postures forward once again. We then stood in place for what seemed an eternity waiting for the depressing of what was now the camera's "take the damn photo" button. Nothing whatsoever happened again.

I ran over, with the rest of the family in place, frozen in time with smiles at the ready, the Washer Woman never once falling out of character, but the problem was not a surmountable one. The camera had run out of juice. We tried turning it off and back on several hundred times at Ang's insistence, but it was too dead for one last shot.

Ella handed the camera back to me. "Well, that is too bad, that is a great shot of your family with the Washer Woman in the background. My husband has a great shot of the two of us in that exact spot. He was a photographer."

"Where are you from?" I asked.

"Oh, originally from Germany, but that was a long time ago. Where are you folks traveling from?"

"We drove from California to Las Vegas and then rented an RV from there. We've been traveling the Grand Circle." I listed the parks we had been to.

"Oh, that sounds like an amazing journey. I did a similar trip with my husband in the early 70s. He was a photographer. I am retracing the trip in memory of him."

Everest interrupted, "Hey, Dad! Can Bryce and I walk back to the RV?"

"Sure, son. Hold on a moment, Ella. Here are the keys, no messing around and lock yourself in when you get there."

"Sure, Dad." Ev and Bryce ran back up the short trail to the motor home.

"What were the parks like back then for you?" Angela asked.

"It was a very good time… and a very hard time for us." My husband was a vice president at a company in Colorado. Then one day he came home with some results from the doctor. He had developed a form of colon cancer. It changed everything. He was forced to leave his job and we poured everything into making him well again. We lost our home and the entire time we just tried to not give up the hope he would survive it."

"We had to head up to Oregon to visit a doctor, a specialist. At first we were going to drive straight to Oregon. Just head up there and head straight back. But somewhere in the planning, we changed our minds and decided to make the trip something more than just driving straight to the specialist. We took what little equity we had left from selling the house and bought a motor home, more of a minivan with a stove really. It wasn't considerable but the thing didn't bother us much. We traveled to many of the same places you just described. Zion, Bryce, Arches, and here, plus Yellowstone and the Tetons."

"It was here at this arch that my husband regained himself a bit. He was strong, a very strong man, never complained. But you could see it in his expression, he wasn't himself, at least until this trip. He started taking pictures. He had a nice box camera, cherry wood frame, a special lens, he would take these 5 x 7 negatives. He had the camera since he was a boy, his father gave it to him. It was the one thing he wouldn't part with."

"He shot Mesa Arch at sunrise, standing nearly right here, where we are standing. The photo resonated with people. He opened up a photography studio and shot much of the Southwest. It was his calling. It gave him the will to live and that transferred into his photos."

"Did you ever make it to Oregon?" I asked a little puzzled.

"Oh yes, sorry! I got off track! Yes, we made it to Oregon and he went through chemo and his cancer went into remission. It was such a relief. We then set up a little studio in Boulder, Colorado and each season we would take some long outing to photograph some more of the world. Our little motor home, Tom and myself, puttering around, catching the Southwest, sometimes at its finest."

"Was he a photographer I would know?" Ang asked.

"No, he was never that famous, but we made enough money from his photography to live a good life. Even though his cancer went into remission, I think he knew his time was coming to an end. His brush with death inspired him to capture the essence of a scene. There was a soulfulness to his photography. One year we came back to this spot and he took a picture of the two of us, sitting and holding hands, here at Mesa Arch with the sunrise behind us. He made a large copy, about a meter wide and gave it to me just before he died. It was just the one shot, he usually took many, but this time he just took the one. The picture hangs in my living room over the fireplace. It is a perfect picture. The lighting is just so…I sometimes catch myself just immersed in it, the two of us together. It was the last picture he took of us."

"Soon after he gave it to me, his cancer returned and it took him. I think he knew when he took it; I can see it in his eyes when I look at the picture. It's not a sadness I see, it's a look of subtle confidence. As if he knew he would be leaving this world but was at peace with it and knew that one day I would be too."

Ang wiped a tear from her cheek and came in closer to Ella. "I'm really sorry for your loss," Angela said.

She put her arms around Ella and gave her a deep hug. I did as well. It was such a touching moment for us. Ella didn't cry but instead gazed calmly beyond to the Mesa Arch and the distant Washer Woman. As I drew away I saw a sense of knowing in her gaze, a sense of peace. She was looking at a scene that was hanging in her living room, a scene she had lost herself within on countless nights, staring at it over and over. It had become a beacon to help reconcile her loss. It was at times her entire world, that moment at the Arch with the sun's morning glow and her husband looking back at her, telling her it was okay. The scene was etched in her mind and now it was before her in real life, a memory imprinted on the canvas of reality.

We thanked Ella for her story and for taking the photos and began walking back to the RV and our kids.

"That was an amazing story," Angela remarked.

"Yeah, it was. I was a little surprised she opened up so much to us," I said.

"Oh, I don't think she cared about that. It was probably good to tell someone about her husband. I know I'd be happy to tell someone my wonderful story. It was so romantic; what a beautiful lady."

Ella had been slowly retracing the journeys she had taken with her husband for these past weeks, reliving the happiness they had shared, the moments of laughter, the near disasters, and their incredible stories, if only to them. She passed through towns that in some ways had changed and in others remained exactly the same. In the end, her pilgrimage had led her to this spot, culminating to gaze at the thing that summed up everything they were, everything they had together. In some way, I don't think she was traveling alone in her journey. The essence if not the spirit of her husband was with her.

174

Arches
National Park

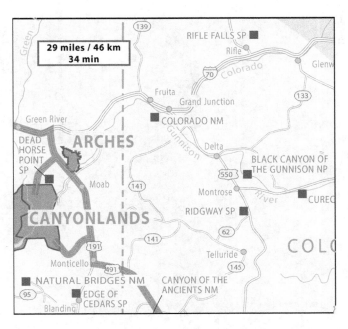

"*Wilderness is not a luxury but a necessity of the human spirit, and as vital to our lives as water and good bread. A civilization which destroys what little remains of the wild, the spare, the original, is cutting itself off from its origins and betraying the principle of civilization itself.*"

—Edward Abbey, *Desert Solitaire*

ARCHES NATIONAL PARK

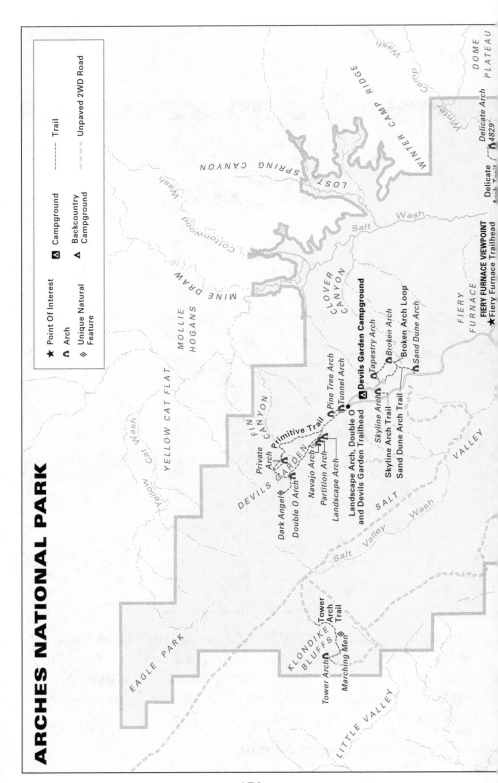

Legend:
- ★ Point Of Interest
- ∩ Arch
- ◈ Unique Natural Feature
- ◪ Campground
- ▲ Backcountry Campground
- ----- Trail
- ==== Unpaved 2WD Road

EAGLE PARK

YELLOW CAT FLAT

Yellow Cat Wash

MOLLIE HOGANS

MINE DRAW

Cottonwood Wash

LOST SPRING CANYON

Salt Wash

WINTER CAMP RIDGE

Camp Wash

DOME PLATEAU

Delicate Arch ∩ 4829'
Delicate Arch Trail
Delicate Arch Trailhead

CLOVER CANYON

FIN CANYON

DEVILS GARDEN

Primitive Trail

Private Arch

Dark Angel
Double O Arch
Navajo Arch
Partition Arch
Landscape Arch

Pine Tree Arch
Tunnel Arch

Landscape Arch, Double O
and Devils Garden Trailhead

Devils Garden Campground ◪

Tapestry Arch

Skyline Arch
Skyline Arch Trail
Sand Dune Arch Trail

Broken Arch
Broken Arch Loop
Sand Dune Arch

FIERY FURNACE

FIERY FURNACE VIEWPOINT
★ Fiery Furnace Trailhead

SALT VALLEY

Salt Valley Wash

KLONDIKE BLUFFS
Tower Arch Trail
Tower Arch ∩
Marching Men ◈

LITTLE VALLEY

176

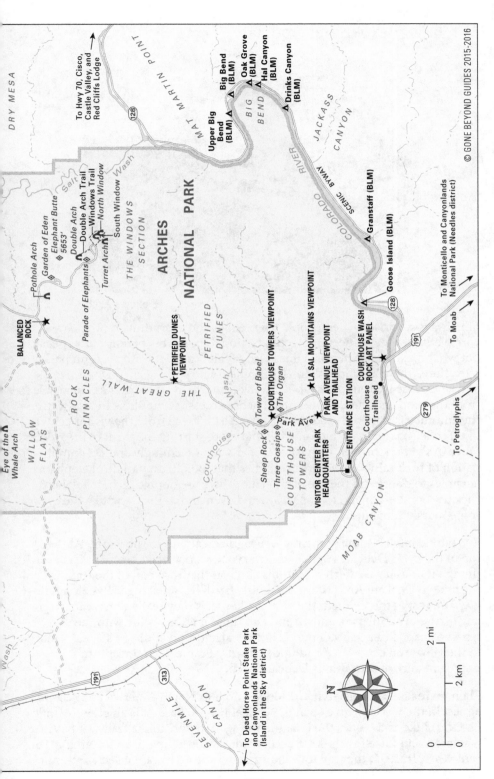

© GONE BEYOND GUIDES 2015-2016

What Makes Arches Special

Delicate Arch

I'm always surprised when people tell me they did everything on the Grand Circle but have never been to Arches National Park. This park is truly special, but what makes it so special is that it isn't pretentious. It's simply a fun park to explore. There are more than 2000 arches of all sorts of shapes and sizes, and a new one is around just about every turn. Many of the arches are visible from the road and there are dozens that are accessible via short hikes. Even the entrance is fun. The road climbs up a tall cliff face from the visitor center like a roller coaster gaining some height before starting the thrill of the ride. Once in the park proper, the visitor is met with a seemingly endless combination of rock rainbows. There are arches that look like a parade of elephants, keyholes to doors and the eye of a needle. There are double arches, balanced rock towers standing on top of arches and even arches that look like the eye of some massive creature.

The park contains some of the most recognized arches in the world. At the top of the list is Delicate Arch. Most everyone who visits takes this hike, even though it does have a fairly strenuous climb at the front end of the trail. Even the hike to Delicate Arch is fun. It's a little hard, has amazing views along the way and just at the moment the weary hiker feels they really don't want to go any further, you turn around a bend and there it is, big as life with the often-snowcapped La Sal Mountains in the background adding a surreal context to the view. You can even stand under nearby Frame Arch to capture a very unique picture of the famous Delicate Arch.

Then there's Landscape Arch, the longest arch in North America and second largest in the world, with a span of 306 feet base to base. It is an easy 1.6-mile (2.4 km) hike and baffles the imagination with its threadlike frailty. It has in fact lost a bit of itself with three decent stone slabs falling from the arch in recent years. In 1991, the trail to walking under the arch was closed as a result.

There is something wonderful and even magical about stepping through an arch. For everyone who comes, the arch draws them in, invites them to stand underneath these bows of rock and step through them to see what they look like from the other side. Watch your fellow visitor. They walk up to the arch, look up underneath it and then carry through to see it from the other side. Arches fascinate, and at Arches NP, there is a lot of fascination. Nowhere in the world is there a place quite like this park. The arches are an invitation, every one of them.

Staying in Arches National Park

If you do come during peak months and didn't get a reservation, plan on staying outside the park. Since Arches is such a close neighbor to Canyonlands, refer to the Staying in Canyonlands section regarding information for lodging and campgrounds outside the park.

Tower of Babel

There is one campground in Arches, eighteen miles (29 km) from the park entrance. The Devils Garden Campground contains 50 sites, all of which can be reserved in advance between March 1 and October 31. You can reserve sites online at www.recreation.gov or by phone at (877) 444-6677.

The sites do book up early during peak times and can be booked up to six months in advance. One tip if you aren't seeing availability is to keep checking. In fact, check as if you have OCD. Folks do cancel, but the sites will be gobbled up within ten minutes. If you really want to stay in Devils Garden during peak times, bring equal measures of tenacity and resilience. There is a good reason to stay in the park—accessibility. Hiking trails are right off the campground, leading to more than a dozen arches within a relatively short distance.

Devils Garden Campground does have potable water plus the usual round of amenities, including a picnic table, grill and both pit and flush toilets. Some of the sites accommodate longer RVs up to 30 feet. There are no showers or RV dump station in Arches. Sites are $25 per night. During the winter months, (November 1 to February 28) sites 1 –24 are available on a self-serve basis.

Arches Geology

The Arches

The first question one might ask is why are there so many arches in Arches National Park? Seriously, nowhere else on the planet are there over 2000 catalogued arches and countless remnants of previous arches in one place. Arches of sandstone rock can be found all over the Colorado Plateau, yet here, there must have been ideal conditions to help create so many of these sweeps of curvaceous wonder. The truth is there were a number of forces at play to create the ideal environment for these wonderful rock formations. Like the ingredients of Canyonlands, geological oddities, salt, stability, and just the right amount of erosion have played a part.

The area around Arches NP was at one time an inland sea, spreading from horizon to horizon. Starting 300 million years ago, these seas would come, dry up, and return, twenty-nine times in all. Each time the waters evaporated, they left behind salt beds that eventually grew to more than five thousand feet thick. This is once again the now hopefully familiar Paradox Formation. The salt was then covered by a tremendous amount of rock and sand. Just as we learned earlier, the salt, which is less dense than the rock and now under intense pressure from the rock above it, started to flow very slowly. It was forced westward, blocked by faults and eventually collected into a dome 2 miles (3.2 km) high, 3 miles (4.8 km) wide and 70 miles (113 km) long. Since the salt was less dense than the rock, it was able to float through the rock layers above it but never reached the surface. This took 75 million years.

Then the salt finally reached equilibrium with the rock above it and stopped flowing. Then, on top of all that salt and rock, over a mile deep of additional rock was deposited. When the Colorado Plateau was itself pushed upwards, water and lots of time eroded away all but a thin layer of the rock above the salt dome. This thin rock layer around the salt dome cracked, and when the rock layer was finally exposed to the surface, the salt underneath was exposed to the elements. It slowly washed away, and the dome of rock collapsed and formed what is now known as Salt Valley. At the valleys edge, this geological activity created long thin, vertical monoliths of rock called fins.

Okay, so what does this have to do with perfect arch creation? On either side of Salt Valley, the fins of rock continued to erode. With the absence of any earthquakes in the area, these narrow fins were left to the devices of water erosion and became perfect for arch creation.

The erosion of the fins is the same. Water eats away at some of the calcium carbonate cement in the rock until a hole is formed. Then erosion and gravity weighing on the now unsupported rock slowly enlarge the hole over time. Since there are no earthquakes in this area, the hole is allowed to enlarge to unbelievable spans, creating the delicate and immense arches you see before you.

As you travel deeper along the main stretch of Arches NP, you are actually traveling up the northern edge of Salt Valley. The conditions here were perfect, the deposit of a large amount of salt, years of erosion, the cracking of the rock layer into nice slabs that became vertical fins of rock perfect for arch making. This area is amazing in its perfection of arch creation. Nowhere on this earth have geologic conditions come together so well for this rather marvelous phenomenon to occur.

Petrified Dunes

If you think about it, there really isn't any such thing as a petrified dune, so why is there a spot in Arches with such a namesake? Well, they do look like sand dunes frozen into place and yes, they were in fact at one time sand dunes before being covered with other sedimentary layers. In reality, they are simply rock formations eroded from the sand dune beds of 65 million years ago. Petrified sand dunes are simply sandstone, so these are simply sandstone formations that look like dunes of sand.

Still, given the connection of these current formations to their sand dune past, perhaps there is something else going on here. Perhaps these are ghost dunes forced to continually resurrect themselves in dune-like shapes, perpetually stuck as geologic echoes of happier times when sands could roam freely and openly here in Arches. On a walk among these formations, is that just the wind you hear or the cries of long dead dune souls yelling out against some ancient curse to be freed! It's probably just the wind and perhaps too much sun, but you will never know for sure.

Arches History

The history surrounding Arches NP is similar to Canyonlands NP in that the chronicle begins with early ancestral peoples and includes a nod to Mormon influence followed by a small group of recent advocates who helped in the formation of the park. Still there are differences in the amount of inhabitation, in the hardships of the parks most famous settler, John Wesley Wolfe, and of the tenacity of one man who helped bring both Arches and Canyonlands to the attention of the United States.

Early Inhabitants

The most interesting aspect of early inhabitation is that there isn't much evidence that much occurred. The hunter-gatherer period during the Ice Age of 10,000 years ago shows some evidence that they hunted in the Courthouse Wash and Salt Valley. There are pockets of chert and chalcedony quartz that were used for making stone tools in these areas and the honing of rock into sharp dart points. Crude knives and fur scrapers can still be found as debris piles in these areas.

While common in the Mesa Verde National Park, Arches was much farther north for the ancestral Puebloan territories. As such, there was little inhabitation by these agriculturalists and hunter people of two thousand years ago. There are a scant few dwellings in Arches, thought to be for seasonal use. While evidence of habitation during this period is scarce, there was a fair number of rock drawings created during this period. With the prolific arches in the area, it is easy to imagine this area held a special significance for the Puebloan people. It is difficult to know whether their lifeway was better suited to the lands farther south, or if they refrained from inhabiting the area consciously because of the arches themselves.

Puebloan people began to leave the region about 700 years ago for a number of reasons, mainly because of consistent drought. Other tribes such as the Ute did make their way into the Arches region. The petroglyph panel near Wolfe Ranch depicts a hunting scene with humans on horseback. The Utes were introduced to horses by the Spanish in the late 1700s. While there is no evidence beyond the rock art, it is possible that this was a seasonal site for the Utes. It brings one to ponder; did they visit Delicate Arch with the same passion as folks do today? It is easy to imagine the hike up to Delicate Arch as a playground for young Ute children, playing hide and seek among the rocks. Perhaps a group of older boys hunted smaller game in the hopes of coming back to the tribe with a feeling of accomplishment and pride. These are likely products of imagination, something perhaps to help take your mind off the steep trails as you head to Delicate Arch.

John Wolfe and Other Settlers

Wolfe Ranch Cabin

Moab and the surrounding area was settled more slowly than other U.S. Southwest territories. The original inhabitants were often hostile and the terrain itself was as rugged as it was arid. Dry summers, cold winters, little water and hostile Indians kept many settlers away. It wasn't until 1877 that

182

Moab itself was established—a good 33 years after Brigham Young started his settlement of Utah. By 1883 the Denver and Rio Grande Western Railroad was completed, and along with it came a welcome increase in stability for the early pioneers.

John Wesley Wolfe was a Civil War veteran who suffered from a leg injury during the war. His injury was painful, especially during the harsh Ohio winters, so he decided to look for a warmer, dryer climate. The tamer lands and warm climes of Moab spoke to John. He settled in the Salt Valley region with his son Fred in 1888. Wolfe built a cabin on the banks of Salt Wash, which was as isolated from Moab as it is today. What the land did have was water. John and his son dammed the wash and used it to irrigate a garden. The water wasn't suitable for drinking, which came from a spring some three quarters of a mile (1.2 km) away.

John and his son were comfortable with their "make do" lifestyle. They built a very simple one-room cabin. They grazed a few cattle under the Bar DX brand on his 100 acres and even built a corral for them. Here is an excerpt of a letter from John to his family back home:

We have started a cattle spread on a desert homestead. We call it the Bar— DX Ranch. Fred and I live in a little log house on the bank of a creek that is sometimes dry, sometimes flooded from bank to bank with roaring muddy water. We are surrounded with rocks—gigantic red rock formations, massive arches and weird figures, the like of which you've never seen. The desert is a hostile, demanding country, hot in summer, cold in winter. The Bar—DX Ranch is a day's ride from the nearest store, out of the range of schools.

John was married for the duration he lived with his son, and while he continually promised to return, he spent another eighteen years at the ranch. His wife refused to go west and never did join her husband in Utah. In 1906 Wolfe's daughter, Flora Stanley, her husband Ed and their two small children Esther and Ferol came out to live with her father and brother. John sent money from his pension check for the train ride out to Utah and met them at Thompson Springs (now Thompson, Utah).

John put the family in his wagon and rode them the 30 miles (48 km) back to his ranch by horse. The tiny log cabin with only a dirt floor brought his daughter Flora to tears. John promised to build a new cabin and a dugout cellar in the spring of 1907. This cabin was built from logs carried from the banks of the Colorado River, six miles (10 km) away and included a proper floor. In spite of these new digs, the newcomers stayed on the Wolfe Ranch for less than two years before moving to Moab.

John Wolfe sold the ranch to Tommy Larson in 1910 and returned to Ohio. There he lived out the rest of his life, dying on October 22, 1913 at the age of 84.

Tommy Larson sold the ranch to Marvin Turnbow and his partners Lester Walker and Stib Beeson. In 1927, Turnbow helped as a camp hand for the U.S Geological Survey and for many years both USGS maps and National Park Service maps listed the cabin site as "Turnbow Cabin." The ranch was sold to Emmett Elizondo in 1947, who later sold it to the National Park Service. John Wolfe's granddaughter, Mrs. Esther Stanley Rison, and his great-granddaughter, Mrs. Hazel Wolfe Hastler, visited the cabin in 1970, providing details for the historical record. The ranch site was renamed "Wolfe Ranch" shortly thereafter.

Park Founders and Advocates

The Salt Valley and the surrounding territory of Arches NP were mainly off the national radar until the turn of the twentieth century. It had not been part of the earliest expeditions by the hardy Jesuit priests and was not explored during John Wesley Powell's or Fremont's many ventures into the Southwest. For the most part, the land of the Arches fell into that of southwest lore, the truth known only to those in Moab and other locals. In 1911, Loren "Bish" Taylor began to describe the wonders of Moab as editor of the local Moab newspaper. Loren loved to explore the local area and had taken over the Moab newspaper at the tender age of 18. He wrote about all of Moab, including the rainbows of rock within Arches, through the 1940s.

Another early proponent of Arches was John "Doc" Williams, Moab's first doctor. John did a fair number of "house calls," going from ranch to ranch on horseback. On his rides through Salt Valley, he often climbed out of the northern end of the valley to a spot now known as Doc Williams Point. On many rides, "Doc" and "Bish" rode and explored the regions together.

By 1923 word of the unique lands and numerous arches spread to the board members of the Rio Grande Western Railroad, who were looking for additional tourist stops to attract rail passengers. They were impressed with the what they heard about the area and began a campaign to get the U.S. Park Service to include the land in its collections. Little did anyone know the magnitude of the unique qualities park or the true number of arches. At the time, they thought there were only 90 arches within the park and not the 2000 arches by current count. On April 12, 1929, President Herbert Hoover signed 1,920 acres in the Windows and 2,600 acres in Devils Garden as Arches National Monument.

The formation of Arches as a national monument in the early 1920s helped shelter the park from the flurry of uranium exploration in the mid 1940s and 1950s. While that put some additional burden on what would become Canyonlands NP, it also helped limit the damage of that park to some extent. In 1949, Bates Wilson became the custodian of Arches and Natural Bridges   National Monuments and helped bring much-needed attention to the Canyonlands area. He was an influential voice in the creation of Canyonlands NP. He also had a large hand in shoring up Arches.

When he began his stewardship of Arches in 1949, the park had no paved roads, no campground, no trails, and no visitor center. By his retirement in 1972, the park had doubled in size, gained more amenities for the tourist and had gone from being a national monument to a national park.

Bates managed one park ranger from 1956 to 1957 who had a knack for describing the soul of the desert while not being shy about his feelings toward preservation over tourism. Edward Abbey lived in "a little tin government housetrailer" near Balanced Rock. He was part of a movement of environmental activism that continued into the 1970s and even today, bringing to bear the creation of the Environmental Protection Agency and national awareness toward protecting the environment. The activist movement did a lot to help reduce air and water pollution and set up recycling programs to reuse resources. Prior to this movement, the nation's concerns were growing regarding what was then a relatively untethered industrial condition. While there is always more that can be done to minimize water, air and soil pollution, the efforts of this movement have created an overall improvement in environmental conditions.

Edward Abbey's work included Desert Solitaire, an eloquent and personal account of his time spent as a ranger at Arches. Edward's book saw the move toward expanding national awareness toward parks like Arches and the resulting infrastructure needed to support the increased volume of tourists. He wrote of his concerns of creating park policy that strayed from preservation, that by the simple act of increasing the number of cars and people coming to the park, we would destroy them. It is interesting to note that park policy continues to struggle with this notion today, finding a balance between making the treasures available to the nation while protecting them. It is hard to say whether Abbey's books helped his cause or accelerated the amount of traffic to the park. His books brought national awareness through descriptions that beckoned the readers to see for themselves the lonely and magnificent call of the desert.

Things to Do in Arches NP

Unlike Canyonlands, Arches NP is both more accessible and smaller in size. Many of the popular formations are short hikes from the parking lot and consolidated so that you can see a number of different arches and other features within one stop. This does have its drawbacks. Parking during the peak season can be a challenge. Oftentimes you will find yourself parking your RV a good five minutes from the trailhead by foot. Once on the trail, you will find yourself among many who have come to see the same arches and views. If you are looking to have the park to yourself, remember that many of your fellow tourists are staying in nearby Moab. This means that early mornings and dinnertime are typically gentler and more peaceful times to explore.

Courthouse Section

Courthouse Wash Panel

Moderate to Strenuous - (5.5 miles/ 8.9 km), one way, allow 3 hours one way

Courthouse Rock Art

The Courthouse Wash Panel is one of the more colorful and intriguing petroglyphs in the area. It shows humanoid figures with trapezoidal forms representative of Barrier Canyon Style rock art. The anthropomorphic figures are ordained with abstract, almost alien, heads. While still full of color, the panel was vandalized in 1980 when someone splashed bleach on it. As disappointing as this is, the National Park Service was able to perform some restoration, although not to its original grandeur.

The panel sits just inside the outlet of Courthouse Wash into the Colorado River. There is parking off Highway 191 and the panel sits less than a quarter mile (1.2 km) upstream from this lower trailhead. The route described here is from the upper Courthouse Wash Trailhead accessed from the main park road. Come into the park and look for the Courthouse Wash parking area on your right, just across the obvious bridge. The hike is a delight, winding gently down the Courthouse Wash either alongside it or by walking in the creek itself. It can be a sandy walk, and there are pockets of non-life-threatening quicksand as you cut through tall canyon walls to the lower trailhead. The route is one way and is best pre-planned with a shuttle car waiting at the lower trailhead. Otherwise, admire the panel and return by walking back upstream . There are several side canyons to explore along this hike, the first encountered that cuts in a northerly fashion is a favorite.

Park Avenue

Easy – (1.0 mile / 1.6 km) one way, allow 30 – 60 minutes one way

Park Avenue

Park Avenue has a small elevation change as it descends steeply into a wide canyon with amazing thin-walled fins of rock that sheer upwards hundreds of feet into the air. The scenery is best described as epic southwest, as grand as anything the Colorado Plateau has to offer. Once in the canyon, the walk is easy enough, allowing one to take in the view of the Courthouse Towers, including The Organ, a massive sandstone fin tower. Other notables are Sheep Rock, which looks like a lamb on a rock, and the Three Gossips, which resemble three figures standing around. If you are of the paranoid type, the Three Gossips are definitely talking about you! If you look to your left of Sheep Rock, you can see a newly forming arch that some have nicknamed "Baby Arch." Sheep Rock itself is thought to have once been part of a double arch. See if you can make out the remnant towers that have sparked this theory.

The area is well marked and is one of the first pull-offs as you enter the park. To get back to your car, either return the way you came or arrange for a shuttle car to pick you up at the end of the trail. The Park Service discourages hikers from walking on the park road.

Balanced Rock

Windows Section

Once past the Courthouse Towers and Park Avenue, look for the North and South windows ahead of you to the right. This section, called the Windows, contains a number of easily accessible arches that are both dramatic and awe-inspiring. This is a very popular destination and is best done early.

Balanced Rock

Easy – (0.3 mi / 0.5 km), round trip, allow 15 - 30 minutes

Balanced Rock is one of the more iconic landforms in Arches NP and the Southwest. It has been photographed and copied in movie sets so many times, it will likely be a familiar form when you first see it. The landform itself is a 128-foot tower of different layers of sandstone that are eroding at different rates. The capstone is eroding slower, which makes for the look of a large rock balancing on a smaller pedestal. Balanced Rock can be accessed just before turning right into the Windows Section.

The Windows

Easy – (1.0 mile / 1.6 km), one way, allow 30 - 60 minutes one way

North and South Windows

The Windows Trail, starting at the Windows parking area, is an easy climb up a well-graded path that leads to three huge arches, the North and South Windows and Turret Arch. There is a slightly longer and often pleasant primitive loop that can be used to get to these arches as well. The primitive loop trail starts at the South Window viewpoint.

Garden of Eden

Garden of Eden is officially a viewpoint, and there are no trails per se. The area is a formation of balanced rocks and broken arches from years past. Much of the area is

Garden of Eden

slick rock and fine for scrambling around if you want to get off the beaten path. Be mindful of walking on any cryptobiotic soils, which are fragile black soil crusts that are precursors to allowing larger grasses and plants to survive in the desert. It takes about forty years for this soil to recover from a single footprint.

Parade of Elephants

This ensemble of rock arches and fins does indeed look like a parade of sandstone elephants walking together. The Parade of Elephants is just on the other side of the parking lot from the Windows. This landform is popular with the little ones and well, just about everyone else. It's a very cool rock formation.

Parade of Elephants

Double Arch

Easy – (0.5 mi / 0.8 km), round trip, allow 15 - 30 minutes

Double Arch is one of the more magical landforms within Arches NP. Not

only is it a true double arch, but also both arches are massive and seem to interconnect with each other from certain angles. It is tough to make out the nature of this landform from the road, and it is easily overlooked by folks who just got back in their vehicle from the Windows trailhead. That said, this is not a formation you want to miss; it is one of the highlights of the park. The trail from the parking lot is sandy and flat. It is possible to scramble up into the bases of both arches.

Double Arch

Delicate Arch Section

Further north into the park, you will see a turn-off to your right for Delicate Arch and Wolfe Ranch. Delicate Arch is a must-do for most folks, though it can be a bit strenuous, especially for the younger crowd. It is arguably the most famous natural arch in the world and as such does have a viewpoint that one can drive up to. The viewpoints give a thumbnail view of the arch. To really see Delicate Arch, you have to hike to it.

Wolfe Ranch and Ute Petroglyphs

For those hiking up to Delicate Arch, the Wolfe Ranch and nearby Ute petroglyph panel are found just as you begin. Both are great and welcome visits on the return from Delicate Arch. If you are coming just to see these historical artifacts, Wolfe Ranch and the Ute petroglyphs are accessed from the Wolfe Ranch parking lot. Both are explained in greater detail in the Arches history section within this book.

Ute Petroglyphs

Delicate Arch

Strenuous – (3.0 mi / 4.8 km), round trip, allow 2 - 3 hours

Delicate Arch

The hike up to Delicate Arch is not as strenuous as some will tell you. Granted, there is no shade, so bring plenty of water and wear a hat and sunscreen. There is a fairly decent 500-foot ascent on slick rock after a half mile (0.8 km) of easy hiking. Once you summit the ascent, the trail levels out for the most part and is fairly straightforward. There is a rock ledge about 200 yards long that is navigable for two-way traffic. The nice thing about this hike is that the arch is hidden from you until you are right on it. You turn a corner and bam, there it is, Delicate Arch.

The arch is a juxtaposition of themes for the viewer, with the often-snow-capped La Sal Mountains in the distance framing the fiery and dry sandstone in the foreground. Front and center to it all is the showpiece, the most famous arch in the world. The lighting can be nothing less than spiritual at sunset, though be prepared to share your life moment with your fellow hikers during peak season.

Fiery Furnace Section

Fiery Furnace

Fiery Furnace is a special section of Arches. The area itself is a labyrinth of rock, containing no trails, and lots of scrambling, wedging, and the need for equal helpings of agility and endurance. It is best seen through the park's ranger-led programs, as this minimizes the damage that has been caused of late through too much hiker love. You can access the area on your own, but only if you obtain a permit at the visitor center and watch a minimum impact video. The fee for a permit is $4 for each adult and $2 for children 5 through 12 and can be purchased at the visitor center. For both the permit and the ranger-led programs, children under five are not permitted.

Fiery Furnace

The ranger-led tour is a tremendous amount of fun for an active family but isn't for everyone. Once you start on the hike, you are committed to completing it. The hike includes squeezing through narrow gaps, scrambling up at times, jumping over small gaps and navigating through a maze of rock containing the usual assortment of narrow ledges, loose sandstone and broken rocks.

This ranger-led program contains a fair number of historical and geographical descriptions from likely one of the most passionate advocates of the park you will meet. Bring good hiking shoes, plenty of water and a backpack to store everything because you will be using your hands from time to time to make your way through the terrain.

Tickets for the ranger-led program are by reservation during the peak season up to six months in advance through www.recreation.gov. Like the campground in Arches, this program is quite popular and requires a bit of planning, tenacity and patience to get the spot you want. Tickets during November and early spring can be obtained at the visitor center. Costs are $10 for adults and $5 for children 5 through 12.

Devils Garden Section

Sand Dune Arch

Easy – (0.4 mi / 0.6 km), round trip, allow 15 - 30 minutes

Sand Dune Arch is a secluded arch that is an easy hike along an orange red sand path. The arch is between two large fins, giving a sense of isolation within a very short hike. During windy days, be prepared to get a little sandblasting exfoliation, especially around the shins.

Sand Dune Arch

Landscape Arch

Easy – (1.6 mi / 2.4 km), round trip, allow 60 minutes

What makes Landscape Arch so popular is that it defies logic. It is fragile, seemingly ribbon thin in spots, yet it is the longest arch in the park and the second largest in the world. Landscape Arch is so fragile it prompted the Secretary of the Air Force to put a stop to supersonic jet flight over or even near national parks in 1972 after an outcry from local citizens. The arch measures 306 feet from base to base and can be accessed via a fairly flat gravel trail.

This trail can be a destination in itself or the beginning of the longer hikes to Double O Arch and the Devils Garden Loop. There are nice spur trails down to the Tunnel Arch and quaint Pine Tree Arch.

Landscape Arch

Devils Garden Primitive Loop

Strenuous – (7.2 mi / 11.5 km), round trip, allow 3 - 5 hours

This is the longest maintained trail in the park and covers many of the north canyon fins and arches of Salt Valley. Expect a fair amount of scrambling and generally rugged terrain as you span farther into the canyon. The hike is worth doing, weaning out many of the visitors looking for shorter hikes and providing views of eight arches total, including the solemn Navajo Arch and the remote Private Arch.

In Devils Garden

Double O Arch

Strenuous – (4 mi / 6.4 km), round trip, allow 2 - 3 hours

Double O Arch is listed in case you don't want to do the more primitive loop portion of the Devils Garden Loop or some of the other spur trails to other arches. Double O is an arch on top of an arch, hence the name. It is one of the cooler landforms in the park, looking like a fin of sandstone Swiss cheese. Dark Angel, a monolithic tower of darker sandstone, is off a spur trail another 0.5 mi (0.8 km) further on.

Double O Arch

Hopi Prophecy

After swatting a fly inside the RV...

[Bryce]: You know, Dad, the relationship between humans and flies has never been a good one.

[Me]: How so?

[Bryce]: Well, how many times do you encounter another species and worry about getting squashed?

Nearing the Tower of Babel in Arches NP

Despite completing a worthy family hike of Delicate Arch, there was a hardened silence in the RV. I drove, equally lost within my own thoughts through Arches NP back toward our campsite. The views were spectacular and surreal, but that didn't matter, they played for no one. Our minds were on something that had happened earlier on the trail. Bryce finally broke the silence, spilling his thoughts from beginning to end, without a pause.

"I just didn't understand those kids back at the hike. Dad, did you see those kids? I mean, you know, they were climbing on the petroglyphs. They littered, they went off the trail, they were trying to catch the lizards and feed the squirrels, it was like they did everything wrong. Don't their parents know it's not right to, you know, feed the animals and dump your trash on the trail and climb on the ruins? It's not cool! It's not right for everyone else. How are people in the future going to enjoy all this stuff if they let their stupid kids climb all over these ruins?"

He was nine and while a part of me realized he was simply parroting what we had taught him, I could not have been prouder. Toward the end of our hike, we had unwittingly paired up with what looked like a single mom and her two boys. The mom was heavyset and had trouble keeping up, even though we were on a flat stretch of ground. The kids, about 7 to 9 years old, were generally hellions. We watched in complete dissatisfaction as they climbed past the barriers to touch the petroglyphs near Wolf Ranch. While I hesitated whether to say something, Bryce didn't. "Hey, you aren't supposed to be climbing up there you know!" he shouted. The boys looked at Bryce and were about to mouth back but saw their mom, who belatedly echoed Bryce's sentiment. The mom looked at me with a harsh eye as she and her tribe passed us.

An older man was standing at the petroglyphs and overheard the whole thing, watching without speaking. He had a graying mane of hair, braided in the back, a weathered face that only sun and wind could sculpt, and clear, sharp eyes. He wiped a swig of water from his mouth as he approached us.

"That's a lot of Junior Ranger badges you have on your hat son," he said to Bryce. Bryce engaged shyly at first, but the man drew him in.

"Did you get all of those yourself"? he asked.

"Yep. I got the one for Bryce Canyon in one day," Bryce said.

Our whole family was now gathering to hear the conversation. "That's great! You know we need more rangers like yourself. You seem to know not to litter and go off trail. You are a good steward of the park. Maybe one day you will want to join us rangers."

"Are you a ranger?" Everest asked, surprised. He wasn't wearing a uniform.

The man chuckled, lighting up his whole face as if it was the sun itself smiling at you. "Yes, well, I am, but I'm off duty at the moment. I just came up here to study these petroglyphs. Any idea what these Ute petroglyphs mean, Bryce?"

"Um, they look to me like a hunting party. It looks like there are Indians on horses and they are hunting some deer."

"That's a pretty good read, Bryce. Have you seen Newspaper Rock yet?"

I interjected. "No, not yet, that's a great set of petroglyphs. We plan on seeing it on our way south. We haven't been to Needles yet."

"Good good. You should absolutely see them. It's worth the drive, if only to see the petroglyphs." The man was about to close the conversation and move on but he looked at Bryce, paused for a second and then stated, "Bryce, I like how you spoke up for yourself back there. These petroglyphs have been around for almost 400 years and this park is here to help make sure that they can be enjoyed by many who come after us. There is a saying, well not so much a saying but an ancient story, that humans will be asked to decide, to choose. There will be those who respect the land and those that don't. Those that don't respect the land will find themselves wishing they had, as Mother Nature has a way of self-correcting if we don't."

I looked at the ranger inquisitively. "Are you talking about the Hopi Prophecy by chance?" I had studied creation and destruction myths in school and what he said sounded familiar.

He looked back at me with equal curiosity. "Yes, actually, I was. I kind of tone it down for folks, especially our Junior Rangers". He patted Bryce on the head lightly. "I don't want to say anything that parents might find offensive."

"On the contrary, if you are familiar with the story, I'm sure the boys would be open to listening to it. Boys?" I gave a quick nod in the direction of my sons.

Bryce looked up at the ranger and said with some seriousness, "Are you a Hopi Indian? I'd like to know the Hopi story. Sure!"

"Well, my young friend. No, I am not a Hopi Indian, my name is Ralph and I'm from Flagstaff. But I did live with them for some time, teaching at a school in a place called Seba Dalkai. I learned a few things while I was living there."

"The Hopis have passed down their beliefs from one generation to the next through telling the next generation. They did not write anything down. Some of their stories are pretty remarkable. They believe that the human race has lived through four worlds. In other words, there were three other times when we grew as a race and society. However, each time the humans could not find a way to live in harmony with the earth and as a result, Nature cleansed the earth of all but a few humans who started the next world.

"Are you talking about the flood and Noah's ark?" Everest asked.

"Well, yes, that was one reset that Mother Nature did. For the Hopi, it was the end of the third world and the beginning of the fourth world. It is kind of amazing actually, all of these stories are myths, right? It's hard to say whether they happened or not. The great flood is not only in the Bible, it is a story told by many cultures and tribes spread over nearly every continent. It's pretty amazing that this "myth" is so much a part of nearly every culture. It happened so long ago that it seems hard to believe that it might have actually happened."

"The Hopi believe we are in the Fourth World. They were given predictions to indicate when that world would end and the Fifth World would begin. One of the first signs was that they would encounter white-skinned men. Of course they did, but can you imagine the telling of this story up until that time? They had never seen white-skinned men before."

The ranger continued, "The signs included that the land would be crossed by snakes of iron. Any idea what that could be?"

"Big iron snakes"? Bryce asked.

"No", he said gently. "No, these were the trains."

"Oh yeah!" Bryce and Everest both nodded.

"How about this one. They predicted that the land would be crisscrossed by a giant spider's web. What do you think that is?"

Bryce shook his head.

"Those are the power and communication lines. They cross the deserts like the fine web of a spider, right?"

"Okay, see if you can guess this one. The land shall be crisscrossed with rivers of stone that make pictures in the sun."

"Are those the roads?" Everest asked.

Ralph pointed at Everest as if he had just won something. "My goodness! That's it! Roads. The rivers of stone. Well, these signs kept coming true and part of their oral tradition was that if enough of the signs started coming true, it was time to tell outsiders, folks that weren't Hopis, about the Hopi Prophecy."

"I learned a great deal from a person I met. His name was Thomas Banyacya. He was a Hopi shaman and he was the one who told me the prophecy. He and his people felt it was time to share the story with folks outside the Hopi people. This man shared it with me in the hopes that I could one day share it with others".

"What's a shaman?" Bryce asked.

Everest looked at me. "It's a medicine man. Right, Dad?'

"Not really", Ralph answered. "The Hopi themselves are a spiritual people and live in the northern corner of Arizona. They chose where they live to help them live humbly, to help them not get too distracted. They have remained their own people because they believe they are the people of balance, the people of peace. The word Hopi means, "People of Peace". The shaman is typically the spiritual leader of the people. I guess you could say the pastor at your church is your "shaman" in a way. Each Sunday, he is the person you go to listen for guidance and to ground you in your beliefs, a person you could go to maybe if you were having trouble spiritually."

"Shamans can also heal and are typically the best connected naturalists in an area. They know the land, the plants, and the animals better than anyone does. They know the plants that will heal and the plants that can harm you. For that, they get this term of medicine man, but in my mind they are much more."

"Wow, how did you meet this guy?" Bryce asked.

"Well, I met him on the Hopi reservation. It was a long time ago, in the 80s. Mr. Banyacya was one of the four elder leaders who were appointed to tell the story of the Hopi. He even drew me a map to the prophecy rock and I've actually seen it with my own eyes."

"Meeting with Mr. Banyacya was pretty much a highlight in my life. He was considered the Gandhi of the Hopi. He worked for most of his life promoting world peace. He was able to speak before the United Nations, but I saw him before this. He was chosen shortly after the atomic bombs were dropped in Japan along with three other leaders to spread the interpretations of the prophecy. Up until that time, the prophecy was kept secret and told orally from one generation to another. In 1948, there were enough predictions that came true for them to feel it was time to tell the prophecy."

"What happened in 1948?"

"We dropped the big one," Ev said glibly.

"They dropped the bomb in 1945, I thought," Ang said.

"Exactly. We dropped the bombs on Hiroshima and Nagasaki in 1945. I guess it took the Hopis a few years to decide it was really time to bring their prophecy to the outside world."

"So going back to the Prophecy Rock, the Hopi Prophecy is drawn on a large rock near Old Orabi. It is pretty amazing, the world's destiny on one rock in the middle of the desert, at least according to the Hopi."

"Is it like a bunch of words telling a story?" Bryce asked.

"No, it's a picture carved into the rock, pretty basic really. There are lots of details and I don't remember them all but it goes something like this. There are two paths. On one path, it shows a man supporting himself by two canes. This symbolizes that he has grown to be of a very old age. On this path, corn is growing. Since corn is difficult to grow in the desert, it symbolizes that this man is in touch with his environment, he has learned to live with it. He is in balance with his surroundings. The line this man is on continues around the rock to the other side, symbolizing this path goes on for a long time.

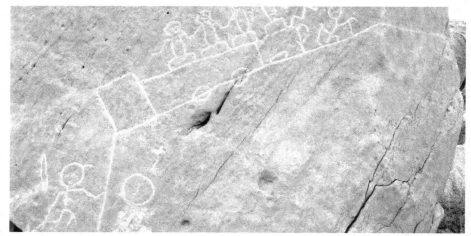

Hopi Prophecy Rock

The other path shows three men. They look like they are squatting. There is a fourth person whose head and hands are detached from his body. This symbolizes that these people think too much, they have surrounded themselves so much with material comforts that they have lost touch with themselves. They connect more with what they see, touch, and taste and have lost their connection with their hearts and with what they feel. They have stopped listening to the world around them and instead listen only to the devices they've created and the thoughts in their own heads. The prophecy tells that we as a society will become immersed with our devices, with our things and that we will in the process forget our connection with the world as a whole. The line these people are on goes straight for a bit and then abruptly becomes a jagged zigzag line of sharp angles, ending after a short time."

Everest looked agasp with his eyes open. "That totally sounds like us! Are we the headless people?"

"It is pretty amazing how the prophecy turned out. We are a society completely disconnected from the beauty of a sunrise or admiring the simple grandness of a tree. We don't take time to watch clouds drift above us or watch a bug make its way across a leaf. We've forgotten how to talk to each other, to give even a simple nod; we've forgotten that a smile is a great default face to put on. We've forgotten how to be at rest with ourselves; we must always be doing something. We've plugged into things that, for the most part, tell us nothing of real importance. I mean, really nothing. Do you kids play on the computer?"

Bryce looked at me as if looking if it was okay to answer. We were guilty of allowing our children perhaps too much screen time. "Yes," he said finally.

Ralph asked, "What do you play?"

"Minecraft mainly. Other video games," said Bryce.

"And YouTube," said Everest.

"What do you watch on YouTube?" Ralph asked.

"Mostly mindless stuff, movie parodies. I have to admit, you are right. It's not high quality stuff," Ev stated.

"You aren't alone. The entire country is staring down at their devices, and we disconnect even from ourselves. We lose focus after just a few minutes. We have a great deal of difficulty simply…being. We use these devices to occupy ourselves, to distance ourselves, from ourselves. How many times a week does someone bump into you because they were paying more attention to their devices than to where they were going? How many times have you done this yourself? The Hopis saw that coming long before we did."

Ev chimed in. "So we're doomed, right? I mean obviously we have chosen to embrace the iPad over growing corn in the desert. We are all waiting for the jagged end of times, is that it?"

"The Hopi prophecy does state that there is a choice. There are a couple of other pieces to the rock that I haven't mentioned yet. There are two circles and one-half circle. The two circles represent the first two World Wars. Without getting into too much detail, the oral traditions spelled out what would mark the wars, including use of planes in WWI and the use of the bomb in WWII.

The third half circle is called the "Mystery Egg." No one knows what will happen, but something will. That something depends on us. If we continue to be destructive, to live as if there will always be resources, if we are not mindful of the planet we live on, Nature will bring balance, but it won't be pretty. The earth will be purified. If enough humans are able to live with our hearts, Nature will still test us, because of the destruction we have already caused, but this test will in the end strengthen us."

"What kind of destruction will the Mystery Egg bring?" Bryce asked.

"There's a bit of unknown here and some tellers of the prophecy differ in their interpretation. One source said the second world shaking, the Second World War, would be recognized when man used the Hopi swastika in war, which the Nazis did. The third world shaking will be recognized by a red cover or cloak. What that means though is anyone's guess."

"Do you believe in the Hopi Prophecy?" Asked Ev.

Ralph paused for a second, glanced at Ang and then looked directly at Everest and Bryce. "I'm not sure it's something you need to believe in order to understand. The message is pretty beautiful. It simply says we should live in a mindful way, guided by our hearts rather than the Internet and TV ads. For me, it says to put down the machines we've made every now and then and simply go out and look at the stars. Once in your life watch the moonrise, it's a tremendous thing to see. Go to the ocean and just listen to the waves, become lost in them, immerse yourself in the sound they make. Try to make it through a day being genuinely nice to everyone you meet. Listen to your own heartbeat, every now and then follow the patterns of your own breath, and remind yourself that you are alive! Find some solace without an iPad in your hand; relearn how to just be comfortable in your own skin. If people are singing, sing along with them. If people are dancing, join in. Live! This is the core of what the Hopi Prophecy is saying. Get along with your fellow human beings and live with great respect for the planet that we live on."

"That is what the Hopi Prophecy is saying, and do I believe? Well, we do seem to have lost our way. There is always some disaster or war or famine somewhere. Bees are dying, there's a huge globbish mass of floating plastic in the oceans, we've overfished the seas, the polar ice caps are melting at a phenomenal rate; yes, we have certainly messed things up. The Hopis foresaw the white man coming, saw them intruding on their lands. They foresaw the trains, the wagons, the electrical lines, the World Wars. Who's to say they aren't right about what's to come? It certainly is something to think about and acknowledge. Regardless of whether it's true or not, which path would you rather live on, the one that lasts a long time or the zigzag path"?

Both of my boys looked at me and said nothing. I smiled and stated the obvious. We all want to have a happy long life. After a bit more conversation, I thanked Ralph and we completed the walk back to the RV. From there, apart from some the discussion from Bryce, we drove silently back to the campground lost in our encounter with Ralph and the disrespectful boys. After dinner, both Everest and Bryce talked quietly among themselves and then came over in unison.

"Hey, Dad." Everest said. "Would you like to take a walk outside, catch some stars or something"?

Bryce was just behind his brother looking up at me with his big eyes.

"Sure, boys. Can Mom come along too?"

"Sure!" the boys exclaimed in near unison. We turned off the lights to the RV, locked up and stepped out into the warm summer night. In this river valley, the cliff walls rose darkly on either side until they met the stars. We found a little beach of sand by the Colorado River and just sat with our flashlights off. We sat and we listened. We listened to the soft currents of the river mainly, to the night critters in the distant bushes, to the wind. We watched the dry desert clouds drift lazily, darkly, under the Milky Way. There was little said and little that needed to be said. In terms of moments I return to, when the stresses of life start to consume me and I need to escape for a moment, I return to this one often. I watch the clouds go silently by and listen to the soft strength of the Colorado. The moment was simple, it was understated and it was by far one of the most content and memorable events of our trip.

Mesa Verde National Park

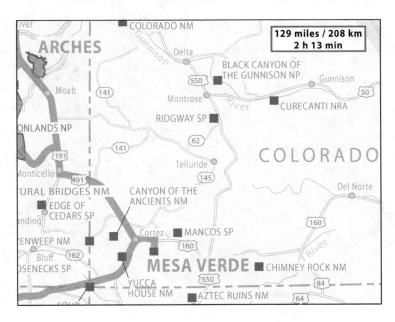

COLORADO NM
ARCHES
Delta
129 miles / 208 km
2 h 13 min
BLACK CANYON OF
THE GUNNISON NP
Gunnison
Moab
550
Montrose
CURECANTI NRA
50
141
RIDGWAY SP
ONLANDS NP
62
COLORADO
141
191
Telluride
145
Monticello
491
Del Norte
URAL BRIDGES NM
CANYON OF THE
ANCIENTS NM
EDGE OF
CEDARS SP
nding
160
ENWEEP NM
Cortez
MANCOS SP
Bluff
162
160
River
OSENECKS SP
MESA VERDE
CHIMNEY ROCK NM
YUCCA
550
84
HOUSE NM
AZTEC RUINS NM
64

"On account of their sheltered position not only the stone walls, but also in many cases the beams that support the floors between the different stories, are wonderfully well preserved. Among the fine, dry dust or the fallen blocks of sandstone that have filled the rooms, we find still in a wonderful state of preservation the household articles and other implements once used by the inhabitants of the cliff-dwellings. Even wooden articles, textile fabrics, bone implements, and the like are often exceedingly well preserved, although they have probably lain in the earth for more than five centuries."

—Gustav Nordenskiöld, *The Cliff Dwellers of the Mesa Verde*

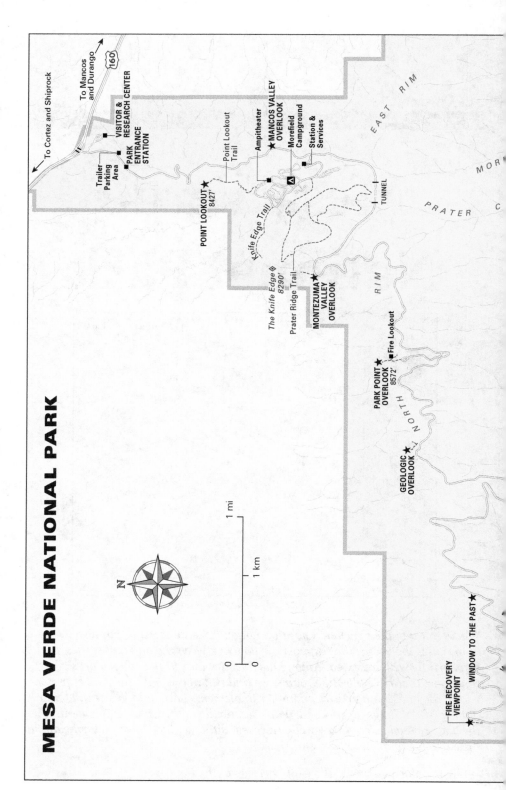

MESA VERDE NATIONAL PARK

To Cortez and Shiprock

To Mancos and Durango

160

VISITOR & RESEARCH CENTER

PARK ENTRANCE STATION

Trailer Parking Area

POINT LOOKOUT
8427'

Point Lookout Trail

Ampitheater

MANCOS VALLEY OVERLOOK

Morefield Campground

Station & Services

Knife Edge Trail

The Knife Edge
8290'

Prater Ridge Trail

MONTEZUMA VALLEY OVERLOOK

TUNNEL

EAST RIM

MOR

PRATER C

RIM

Fire Lookout

PARK POINT OVERLOOK
8572'

NORTH RIM

GEOLOGIC OVERLOOK

FIRE RECOVERY VIEWPOINT

WINDOW TO THE PAST

N

0   1 km   1 mi
0

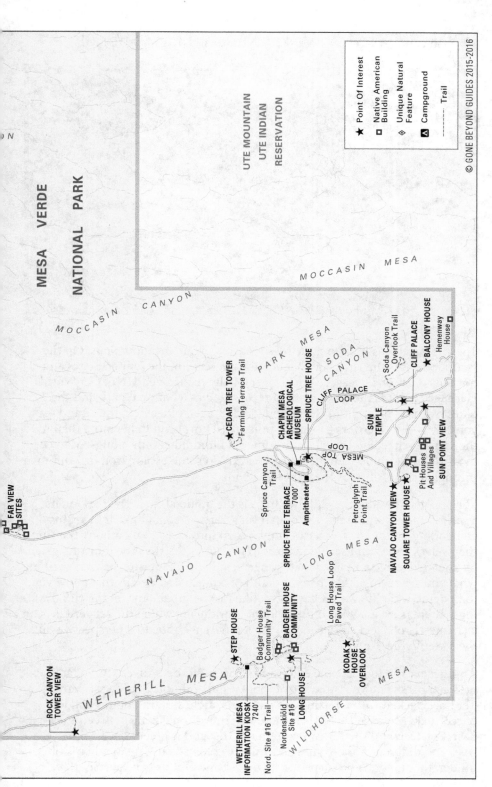

MESA VERDE NATIONAL PARK

UTE MOUNTAIN
UTE INDIAN
RESERVATION

MOCCASIN MESA

MOCCASIN CANYON

PARK MESA

★ CEDAR TREE TOWER
Farming Terrace Trail

CHAPIN MESA
ARCHEOLOGICAL
MUSEUM
SPRUCE TREE HOUSE

SODA
CANYON

CLIFF PALACE
LOOP

Soda Canyon
Overlook Trail
CLIFF PALACE
★
★ BALCONY HOUSE
Hemenway
House

SUN
TEMPLE

SUN POINT VIEW

MESA TOP LOOP

Spruce Canyon
Trail

SPRUCE TREE TERRACE
7000'
Ampitheater

Petroglyph
Point Trail

NAVAJO CANYON VIEW ★
SQUARE TOWER HOUSE ★

Pit Houses
And Villages

FAR VIEW
SITES

NAVAJO CANYON

LONG MESA

ROCK CANYON
TOWER VIEW

WETHERILL MESA

★ STEP HOUSE

Badger House
Community Trail
BADGER HOUSE
COMMUNITY

WETHERILL MESA
INFORMATION KIOSK
7240'
Nord. Site #16 Trail

Nordenskiöld
Site #16
LONG HOUSE

Long House Loop
Paved Trail

KODAK
HOUSE
OVERLOOK ★

MESA

WILDHORSE

Point Of Interest ★

Native American ▢
Building

Unique Natural ◇
Feature

Campground ◣

Trail ------

© GONE BEYOND GUIDES 2015-2016

What Makes Mesa Verde National Park Special

Cliff Palace

There is good reason to include Mesa Verde in your vacation plans. On the facts alone, it is the largest archaeological preserve in the United States and is not only a national treasure but also a globally recognized UNESCO World Heritage Site. It is the eleventh area recognized as a national park and the oldest within your tour of the Grand Circle—even older than the Grand Canyon NP. The park covers 81 square miles (210 km2) and holds more than five thousand archaeological sites and some six hundred cliff dwellings. Many of the dwellings can be seen by car, or you can do some exploration on your own through a series of trails the park has set up.

The real gem besides the cliff dwellings is the guided tours. The park offers a series of tours where the visitor can get a very personal look at the ruins. Depending on the tour, you can climb down into kivas, walk among the ruins themselves and even use cliff ladders to get out of the site. The tours are given by knowledgeable and passionate rangers, who do a fantastic job of describing what you are seeing. They bring a depth of context and details that allow you to imagine what life would have been like for the inhabitants of the cliff dwellings. There is even a 90-minute twilight tour during which the ranger takes on a character role, locked in time, giving a different contextual perspective on the Mesa Verde experience.

Another reason to make the extension to Mesa Verde is diversity. So far, the national parks you've visited are of the "Grand and Epic Southwest" variety. They are packed with amazing canyons, fins, arches, rivers, buttes and lots of red rock. Mesa Verde NP is located in a transitional zone between the desert plateau and the Rocky Mountains. The land is greener, with more trees and different flora from what you have seen so far. The weather is often milder, though don't be surprised if you get one of those famous Southwest afternoon thunderstorms. It is a welcome reprieve from the red rock simply because it's different. In addition, a drive out to Mesa puts you in the state of Colorado and makes it an easy drive to Four Corners, which is cool to visit in its own right. Mesa Verde is a welcome addition to a family vacation. It is immersive, educational and relaxing, all at the same time.

Staying in Mesa Verde NP

Whether you are camping, RVing or looking for lodging, the park itself accommodates everyone. There are plenty of rooms and campsites within the park, which is good as the park involves a fair amount of driving. For folks looking for a room, Far View Lodge is your ticket. For RVers and campers, there is Morefield Campground.

Far View Lodge

The Mesa Verde NP offers lodging facilities inside the park at the Far View Lodge from mid-April to mid-October. Far View is quiet, peaceful and perched high up in the park, giving views into three states. There are no TVs, no arcade rooms and no sports bars adjoining the property, just serene lodging. The downside of this place is the rooms are 50s style, basic and in need of refurbishment for the most part. The lodge offers a standard room and a kiva room. While the kiva rooms offer finer furnishings, they only come with two double or one king options only. Most of the standard rooms have two double or one queen, however there are a few standard rooms with two queens. All room come with exceptional views from your private balcony.

Morefield Campground

Likely the best part of this campground is there are plenty of spots to choose from, and they rarely fill up completely. The Morefield Campground is located just 4 miles (6.4 km) past the Mesa Verde entrance and has 267 sites, 83 of which are designated for RVs. The campground is distributed across three loops with the Ute loop being the loop designated for RV sites. There are 15 full hookup sites that are typically reserved in advance.

Each site comes with the standard amenities, including a picnic table, fire pit and grill. The site is located within a scrub oak canyon filled with grasses, wild flowers, deer, wild turkeys and other fauna. On one early morning RV dumping station stop, we saw a herd of deer galloping and playing in the hill across from the station. The scene was a true spirit lifter during a typically unwanted chore.

While there are usually enough open campsites, some are only barely worthy of even a small RV. More than a few sites lean to one side, which makes cooking a challenge and sleeping uncomfortable. Keep your eye out for level sites as you drive through the loop to choose where you will stay.

Please stick to the Ute Loop, which is designed for RVs. The other loops are built more for cars than RVs, plus every tent camper will look at you funny as you drive within their "tents only" loops.

There is more to Morefield than just a large campground. There are very pleasant hiking trails that start at the campground, including the Knife Edge Trail, which is a short old road that leads to great sunsets. At the entrance of the campground is a decent dumping and filling station. Just above the campground is a full service concessionaire station. There you will find many creature comforts, including free showers, which are clean and private. There is a coin-operated Laundromat, a grocery store, a gas station and a gift shop as well. This is where you will check in to reserve your campsite. Both the site and shops are run by Aramark, and they will be happy to fill you in on the details.

One other thing to keep in mind is the overall layout of Mesa Verde. There is one road into the park, which ultimately dead ends at the ruins. The campground is near the beginning of park's entrance, and it is a windy 15-mile (24 km) drive just to get to the ruins from your campsite. If you have purchased a tour, be sure to factor in the drive time.

Mesa Verde Geology

The main event when it comes to Mesa Verde are the cliff dwellings; however, if you think about it, the inhabitants didn't live in cliffs, they lived in alcoves that were created within the cliff walls. The alcoves are what drew the ancestral inhabitants to the Mesa Verde area and as alcoves are geologic formations, the geology of Mesa Verde suddenly becomes pretty important.

In fact, even the term mesa is a geologic term. A mesa, such as the one found in Canyonlands' Island in the Sky District, is defined as a flat-topped landform with straight cliff-like sides. The term mesa is Spanish for table and thus Mesa Verde means "Green Table." That said, even though the national park is called Mesa Verde, it isn't a mesa per se in geologic circles. Sure, it has a flat top, more or less, but it doesn't have straight cliff-like sides. No, the sides of this so-called "mesa" are sloped, which in the world of geology is known as a cuesta. What you can do with this information is anyone's guess. If you go around calling the place "Cuesta Verde," normal people will look at you funny and the two percent who might understand what you are saying will likely judge you as a geologic elitist. Best to just keep this information to yourself and relay it only when the there is a significant lull in the campfire discussions.

Let's get back to the main geologic feature, those alcoves. Alcoves at Mesa Verde are formed through a rather simple process. The first thing to know is that the mesas of Mesa Verde are composed of a layer of sandstone sitting on top of a layer of shale. In the rock world, sandstone is very absorbent; however, shale is not. So, you essentially have a big sponge

Example of an alcove. Hard shale floor under a thick layer of softer, absorbent sandstone that is slowly eroded away by water.

sitting on top of a hard surface. The second thing to know is that the mesa is tilted, not much, mind you, only about 7 degrees. The third thing to know is that gravity works in Mesa Verde just like it does everywhere else.

If you put these three things together, you can understand the creation of an alcove. When it rains, the water becomes absorbed by the sponge-like sandstone. The water slowly settles downward through the sandstone until it meets the shale layer. Since all that water needs a place to go and since the land is titled 7 degrees, it naturally follows the path of least resistance by going downhill. The water continues to travel through the sandstone along the top of the shale until it finds an outlet at one of the canyon edges.

From there the water travels down the canyon as a trickling seep. The seeps of Mesa Verde remove a tiny fraction of the sandstone as the water continues downstream. The sandstone is chemically dissolved and physically transported away over time into the creeks and rivers below. As the alcoves become larger, they start to eat inwardly into the cliff wall. Over time, larger rocks fall, which opens the alcove up even more. The water from the seeps slowly erodes away even these larger sandstone rocks that have fallen. The end result is a large, arched alcove that is suitable for habitation.

There are a couple of other interesting tidbits about the relationship of seeps and the residents of Mesa Verde. The sponge-like property of sandstone meant the seeps could provide the inhabitants with a year-round supply of water. The seeps not only allowed folks to survive, but also allowed for agriculture. With agriculture, the residents were now sustained in one place and didn't have to roam for food like their hunter-gatherer forefathers. The alcoves also gave shelter from elements and some protection from enemies. Once again, the right conditions, a little water and an abundance of time proved to be the right ingredients to start a civilization.

Mesa Verde History

The history and culture of the Mesa Verde people has been studied in great depth. There has been so much focus and detail that it can be a bit consuming to a visitor. If we can start with the bigger picture, perhaps it will help to frame the context of Mesa Verde history.

About 1,400 years ago, in other parts of the world, China was printing its first books, Vikings were invading Northern Europe and all of Europe was still recovering from the decline of the Roman Empire. Meanwhile

Kiva in Balcony House

in North America, there was a group of people who decided to call Mesa Verde home. They found water, food and shelter. Over the course of 700 years they stayed in this one place. They integrated with the land, developing such a deep tie to their surroundings that they could listen to it and learn from it. The plants, the sky, the flow of water, all of it became extensions of their own eyes and ears. The land became a part of who they were as a society. They developed laws, customs, spiritual bonds and methodologies of all sorts that helped them get continuously better at not only living but also thriving. During this time they continued to find improvements in everything they did, including the way they made their clothes, stored their food and water, cultivated food and hunted. Their shelters improved as well, becoming elaborate multi-story communities with areas set up to trade, sleep, socialize and commune with their beliefs.

Then, they left. They didn't depart all at once; they left over one or two generations. Mesa Verde was no longer called home for reasons that are not truly known. They left and went south as separate groups, leaving their homes and most of their belongings behind. Today, there are twenty-four tribes that have a special relationship with these Mesa Verde ancestors, that look upon their own people and at themselves and call the inhabitants of Mesa Verde a part of their ancestral record.

From 1300 CE to the late 1800s, the cliff dwellings of Mesa Verde were known only to the local tribes. In 1859, the area was named "Mesa Verde" by European settlers. By 1874, the ruins were discovered and the first photographs taken. As early as 1886, folks felt the place was special enough to become a national park, and in 1906, it did, under the pen of President Theodore Roosevelt.

From its declaration as a national park through today, the cliff dwellings and surrounding areas have been excavated and preserved to both understand and maintain this culturally significant place. In 1978, Mesa Verde was named a Unesco World Heritage Site. Today, the park is shared by more than 600,000 visitors each year, allowing an up-close look at these fascinating ruins of a civilization that was called home to a society of people for more than 700 years.

Mesa Verde's First Inhabitants

The Modified Basket Makers (550 to 750 CE)

The initial inhabitants settled in Mesa Verde some 1,400 years ago. The land was higher than surrounding land, so they could easily spot intruders from a distance. It held alcoves in cliff walls, which meant shelter with even further protection. There was water, constant water, year round, which was essential. In addition, there was enough game to hunt. It was an ideal place to live, to raise children, to grow a civilization. It is really unknown how many came to this place at first, perhaps several families, maybe even several groups that agreed to live together. They came with some crudeness, more hunting and gathering practices, but with some advancements. They could make baskets to carry things; they knew well how to use the atlatl and spear. They could hunt and bring home food for their families on a consistent basis.

The place of Mesa Verde allowed them to achieve more. They settled and learned how to make crude clay pots, which reduced the number of baskets needed, which wore out quicker. The pottery helped in so many ways, carrying water, cooking food more evenly; it was a paradigm shift. They learned to grow beans and by the end of this period replaced the spear and the atlatls with a new invention, the bow and arrow. It made hunting easier as well as provided more hides for clothing. This led to more time for social events, both for celebration and for spiritual congregation. There were items of ordinary use and items of significance, such as robes made of turkey feathers.

Developmental Pueblo (750 to 1100 CE)

By this period, the once small group was now a civilization. Buildings were architected and constructed, most facing south for warmth and with windows shaped like U, E and L shapes. The rooms were close together, wisely thought out as this provided both protection and greater warmth. The connection of the people was deeply rooted in the spirit, and religious celebration was commonplace.

During this time, the crude pottery of their forefathers was advanced upon, becoming pitchers, bowls, jars, and other implements of dishware. They began to see beyond pottery as merely utilitarian and to use it for decoration. The pottery was tastefully decorated with white clay inscribed with black patterns. Painting of interior rooms became a thing; society was alive and vibrant with artistry and color.

The scientifically minded were also busy. Their buildings became more sophisticated to meet the growing population. They built upward, creating towers and multi-story buildings. Their architecture was unrivaled, to be sure. The Square Tower House was the tallest building in North America until the mid-1800s. They created reservoirs for water and even dams, which allowed for better conservation of water for use during the drier months. This was born likely of need rather than forethought, as the people of Mesa Verde were to endure a 24-year drought that ultimately led to the abandonment of their home for more fertile ground. By 1300 CE, the population of Mesa Verde had gathered up and left a place they had called home for several hundred years.

European Discovery

While the Spanish explorers of 1776 came within sight of Mesa Verde, they did not see the ruins themselves. It was the trappers and prospectors who discovered the ruins, with miner John Moss being the first one credited. Moss saw the ruins in 1873 and was impressed enough by them that he came back with friend and photographer William Henry Jackson.

Cliff Palace circa 1891

Jackson was a prolific and nationally known photographer, publisher, and painter. His work has become an impressive chronicle of the early west, including the Rocky Mountains and Yellowstone. During his life of 99 years he created more than 80,000 photographs. Moss led Jackson to Two Story House, where he took the first photographs of the cliff dwellings of Mesa Verde. These photographs were subsequently published, bringing national attention to the area.

Bit by bit, more of the dwellings were found. The Wetherills settled a ranch southwest of Mancos, Colorado, and developed a relationship with the nearby Ute tribe. The Ute tribe gave the Weatherills approval to winter their cattle in the lower and warmer plateaus of what is now the surrounding Ute Mountain Tribe. Acowitz, a member of the Ute tribe, told of a place of the "old people—the Ancient Ones." He explained that the place was sacred and that the Utes never go there. However, the tale struck the imagination of the cowboys, and on December 18, 1888, Richard Wetherrill and his friend Charlie Mason found and named Cliff Palace, gathering artifacts as they explored. Some of the artifacts were later sold to the Historical Society of Colorado, but much of them were kept.

The Wetherills explored and removed artifacts from several of the cliff dwellings. On one occasion, they brought along Baron Gustaf E. A. Nordenskiöld, a trained mineralogist and scientist. He was the first to bring the scientific method to the collection of artifacts in Mesa Verde, using meticulous field methods in the cataloging of the sites. In 1893, Nordenskiöld published his examinations and photographs as *The Cliff Dwellers of the Mesa Verde*. While his work drew more attention to Mesa Verde, not all of it was positive. In addition to writing the book, he shipped about 600 artifacts out of the country to Sweden, where they now reside in the National Museum in Helsinki, Finland. This initiated concerns for the need to protect Mesa Verde and the cliff dwellings.

Creation of a National Park

The area saw increasing foot traffic, artifact removal and even destruction of the ruins themselves. From Nordenskiöld's shipment in 1893 to 1906 when the area finally became a national park, Mesa Verde saw its worst treatment. Looters broke through exterior walls simply to allow more light in. Beams were used for firewood until nearly all of the roofs were lost. The Cliff Palace was damaged extensively. Some of the objects went to museums, but many were simply lost to private collections.

Fortunately, there were folks getting the right attention to the park. Virginia McClurg was tireless in her efforts to protect the history of Mesa Verde. She gave speeches worldwide and formed the Colorado Cliff Dwellers, an organization developed to reclaim the artifacts and promote preservation. Along with fellow activist Lucy Peabody, the women lobbied with members of Congress for Mesa Verde's protection.

J. Walter Fewkes, an ethnologist at the Smithsonian Institute, documented a report to the Secretary of the Interior on the horrible shape of the ruins. Their call was for the preservation and creation of a national park; however, there was a bill as late as 1904 that discussed who would have the rights to remove artifacts. At times, it seemed Mesa Verde would not receive the protection it needed. However, through years of lobbying, the efforts of these people finally paid dividends. On June 29, 1906, President Theodore Roosevelt signed legislation declaring Mesa Verde a National Park. It was the first cultural national park set aside by the National Park Service. In 1978, Mesa Verde was further recognized by the United Nations Educational, Scientific and Cultural Organization (UNESCO) as a World Heritage Cultural Site. The shipment of artifacts by Nordenskiöld remains in Helsinki at the National Museum of Finland.

Things to Do in Mesa Verde NP

Mesa Verde is definitely a different national park. While the themes of all other national parks are about epic landscapes, Mesa Verde is one of cultural immersion. While one can find hiking trails, car tours and self-guided exploration, the true connection occurs with a good guide. The park rangers are those guides and they aren't just good, they are amazing. There are several guided tours for the visitor and they are uniquely special and worth doing. The rangers will draw in context from their own experiences of the park and knowledge of the Mesa Verde people to enrich your understanding. Most people that come to Mesa Verde leave with a sense of awe, wishing they could have stayed longer. The ranger-led tours are that good. You are walking among the largest archaeological site in the United States, former home to a civilization for 700 years and then left. It was then picked up and put under the care of the National Park Service 700 years later to preserve these "works of man."

Before going into the tours themselves, it helps to have a little idea of the layout of Mesa Verde. It has one entrance, which doubles as the park's exit. Near the entrance is the visitor center, which is where you can purchase tour tickets and get your bearings. The road to the ruins is windy, long and thus slow-going for an RV. To that end, it does pay to plan your visit as it takes about 30 minutes just to get to the ruins. The main road from the visitor center branches at the park's Far View Lodge. Wetherill Mesa Road is only open seasonally from Memorial Day to Labor Day, and vehicles longer than 25 feet are not allowed. There are some great sites to see at Wetherill, including Step House and Long House; however, you may need to take these off the plan if you are in even a small RV.

Fortunately, the other road going to Chapin Mesa does not disappoint. Guided tours on this mesa include Cliff Palace, Balcony House and Spruce Tree House. There are also a nice archaeological museum, gift shop, restaurant and hiking trails on the Chapin Mesa route. Plus, the road is okay for larger vehicles, including RVs. One note: do find parking in the designated areas for motor homes. The rangers ticket vehicles that make poor parking choices.

Guided Tours

As stated earlier, taking a guided tour is highly recommended. The rangers are all wonderfully passionate and well versed in what is known of the Mesa Verde inhabitants. There is no bad tour, nor is one better than another.

They are all special. There are some tours that require climbing up a ladder or out onto an open rock face. The wording that the park provides causes the reader to wonder whether they will be putting themselves in danger. In reality, the wording is conservatively written to manage to the largest possible crowd. The climbing activities are easily achievable for most active visitors and are as fearful as climbing up a slide at a children's park. That said, rely on your own judgment in whether the more active tours are right for you.

There are some operating hour logistics to consider. The park runs in two seasons, each having its own operating hours. The summer/fall schedule typically runs from May 24 to November 2, and the winter/spring schedule runs the rest of the year. In general, there are more tours and they are offered more frequently during the summer/fall schedule. The cost of each tour is $3 per person. You will need the ticket to take the tour and can purchase them at the visitor center. There are no refunds.

If you are going during peak season, it will help to have your preferred plan and a backup plan on which tours you want to take, as they do book up. The most popular tours are Cliff Palace and Balcony House. Given the demand, you may be asked to choose only one of these tours per day. Long House gets less traffic and can typically be combined with either the Cliff or Balcony House tours. The ticketing process can in itself take time, as there are a lot of folks there with you. Also, as stated earlier, make sure you factor in about an hour to get to the ruins and find parking.

During the summer/fall schedule, the rangers also offer Cliff Palace Twilight tours. These tours are limited to groups of twenty, last 90 minutes and—as the name suggests—are led in the early evening between 6:30 and 7:15 pm. This is a chance for the ranger to educate in a character that is a historical representative of the park's past. The ranger will stay in character the entire time, which is quite magical given the setting and the early evening hour. For many this is the highlight of their stay. Tickets for the Cliff Palace Twilight tours are $10 per person for all ages.

Tickets can be picked up at the following locations:

- Mesa Verde Visitor and Research Center: (main visitor center near entrance, seasonal hours, but typically 8 am to 5 pm)

- Morefield Ranger Station (near Morefield campground, open during peak season only, limited hours, 7 am to 11 am)

- Colorado Welcome Center (in Cortez at 928 E. Main St., Cortez, CO 81321, Phone: (970) 565 4048. Seasonal hours typically from 8 AM to 5 PM)

One more tip before discussing the tours themselves: Water is the only food item that is allowed on the tours. Food, beverages, candy and gum are not permitted. Tours are an hour long, so fill up prior to your arrival.

Cliff Palace

Cliff Palace is the largest cliff dwelling in the park and in the United States. It is also the most popular tour. Visitors will get a close look at what is considered the former social center of the Mesa Verde communities. The ranger-guided tour lasts one hour and does involve some hiking on uneven stone pathways and steps. There are small 8–10 foot (2.6 -3m) ladders that one needs to ascend a 100-foot (30m) climb. At the visitor center there are somber warnings about these ladders; however, for most people they are similar to climbing a playground slide. The total walking distance is a short quarter-mile (400m) round trip.

There are 150 rooms that make up the dwelling along with 23 kivas, round ceremonial chambers. The dwelling is thought to have housed 100 people. This community was divided into smaller sub communities or polities. It is thought that each polity had its own kiva. The number of kivas in Cliff Palace suggests that this area was a highly social area as the ratio of rooms to kivas is much higher (nine rooms for each kiva built in Cliff Palace versus an average of 12 to 1 for the overall Mesa Verde community).

The structures are made of sandstone, mortar and wooden beams. Sandstone blocks were shaped using harder stones with mortar to seal and maintain structural integrity. In some places, small "chinking" stones were placed in larger gaps. Once finished, the walls were colored with earthen pigments. A sharp eye in Cliff Palace and in the other dwellings will note that the doorways are fairly small. The average man was 5'6" while the height of the average woman was around 5'.

Square Tower House

One of the more prominent dwellings is a large square tower known as the Square Tower House. The Square Tower House was in ruins by the 1800s and has been restored by the National Park Service. It stands 26 feet tall and has four levels.

Balcony House Tour

This one-hour ranger-guided tour is a little more adventurous than the Cliff Palace tour and explores a cliff dwelling sitting on a high ledge facing east. The eastern view meant colder winters, but the tradeoff for those living here was increased security. The ledge was only accessible via a series of small footholds carved into the cliff by the early dwellers. This is believed to be the only way into and out of the dwelling and was thus easy to defend.

Ladder Approach at Balcony House

Modern visitors are faced with a similar challenge, although the National Park Service has done a good job of making the journey adventurous but safe. The visitor will need to climb up a 32-foot ladder at the beginning of the tour. To get back out, one will need to bend low through a 12-foot-long tunnel to climb two 10-foot ladders. As with all of these tours, you will need to feel comfortable that you and your party can climb the ladders.

The Balcony House is smaller than the Cliff Palace, with 45 rooms and two kivas. Don't let the smaller size fool you. Given the Balcony House was harder to get to, it was placed into the park's hands in better shape than some of the other dwellings. Many of the wooden beams can still be seen supporting roofs and sticking out of room walls. The Balcony House gives an intimate look at the Mesa Verde cliff dwellings. Besides the wooden beams and roofs, another favorite feature is a T- shaped doorway that can be seen during the tour.

Long House Tour

The Long House Tour is the longest, most in-depth and engaging tour offered. The tour is 90 minutes compared to the usual one-hour tours of Cliff Palace and Balcony House, includes a tram ride to and from the trailhead

1929 Photo of Navajo Boy at Balcony House

and is on the less traveled Wetherill Mesa. Unfortunately, it is also the hardest to get to for folks in an RV as vehicles over 25 feet are prohibited on the Wetherill Mesa Road. It is only open from Memorial Day to Labor Day each year. This tour is the most strenuous and requires a ¾-mile (1.2 km) hike round trip to access the dwellings.

The tour begins at the Wetherill Mesa information kiosk. Here you will board a tram that travels through a pinyon juniper forest undergoing recovery from a recent burn. Once at the Long House Trailhead, you follow a paved path downhill about 1/3 mile (0.54 km) to reach the ruins. At one point, there is a concrete staircase of 50 steps with railing.

The hike itself adds to the ambiance of discovery. The ruins are not in sight at first, only the tops of mesas and wide canyons. The hike descends through wonderful rock and pinyon juniper forests. In the summer, it is hot and dry and, while this leads to the strenuous aspects of the hike, it may give appreciation for what the early inhabitants faced. Once fully immersed in the surroundings, Long House comes into view.

After a short lecture near the ruins, the tour includes climbing two 15-foot (4.5m) ladders up into the site itself. No longer standing alongside the ruins, you are now inside them, bringing a personal aspect to experiencing the dwellings. The ruins themselves are fairly extensive, with more than 100 rooms, including multistory buildings. Long House is the second largest cliff dwelling in the park. The ranger will point out some petroglyphs along the way as well. The tour ends by taking the same trail back, this time uphill. On a hot day, the 50 concrete steps won't look as welcoming going up as they did going down. The tram will take you back to the Wetherill parking area.

Self-Guided Tours

Spruce Tree House (Chapin Mesa)

During the winter months from November to early March, the Spruce Tree House is not only a ranger-led guided tour but is free. The tours last one hour and are given three times a day. The rest of the year, it is available as a self-guided tour.

Spruce Tree House is the third largest cliff dwelling (Cliff Palace and Long House are larger). It is also the best preserved of the cliff dwellings. The walking distance of the tour is ½ mile (0.8 km) round trip and begins at the Chapin Mesa Archeological Museum. Visitors can meander at leisure along paths that encourage a more relaxed experience. There are around 130 rooms and 8 kivas, which were believed to have housed 60 to 80 people. There are many multistory buildings to view and a kiva that one can enter as part of the tour.

Spruce Tree House

Far View Sites Complex (Chapin Mesa)

Coyote Village, Far View Sites

The Far View Sites are often overlooked on the drive to the more known sites at Chapin Mesa proper. The Far View Sites are unique in that these villages sit at the top of the mesa rather than in an alcove of a cliff. There were at one time 50 villages in the half square mile surrounding this area. The self-guided tour gives a nice walk among five of the villages plus a dry reservoir. The trail is unpaved but level and is ¾ mile (1.2km) long. These surface sites include Far View House, Pipe Shrine House, Coyote Village, Far View Reservoir, Megalithic House, and Far View Tower. This is a great hike if you want to round out the day's experience on your way back to the campground.

Badger House Trail (Wetherill Mesa)

The Badger House Community is a series of four sites on a paved and gravel trail. The sites include Modified Basketmaker Pithouse, Developmental Pueblo village, Badger House and Two Raven House. Like Far View Sites Complex, these sites sit on top of the mesa. The trail is 2.5 mile (4km) if started at the Wetherill Mesa Kiosk or 1.5 miles (2.41 km) if you take the tram to the Badger House tram stop. The tour is both educational and peaceful.

Step House (Wetherill Mesa)

Step House

The Step House is one of the more unique self-guided tours in that one can see clear distinctions pointing to two separate occupations of the site. The first inhabitants were the Modified Basketmakers, which dated to A.D. 626. Evidence of their habitation can be found between the old stone steps on the southern edge of the site and the large boulders to the north. The area was inhabited again in A.D 1226 as evidenced by the masonry structures seen within the rest of the site. Two standouts of the ruins are a pit house and the petroglyphs.

The trail is steep and ¾ mile (1.2 km) long along a winding path. Many visitors that come to Wetherill Mesa combine the Step House self-guided tour with the ranger-led Long House tour. Allow a good half day if you decide this is the right combination for you.

Driving Tours

Cedar Tree Tower (Chapin Mesa)

This short drive off of Chapin Mesa Road gives a good example of a tower site. Here there are several tower sites that were built during the Classic period (A.D. 1100-1300). They are similar in construction to the kiva and are typically associated with them. What the towers were used for exactly remains unknown. Leading theories are mixed between a communication system and something more ceremonial in nature. The tower can be seen from the road and is open from 8 a.m. to sunset daily.

Wildflowers

On the road to the Cedar Tree Tower is a short ½ mile (0.8 km) loop trail that shows farming terraces. Farming terraces were a common and ingenious agriculture method for the Mesa Verde people. The farming terraces were built on slopes as level areas blocked on the downhill side by rocks that acted as check dams. The dams slowed the downhill migration of rainfall and snowmelt, providing needed moisture for planting. A closer look reveals they built the terraces around narrow drainage areas that helped gather and divert the water to these terraces. It was a great use of rock, water and gravity combined into a simple but effective feat of engineering.

Mesa Top Loop Road (Chapin Mesa)

If walking tours are not in the plans, you can still enjoy the 700 years of Pueblo history through the Mesa Top Loop auto tour. There are twelve accessible sites along the 6-mile (10km) driving tour. Some of the sites include short paved trails. The tour does an excellent job of taking the visitor through the history of Mesa Verde. Highlights include Sun Point Overlook, Square Tower House, and views of Cliff Palace from Sun Point and Sun Temple. There are

House of Many Windows

similar overlooks along the Cliff Palace Loop Road. Both auto tour sites are open from 8 a.m. to sunset.

Shuttle Tour

ARAMARK concessionaires offer guided bus tours of the Mesa and Cliff Palace loops. Allow a half day for the tour, which departs from the Far View Lodge at 8 a.m. and 1 p.m. from mid-April through mid-October. Cost is $36 for kids and $48 for adults. These tours can be reserved and do sell out. The ARAMARK tour guides are quite knowledgeable and give a well-rounded experience of the Mesa Verde history, dwellings and its former inhabitants. The admission includes a guided walking tour of Cliff Palace. You will need to bring your own snacks or hold out for the stop at the Spruce Tree Terrace Café. Tickets can be purchased at the visitor center, Far View Lodge and the Morefield Campground.

Hikes

While many of the self-guided and ranger-led tours involve hiking, the following represent actual hikes in the park.

Petroglyph Point Trail

Moderate – (2.4 mi / 3.9 km), round trip), allow 2 hours

Petroglyph Point

This trail begins from the Spruce Tree House trail and is one of the more pleasant hikes in Mesa Verde. The loop starts down below the mesa top, following what feels like an ancient trail used years ago. One winds through narrow rock passages among pinyon juniper forests with views of Spruce and Navajo Canyons. The trail "ends" at the petroglyphs, which are impressive and worth the hike. From the rock art, the trail heads up to the top of the mesa for a level and fairly easy walk back to the parking area. The hike drops you at the Chapin Mesa Archeological Museum, which is well worth a visit in its own right. Across the street is the Spruce Tree Terrace Café to finish off the hike with a well-deserved snack.

A trail guide is available and registration (at the museum) is required.

Spruce Canyon Trail

Moderate – (2.4 mi / 3.9 km), round trip, allow 2 hours

Spruce Tree House from Bottom of Spruce Tree Canyon

Spruce Canyon Trail begins at the Spruce Tree House trail and gives the viewer a chance to experience the ecosystem of the canyon floor. The trail heads to the bottom of Spruce Tree Canyon and then back up along the mesa top in one nice loop. Like the Petroglyph Point Trail, the loop finishes at the Chapin Mesa Archeological Museum, which is well worth exploring in its own right.

Nordenskiöld Site No. 16 Trail

Easy – (1.0 mi / 1.6 km), round trip, allow 30 minutes

This trail found in the Wetherill Mesa section leads to an overlook of Nordenskiöld Site 16.

Prater Ridge Trail

Strenuous – (7.8 mi / 12.6 km), round trip, allow 4 - 5 hours

This loop is the longest of the three trails that start from the nearby Morefield Campground. The trail climbs until it reaches Prater Ridge and then follows along the rim of the cuesta. Like all of the trails near the campground, it is light on ruins but big on nature. Prater Ridge gives expansive views of the Montezuma Valley. This is honestly one of the best of the longer hikes in the park. It makes a complete loop, giving a variety of views of the southern Colorado countryside. If you want to make it a smaller loop, there is an obviously marked cutoff trail that trims the loop by roughly half.

Montezuma Valley Overlook

Knife Edge Trail

Easy – (2.0 mi / 3.2 km), round trip, allow 1 hour

One of the other three hikes near the Morefield Campground, this short there and back trail gives some decent views of Montezuma Valley. The trail starts by passing between the Prater Ridge and an obvious little rock hillock called Lone Cone. There is a bit of elevation at first, but much of the trail is flat asa it follows the old Knife Edge Road. The trail pretty much just ends at a sign that says "STOP!! Trail End" indicating it's time to turn back. This short trail is nicely secluded on most days and provides a great place to take in a sunset.

Point Lookout Trail

Strenuous – (2.2 mi / 3.5 km), round trip, allow 90 minutes

This is one of the three trails that start from the Morefield Campground. The trail does pass by some Ute structures and other ruins as it makes its way to a highpoint called Point Lookout. The point stands as a natural lookout tower for the entire Mesa Verde area. It was used by the United States Calvary to signal fellow mounted forces as well as earlier by the Utes.

There is an elevation gain of about 500 feet, most of it occurring in the first half mile as the trail winds on up via a series of switchbacks. The trail continues on through Oak brush vegetation with a few more switchbacks and then more gently climbs the final half mile to the top. The trail here narrows to a knife ridge, but there is plenty of vegetation on either side. Here there are remnants of Ute structure, inscriptions, initials and other interested artifacts as you reach the top and the great views of the Mancos and Montezuma Valleys.

Wetherill Mesa Bike and Hike Adventure

Strenuous – (9.0 mi / 14.5 km), round trip, allow 4.5 hours

This is likely one of the coolest ranger led hikes in the entire Grand Circle. You get to hike with a ranger for four miles and bike alongside for another five miles. This isn't a tram stuffed full of people and some guy reciting into a megaphone, this is a full immersion bi modal journey into Mesa Verde accompanied by an expert hiking and biking along with you.

The entire trip is filled with great views of cliff dwellings with in depth trips to Nordenskold #12, Double House and even includes a short hike to Long House. Allow about six hours total for the hike and driving time to the starting point from the visitor center. Also bring plenty of water, snacks, sunscreen and a hat. Folks must be in good overall shape for this adventure.

Tickets are $18.00 for adults and $15.00 for kids up to 16 years old. Tours are limited to 15 people. Bike not included (you need to bring your own). There are rental bikes available, call (970) 529-4631 for information on local bike rental places. Also, tour times were limited to Wednesdays and Sundays as of this writing.

The Challenge of Fuzzling

On a Hot Afternoon..

[Everest, giving me a big hug]: Dad, I love you.

[Me, taken back by the moment]: Hey, son! I love you too! Glad to have you on this trip.

[Everest]: Yeah, me too. (Pauses) Can I have the iPad?

Climbing Out of the Mesa Verde Cliff Dwellings

Since this is a guide meant for families, a code word is needed to take on this next topic. You see, dear reader, what I want to discuss next is fairly sensitive and is likely inappropriate for younger folk who might have previously thought storks were part of said matter. It's a worthy discussion to have, as you may be wondering yourself how certain things are accomplished in an RV.

Now, I'm not writing about this subject because of some purported belief that I'm an expert in the area, but more out of the notion that writing about this subject could be a lot more fun than writing about another hike. Certainly, too, it will hopefully make for a better read, so let's just say I'm doing this for both of us.

Besides, on the topic that is about to surface, it is certainly popular, but as there is much taboo surrounding this domain we are going to need a code word. So in the spirit of keeping this guidebook at a PG-13 rating, let's mask everything I'm about to talk about with the verb "fuzzle." As a word, fuzzle is kind of cute; it sounds ambiguously like something you'd see in a parts catalog, as in "hand me that fuzzle" or in a children's book, as in "the fuzzly little fuzzle bears walked hand in hand to the stream." Regardless of what fuzzle could mean, I imagine or at least hope that by now, every parent knows exactly what we are about to talk about. That's right, let's take on the challenges of fuzzling in an RV.

Spousal fuzzling on a family vacation is difficult enough in its own right and especially in this day and age. Say you want to have some fuzzle time in a hotel situation. Back when I was a kid, my dad would ask the hotel receptionist to give us a room on a floor with a malfunctioning ice machine. He would then send my sister and me off to get some ice. In his masterful plan he wouldn't tell us that the ice machine on our floor was broken or that the next closest ice machine was in a separate wing. We would, of course, chomp at the bit for a chance to get a bucket of ice because, let's face it, for a kid, pushing a button and watching ice fall out is about as fun as childhood gets. This clever plan would give my parents time to test out the sheets (or to use our code word, get in some quick fuzzling).

Like the Easter Bunny and Santa Claus, I sadly did not realize his masterful plan until my adult years, but that's not the point. The point is, in those days you could send your kid to another hotel for ice and this was okay. Life was simpler then, safer. In this modern age, many parents, including my wife, are hesitant to let their children out of sight.

For example, my recent plea to allow the kids to independently explore the hotel in Vegas went something like this.

"How about we let the kids go down to the hotel arcade on their own?" I asked Ang as if it was the best idea ever.

"Oh, no. They're too young. I just read about a kidnapping of a child Bryce's age… at Disneyland no less."

"I thought I read that was an urban legend. You know, Everest will be driving a car in a few years. Bryce is a black belt in karate. I can personally attest to his ability to deliver a mean kick to the family jewels."

They are both in good shape and could outrun most predators. I think the two of them are ready, if just for thirty minutes. They could go together. I'm sure they will be safe."

From this point in the debate, there is typically much wrangling that quite frankly is rather dull to read, but eventually Ang brought up a possibility that lay within the realm of the incredibly improbable, such as the following:

"But what if there's an earthquake? We are on the eighteenth floor, after all. The arcade is on the third floor. How will we get to our boys in the chaos?"

By the time she gets to the "earthquake in Las Vegas" section of the dialogue, I realize there is no amount of logic that will prevail here. If I find a rational means to overcome the earthquake theory, she will move to the possibility that killer bees or a freak tsunami might hit the town. The point is, she's the mama bear and in matters of protecting her cubs, reason has no jurisdiction. In these cases, I give up and settle in with the kids as they watch Sponge Bob Square Pants. As Sponge Bob searches for his lost jelly fish net, my mind wanders to thoughts of every couple in the hotel happily fuzzling away like crazed weasels except for us.

As challenging as fuzzling on a family vacation is in a hotel room, fuzzling in an RV is nearly impossible. The main problem here is that the bed is part of the RV. Everything you do in your RV bed is felt by everyone else in the RV. When you turn over in your RV bed, the entire RV moves. If your kids wrestle up in their bunk bed on the other end of the RV, it will feel as if they are wrestling in your bed. This leads to a simple truth. Beds on shocks are not conducive to anything that remotely resembles fuzzling. So even if you are the type of parent who has mastered ninja fuzzling when your kids are dead asleep (something by the way that would never happen in our family, but you folks know who you are), you are in for some new challenges.

You could send your kids out to play, but even then, those shocks on your RV are disturbingly sensitive. Not only will your children wonder why the RV is rocking, so will your neighbors. Moreover, if there is a squeaky strut or shock, forget about it. I mean how in the world could you focus on the fuzzling at hand when there is some stupid noisy shock yelling out to the campground, "Hey everybody, over here! There's a couple trying to fuzzle, turn off your generators and gather round!" Soon you will have the entire campground standing around cheering you on, beer cans and spatulas in hand, while your kids sit confused and a little scared at the picnic table. It's not exactly an event where people would say, "Yeah, that's good parenting."

There is privacy for a couple in the shower, but if you go that route, invest in some yoga classes beforehand as you will definitely need to get your contortionist on if you are going to fuzzle there. The shower space is the afterthought of a small RV. It's where they took space away to give you a bigger kitchen, and it's like trying to fuzzle in an airplane bathroom except without all that engine noise to mask the effort. The shower is a good alternative if you absolutely must fuzzle, but only as a last resort. It will draw the same amount of attention as other areas in the RV, but with less fuzzling option possibilities.

If you don't have children and/or are an exhibitionist in nature, then the RV is perfect for your needs. You really can fuzzle in places that you may never have fuzzled before, and if you park at a remote campsite, you can do so without drawing too much of a crowd. Plus, there's the great outdoors. With a good pair of hiking boots and plenty of water, you can fuzzle on virgin ground. It is truly open territory for you folks. For the rest of us who have kids, morals and perhaps a tad more dignity, our hats go off to you. My only guidance here is be mindful not to disturb the land if you go off trail. Just because you want to have a good time doesn't mean you shouldn't be a good custodian of our national parks. If you pack it in, be sure to pack it out—you know what I'm saying. Plus, it's always good to have a good exit strategy if you take on fuzzling in bear country. Bears are opportunists by nature and live to catch a couple off guard in situations like these. They will not only eat you or worse, the story they will tell their animal friends will become that of legend. It will be passed down from one bear generation to the next. This is not how you want to immortalize yourself, trust me.

To recap, if you are traveling with your children or in-laws, fuzzling in an RV presents its own special set of challenges. It is as noticeable as a tourist in polyester and draws more attention than a generator running during off-hours. Be prepared to forego fuzzling altogether for the duration of the trip, and if you must fuzzle, remember the shower is an option, albeit a limited one. If you follow this guidebook to the letter, the one biggest secret I can give you is the Gifford Pie shop at Capitol Reef and $5 per kid will get you about 20 minutes. If you give more money for ice cream, you get about 5 minutes extra. Fruita is truly an Eden of paradise! To those of you who are reading this in the order of parks visited, I realize you have likely already completed that leg of your journey. I'm confident however in your abilities to improvise your own clever solution. Dear reader, best of luck in your own fuzzling endeavors!

Grand Canyon
National Park

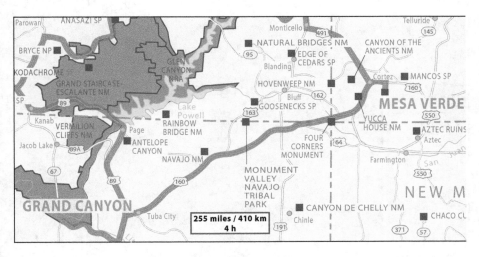

"*We are now ready to start on our way down the Great Unknown...We are three quarters of a mile in the depths of the earth ...We have an unknown distance yet to run; an unknown river yet to explore. What falls there are, we know not; what rocks beset the channel, we known not; what walls rise over the river, we know not. Ah, well! We may conjecture many things. The men talk as cheerfully as ever; jests are bandied about freely this morning; but to me the cheer is somber and the jests are ghastly.*"

—John Wesley Powell, *Down the Great Unknown*

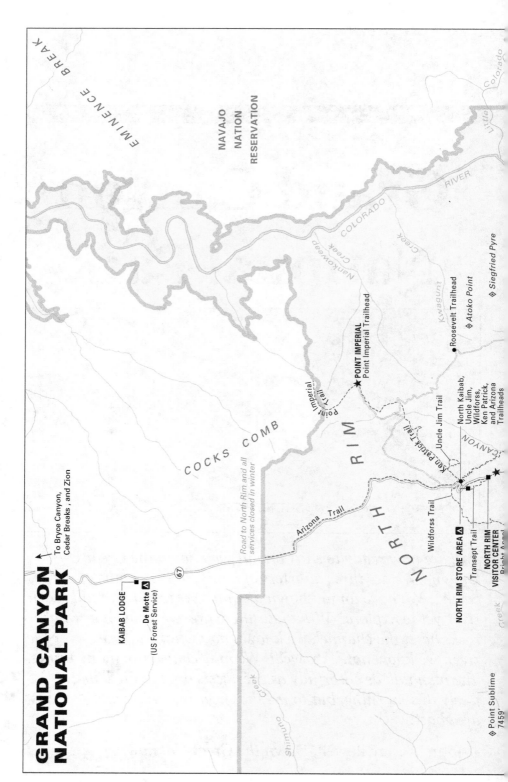

GRAND CANYON
NATIONAL PARK

EMINENCE BREAK

To Bryce Canyon,
Cedar Breaks , and Zion

NAVAJO
NATION
RESERVATION

COLORADO

RIVER

Little Colorado

COCKS COMB

COLORADO

Nankoweap Creek

Kwagunt Creek

◈ Siegfried Pyre

● Roosevelt Trailhead

◈ Atoko Point

POINT IMPERIAL
Point Imperial Trailhead
★

Point Imperial Trail

Road to North Rim and all
services closed in winter

67

KAIBAB LODGE
■ De Motte ⚠
(US Forest Service)

Arizona   Trail

Ken Patrick Trail

Uncle Jim Trail

North Kaibab,
Uncle Jim,
Wildforss,
Ken Patrick,
and Arizona
Trailheads

N O R T H   R I M

CANYON

★

Wildforss Trail

NORTH RIM STORE AREA ⚠
Transept Trail

■ ■

**NORTH RIM
VISITOR CENTER**
Bright Angel

Shinumo   Creek

Creek

◈ Point Sublime
7459'

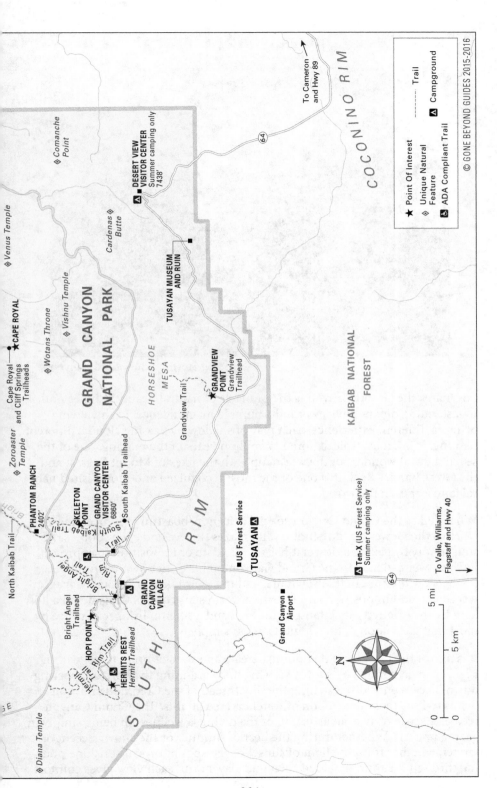

© GONE BEYOND GUIDES 2015-2016

Legend
- ★ Point Of Interest
- ◈ Unique Natural Feature
- 🏕 ADA Compliant Trail
- ------ Trail
- 🔺 Campground

COCONINO RIM

To Cameron and Hwy 89

64

DESERT VIEW VISITOR CENTER
Summer camping only
7438'

Comanche Point

Venus Temple

Cardenas Butte

TUSAYAN MUSEUM AND RUIN

GRAND CANYON NATIONAL PARK

Vishnu Temple

Wotans Throne

★ CAPE ROYAL

Cape Royal and Cliff Springs Trailheads

Zoroaster Temple

HORSESHOE MESA

Grandview Trail

★ **GRANDVIEW POINT**
Grandview Trailhead

KAIBAB NATIONAL FOREST

PHANTOM RANCH
2402'

North Kaibab Trail

Bright Angel Trail

SKELETON POINT

GRAND CANYON VISITOR CENTER
6860'

South Kaibab Trailhead

South Kaibab Trail

Rim Trail

Bright Angel Trail

Bright Angel Trailhead

GRAND CANYON VILLAGE

■ US Forest Service

🔺 **TUSAYAN**

RIM

★ **HOPI POINT**

HERMITS REST
Hermit Trailhead

Rim Trail

Hermit Trail

SOUTH

Diana Temple

🔺 **Ten-X** (US Forest Service)
Summer camping only

■ **Grand Canyon Airport**

64

To Valle, Williams, Flagstaff and Hwy 40

N

5 mi

5 km

0

0

What Makes Grand Canyon Special

Passing Storm in the Grand Canyon

For many, the Grand Canyon is the pinnacle of natural beauty. It hides nothing, standing before the viewer in its humble magnificence. Each viewing brings a different experience, each play of shadow by passing cloud a different lighting. It is a masterpiece, some 17 million years in the making, one of the seven natural wonders of the world, up with the likes of Mount Everest and the Great Barrier Reef. It is one of the most recognized and most visited natural landscapes in the world.

What makes the Grand Canyon special is its non-boastful presence. It overwhelms the viewer but does not try. It amazes the eye and even soothes the soul simply by gazing at it, yet it has no mandate or imposition in approach. Each viewer can take in the Grand Canyon on his or her own terms, meet it wherever they are in their own life, and the view takes in all that baggage, weariness, and imposition and returns a warm sense of life. Considered a holy land by the original inhabitants of the area and a solemn bringer of peace by most that gaze upon it, the Grand Canyon simply is.

It is one of the few places that doesn't create an expectation to travel within it; one can gain much by simply viewing it, by scanning the horizon, peering down its canyon walls, watching the tiny thread of the Colorado and wonder as to how that little ribbon of water created all this. The Grand Canyon creates a sense of awe, an assertion of the divine, a wellness of being simply in gazing upon it. Whether during the heat of summer or the snowy accent of winter, whether from the light of sunset or the spot lit rays of sunshine pouring through the thunder clouds of a mid-day storm, each view gives comfort.

Think of the times in your life when you felt special. Those singular moments when everything went just so, that you risked the impossible and it actually worked in your favor. When you decided to do something not for yourself, but for someone else. You did that something even when it meant that only you would know of the benefit provided, an unconditional presence of selflessness. This is the Grand Canyon, providing inspiration and warm takeaways for 5 million visitors every year, giving of itself, inducing respectful wonder simply by its own manifestation. What makes the Grand Canyon special is that it gives; it gives openly, generously and without asking anything at all in return. You leave a better person having simply looked at it. There are few places in this world that can make this claim.

Staying in Grand Canyon NP

There are two main areas to stay within Grand Canyon National Park. The most accessible, with the most accommodations and amenities, is the South Rim, including Desert View. The South Rim is also the most popular, receiving nearly 90 percent of the park's 5 million annual visitors. The remaining 500,000 visitors head to the North Rim. Of the two, the South Rim is open year round and both offer the most lodging and camping options of any of the national parks described in this book, but is also the most visited.

South Rim

Within the South Rim of the Grand Canyon are six lodges, one ranch and three main camping destinations. If you are coming during the off-season, South Rim contains the only campgrounds and lodging that are open year round. Desert View and North Rim campgrounds close during the fall and winter months. All lodges and campgrounds book up so make sure you reserve far in advance, especially if you are vacationing during the summer months.

Bright Angel Lodge

In terms of great views of the Grand Canyon right from your room, Bright Angel Lodge is a top pick. This is not a five star hotel, the rooms typically show wear from being constantly at capacity. However the staff are exceptional and the views are amazing. The lodge has something for every budget, from lodge rooms with a shared bathroom, private cabins and rooms and even historic cabins. The two historic cabins, the Red Horse and Buckey O'Neill Cabin are double in price and are better suited for couples. The Bright Angel Lodge was designed by Southwest architect Mary Jane Colter in 1935 and has a warm rustic feel inside and out. Rooms are roughly $100-200 per night with a charge of $9 per each extra person.

El Tovar Hotel

This is the flagship of the entire set of lodges in the Grand Canyon and is arguably the best within the Grand Circle parks described. El Tovar opened its doors in January 1905 under the design of Charles Whittlesey, who was the Chief Architect for the Atchison, Topeka, and Santa Fe Railway. Unlike the rustic, grand, Arts and Craft designs of Stanley Gilbert Underwood, the inspirations for the El Tovar came from European decent, which gives the lodge a look reminiscent of a Swiss chalet. This was done intentionally to appeal to the vacationing elite of the era, who saw Europe and its culture as the reference for elegance. The hotel has seen all manner of the rich and famous, from President Theodore Roosevelt to Sir Paul McCartney. If you don't get a chance to stay in the El Tovar, definitely drop in to check it out. It a remarkable and historic place.

Rooms are in line with expectations with standard rooms starting at $207 for one double and $251 for one queen. For families needing two queen beds, set your sights and pocketbook on the deluxe rooms at $337. That said, if you are okay with spending three hundred dollars on a room, time to upsell you to the suite. You are staying at the El Tovar after all and if you get a suite, perhaps you will share the same room as a past famous dignitary. Many of the 78 rooms within this property are suites containing minor differences and ranging from $421 to $513. The suites offer more square footage, a sitting room and some have a private balcony. Extra persons for the standard and deluxe rooms only are $14.

Kachina Lodge

The Kachina Lodge has a much more contemporary feel than Bright Angel or El Tovar but also offers incredible views. The rooms are decent, basic and typically show some wear. Folks staying in this hotel need to check in at the El Tovar Hotel Front Desk. All rooms offer a king or two queens, plus your own bathroom. Street side rooms run at $215 while canyon rooms run $232 with a charge of $9 per each extra person.

Thunderbird Lodge

Similar to the Kachina Lodge in both form and function, the Thunderbird Lodge offers suitable clean basic rooms, some with spectacular views. The pricing structure is also equivalent to the Kachina Lodge. To check into the Thunderbird Lodge you need to head to the Bright Angel Lodge Front Desk.

Maswik Lodge

Maswik Lodge is a large 278 room complex set back from the canyon's edge. The overall design and architecture reflects the 1960's, which is when the facility was built. Maswik is a Hopi name for the kachina that guards all of the Grand Canyon. One thing the Maswik lodge does do is guard the family pocketbook.

South Rooms are an affordable $107 for two queens, with the North Rooms fetching $205. Extra persons are $9. Overall, the Maswik lodge gets consistently good reviews. Whether it's the price to value or the kachina Maswik helping to make for a pleasant stay, folks tend to leave satisfied.

Yavapai Lodge

The Yavapai Lodge is the largest of the lodges at 378 rooms separated into two wings of multistory structures. The best thing going for Yavapai Lodge is its proximity to the nearby Market Plaza, where a general store, deli, post office and bank can be found. It is also within walking distance of the Visitor Center and coin operated laundry. The lodge is a bit more pricy than the Maswik Lodge for this reason, with West rooms containing two queen beds coming in at $147 and East rooms at $181. Extra persons are again $9 each.

Phantom Ranch

The Phantom Ranch accommodates in a manner unlike any of the other lodges or campgrounds. The ranch and the ranche's name was created from the mind of Mary Jane Colter in the 1920's. The cabins are rustic and look right out of a western movie set, built with a nice mixture of wood and native stones.

What makes the Phantom Ranch cabins special is the journey involved in getting to them. One cannot just pull up to the Phantom Ranch and roll the suitcases across the parking lot. The ranch is at the bottom of the Grand Canyon, so the only way to get to it is by mule, foot or via the Colorado River itself. For hikers there are dormitories separated by gender for $47 per night. For families, look into the complete trip combination which includes getting down to the ranch by mule, full meal options (including a steak dinner) and the cabin. Each cabin holds two people, so if you are travelling as a family, expect to reserve two cabins if you go this route. Full details on the ranch can be found here: www.grandcanyonlodges.com/lodging/phantom-ranch/

One thing to note on staying at the Phantom Ranch, you can't simply drop in and you can't announce you have extra folks out of the blue and expect them to get a place to stay. You need to reserve everything ahead of time and if you are hiking down, you need to let the ranch know you are on your way. This is one of the most popular things to do in the Grand Canyon, so plan accordingly.

Mather Campground

Mather Campground is centrally located in the South Rim park area and is run by the National Park Service. There are 319 campsites available that accommodate RVs up to 30 feet. There are no hookups. If you have a larger RV or need hookups, head to Trailer Village.

Mather Campground is named for the national park's first director and is the largest campground in Grand Canyon. There is firewood for sale, there are laundry and shower facilities, and a dump and water station is available. Generators are allowed from 7 am to 9 am and again from 6 pm to 8 pm. Pine Loop is geared toward tent camping, so if you find yourself in Pine Loop, generators are not allowed. Quiet hours for the entire campground are from 10 pm to 6 am.

As in Zion NP, all sites are reservable and assigned. It is highly recommended you reserve your site prior to arriving. Reservations are taken up to six months in advance. You can stay at the campground for up to seven consecutive days and a total of 30 days per year, though if wanting to stay longer than that is a problem you are trying to solve, I'm envious! Check-in starts at noon, check-out is at 11 am. If the site is available, you can renew for another day after 9 am.

The park generally receives good marks from every aspect. It has hot showers for $2 and is close to nearby Market Plaza, which contains a cafeteria, delicatessen and grocery store. It is also close to the shuttle system, which has drop offs at every overlook in the South Rim short of Desert View. You can take the shuttle to the visitor center and Bright Angel Lodge.

Trailer Village

Trailer Village is close to Mather Campground and about ½ mile (0.8 km) from the rim of the Grand Canyon. While it is located within the National Park, it is operated by the Xanterra concessionaire. Here you will find 80 pull-through, paved sites with full hookups. RVs up to 50 feet long can be accommodated. Each site has the usual picnic table, barbecue grill and 30 and 50-amp electrical service. You can also hook into cable TV, water and sewage if desired. The Trailer Village is open all year and starts at $36 a night. It shares the shower and laundry facility with Mather Campground at the Camper Services area, which is located farther from Trailer Village and closer to the Mather Campground. Besides this downside, the Trailer Village otherwise receives similar praise to that of Mather Campground. You are in the center of the park near the rim of the Grand Canyon. It will be difficult to not be pleased with your stay.

Outside South Rim Park Boundaries

The nearby town of Tusayan has a couple of campgrounds. Ten-X Campground is open from May through September and is operated by the U.S. Forest Service. There are 70 sites available with 15 of them reservable through Recreation.gov. Fee is $10 per night. There is one group site that can be reserved for a party of 100 people.

Camper Village is commercially operated and is located about 7 miles (11 km) south of the Grand Canyon Village in Tusayan. It is open seasonally and offers hook-ups and coin-operated showers. The site offers a general store and convenient pizza; however, this should be considered as a place of last resort. It is consistently given bad reviews on the advisor sites. Call (928) 638-2887.

Desert View

The Desert View section of the park is about 25 miles (41 km) from the South Rim proper, tucked away to the east of the park. While it does get a little less traffic than the main South Rim, the Desert View Drive is typically included as part of the journey for many Grand Canyon visits. There are 50 sites available for tents and RVs up to 30 feet long. Unlike the Mather Campground, Desert View is offered on a first come, first served basis. The campground is closed by late fall and opens in the late spring, typically between October and May.

During the summer months, the campground is filled by early afternoon. The site does have a self-serve registration kiosk that accepts credit cards, though there is something kind of quaint about filling out those little campsite envelopes and having to find exact change for the $12-a-night fee.

There are bathrooms and water, but no dumping or water station, and no showers. The Desert View section has many of the same amenities as the South Rim, including its own visitor center, marketplace and Desert View Indian Watchtower, which is modeled after ancient Anasazi watchtowers and is a unique architectural feature within the park.

North Rim

The North Rim receives much less traffic, is harder to get to and has limited seasons of operation. It is a mere 10 miles (16 km) from the South Rim as the raven flies but a 220-mile (354 km) journey to drive from rim to rim. Given that this side of the canyon gets closer to 500,000 visitors versus the 4.5 million on the South Rim, the pace is much more relaxed and steady. Getting to the North Rim is doable in an RV and can be a rewarding way to see the Grand Canyon. There is one main campground and one lodge on this side of the park. The North Rim of the Grand Canyon, including the campground, is not open year-round. They close for winter typically in October and reopen in mid-May.

Grand Canyon Lodge

The Grand Canyon Lodge was originally built from the design of Gilbert Stanley Underwood in 1927/28 but was severely burned in 1932 and rebuilt shortly after, though whether Underwood had a hand in the new design is under debate. It does carry a fair amount of Underwood's style. The lodge is located at Bright Angel Point and is typically an excellent alternative to the hustle and bustle happening at the South Rim.

For families, the best bet is staying in the Western Cabins, which offer two queen beds, full size bath and porch. Be sure to ask for the Rim View Cabins as opposed to the Standard Cabins. Another great option are the Pioneer Cabins, which were recently remodeled in 2009. These cabins offer two rooms with bunk beds or twin beds in one room and a queen sized bed in the other room.

North Rim Campground

There are 74 standard sites available for RVs and tents plus several more for tent only and group sites. There are no hookups, but there is a water and dump station at the campground. Firewood is available for sale at the nearby General Store.

As the campground is run by the National Park Service, many of the same rules apply as they do in the South Rim. Generators are allowed from 7 am to 9 am and again from 6 pm to 8 pm. Quiet hours for the entire campground are from 10 pm to 6 am. All sites are reservable and assigned. It is highly recommended that you reserve your site prior to arriving. Reservations are taken up to six months in advance. You can stay at the campground for up to seven consecutive days and a total of 30 days per year.

Check-in starts at noon, check-out is at 11 am. If the site is available, you can renew for another day after 9 am. There are laundry and shower facilities as well as change machines nearby.

Grand Canyon Geology

If you've followed the route in this book, the Grand Canyon is the last in a long and hopefully worthwhile journey of seven of the best national parks in the United States. You've been on the Colorado Plateau the entire time and, geologically, the same rules apply within the Grand Canyon as they do for the other parks. Sediments were set down through various geologic events, they turned to layers of rock, the Colorado Plateau lifted up these layers just a little while back, and in a geologic blink of an eye, the Grand Canyon was formed.

There are some amazing distinctions that really set the Grand Canyon apart, however. One of the most amazing aspects is that the Colorado River is currently cutting through rocks that are 2 billion years old and are thus among the oldest visible rocks in the world. Let's put this into perspective.

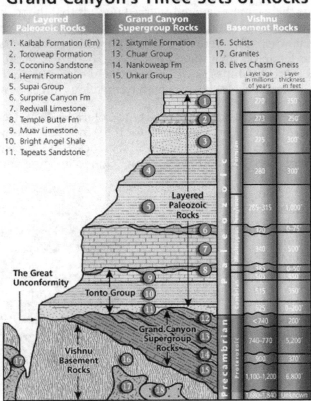

Stratigraphy of the Grand Canyon

The earth was formed 4.5 billion years ago and this strata layer, the so-called Vishnu Basement Rocks, are the oldest rocks in the Grand Canyon and yet are less than half the age of the planet itself. If you average that out among the Grand Canyon's depth of 6,000 feet, every inch down is like stepping back 27,000 years in time. While this is a bit misleading since the rocks don't literally get older in a straight-line fashion, it is still a mind-boggling way to ponder just how old these rocks are.

What is perhaps more amazing is the short amount of time it took to form the Grand Canyon relative to the earth's overall presence. Again, the earth is about 4.5 billion years old. Most theories put the start of the Colorado Plateau uplift at a mere 17 million years ago and the formation of the Grand Canyon itself around 6 million years ago. If we compare this to a human life span of 70 years, the Grand Canyon would have formed during the last month of that person's life.

So why the Grand Canyon? Why did the river cut so deeply that it is over a mile in depth and yet so passionately that the younger rock layers found in Zion and Bryce are all washed away? Theories on all of this differ, and as the Grand Canyon is a geologist's dream come true, each theory is hotly debated. The theory most generally agreed upon is that the rock layers encourage erosion, and when it rains here, it really rains. Since the rocks don't absorb water well, when they were hit with the torrential downpours that hit the area, water was left to do what water does, erode solid rock. In the winters, ice would do its erosional duties as well, freezing and expanding in between rock crevices, breaking apart rock layers with tremendous forces.

The final piece of this theory is the Colorado River itself. While it is considered the principal river for the American Southwest even today, during the late Pleistocene era, when all that locked-up glacier water melted, the river flowed like nothing you can begin to imagine. It provided a conveyer for all that sediment getting washed down from above, pushing the entire canyon full of rock and soil downstream. Without the help of the Colorado River, none of this would have happened. It is, in fact, what makes the Grand Canyon so amazing. It isn't what is there that gives the full picture of tremendous grandeur, it is what isn't there. The Canyon was once solid layers of rock, unencumbered and silent, untouched and buried. The Colorado River helped remove all that space between those layers to create the canyons before you by removing all those unimaginable square feet of rock and taking it somewhere else.

Colorado River

As to the real geology of the Grand Canyon, the geologist's geology, it is well written in many books, online references and the park's several visitor centers. As the center story of the Grand Canyon, the different layers can become quite complex. That said, it is helpful to look at the three main rock groups.

We've already described the Vishnu Basement Rocks, which are also known as the Vishnu Complex. This rock layer is 2 billion years old and is at the bottom of the Grand Canyon. Jumping up to the rim of the canyon, the Kaibab Limestone layer is a mere 230 million years old and is the youngest of the rock layers and the first of the top layer known as the Layered Paleozoic Rocks. This section stratifies down to layers that are around 500 million years old. The layer in the middle is referred to as the Grand Canyon Supergroup rocks and ranges in age from 740 million years to about 1.2 billion years old. There is a gap here between the oldest and lowest section and the one above it of about a billion years. This is referred to as the Great Unconformity and indicates a period of erosion between two periods of deposition.

The great depth of the Grand Canyon was aided not only by the rather rapid uplift of the Colorado Plateau, which allowed for a steeper cut of the Colorado River and its tributaries, but also by the Gulf of California. It is thought that the Gulf of California opened about 5.3 million years ago, which lowered the river's base level, or lowest point. This in turn increased the rate of erosion and cut most of the Grand Canyon to its current depth within a short 4 million years. Similar to digging down at the end of a little stream to allow the water to run out faster, the water picks up speed and takes more debris with it. This was apparently done on the grand scale of a major river. All of this is hotly debated, of course.

Grand Canyon History

From 2 billion years ago to about 11,000 years ago, the history of the Grand Canyon was almost exclusively geological in nature. First evidence of humans in the Grand Canyon dates back 10,500 years. The ancestral Pueblo people followed similar patterns described within all of the Grand Circle national parks, arriving as nomadic hunter-gatherers and shifting over to agriculturally based complex societies over the span of thousands of years. They were thought to have lived in the Grand Canyon National Park area up to 4,000 years ago.

Unique to the northern Arizona region were the Cohonina people, which is where Arizona's Coconino County gets its name. The Cohonina inhabited the areas west of the San Francisco Peaks near Flagstaff, east of the Aubrey Cliffs and south of the Grand Canyon. While they lived during the same period as the early Pueblo people (between 500 and 1200 CE), they exhibited distinctions in their society, mostly in their form of pottery. The pottery of the Cohonina was constructed using a paddle-and-anvil technique, which is a simple but very effective method for producing highly consistent and well-made pieces.

The method starts with a disk of clay and pounding on the clay with a paddle using a curved shaped piece of wood (the anvil) to provide resistance from the inside of the pot. The ceramist works her way around in a circle, paddling the clay into thin walls. The final shapes are decorated with black and gray illustrations.

View of Ancesteral Granary from Nankoweap Creek

The first European to see the Grand Canyon was Francisco Vásquez de Coronado. Coronado and his soldiers had set out to find the mythical Seven Cities of Gold. By the time they reached the Arizona-New Mexico state lines, their supplies were heavily depleted. They found both Zuni and Hopi villages and, after being refused entry by both tribes, forced their way in to replenish themselves. During the Zuni siege, Coronado himself was wounded. During the Hopi siege, they learned of and had Hopi scouts show them the Grand Canyon. The main purpose of visiting the canyon was the Colorado River, which they had hoped would provide a means of traveling back to the coast. The Grand Canyon proved too much for Coronado and his crew as they failed to find a route down to its shores. As a result, they were forced to turn back and head down the Rio Grande.

The Grand Canyon didn't receive another European tourist for 200 years until the two Franciscan priests who visited the Waterpocket Fold of Capitol Reef visited the canyon in 1776. Francisco Atanasio Domínguez and Silvestre Vélez de Escalante visited the canyon along the north rim. There was one other Franciscan missionary by the name of Francisco Garcés who also visited during this time frame. Garcés was as much an explorer as he was a missionary and explored much of the Southwest region of North America, including Baja California, Arizona and Southern California. His demeanor allowed him to establish peaceful relations with many of the tribes, including the Zuni and Hopi. He not only paid a visit to the Grand Canyon but also is credited with giving the Colorado River its name.

There are a handful of trappers who were credited with having visited the Grand Canyon in the mid- to late 1800s, but it was the expedition of U.S. Army Major John Wesley Powell who would put the canyon on the national map as a profound place of wonder. The U.S. War Department had sent Lt. Joseph Ives to the area a decade prior to Powell's expedition to investigate the area's natural resources and find a suitable railroad route to the West Coast.

Ives' group took a steam-boat named the Explorer up the Colorado River from the Gulf of California. The journey took two months and, as can be imagined, was a difficult journey. They traveled some 350 miles (560km) before reaching Black Canyon, striking a rock and being forced to abandon the ship.

Ives declared the canyon "altogether valueless" and was certain that he would be among "the last party of whites to visit this profitless locality." Ives' geologist John Strong Newberry, on the other hand, was awestruck by the canyon's beauty and, after a ten year pause, convinced both the Smithsonian Institution and Powell to take a boat down the river in the Grand Canyon.

Paiute Chief Tau-Gu with John Wesley Powell

Powell's expedition became the stuff of legends.

Powell selected nine men and on May 24, 1869 set out from Green River Station in Wyoming down the Colorado River. Their first expedition was done on a shoestring budget but was still able to bring back much of the first scientific examination of the canyon. In the Canyon of Lodore, one of the four boats capsized, spilling most of the crew's food rations and even some of their scientific equipment, which subsequently shortened their expedition to one hundred days. The expedition was filled with much hardship and raw adventure, including constantly being cold, wet and hungry. Three men of Powell's crew finally decided to turn back and exited the canyon only to be killed by a band of Paiutes.

While the first expedition was rife with danger and lacked resources, Powell brought back enough to whet the appetites of both the scientific community and the nation. He returned two years later with redesigned boats, a chain of supply stations along the route and better funding. Hugely lacking in the first expedition, this second one had a photographer and multiple artists. Nationally acclaimed naturalist painter Thomas Moran joined the expedition in the summer of 1873, offering his artistically soothing works to the growing collection of pictorial artifacts. His "Chasm of the Colorado" hung in the lobby of the Senate in 1874 and now hangs in the Smithsonian American Art Museum.

Powell's work brought focus to the entire Canyonlands regions of the Southwest, with the Grand Canyon being the crown jewel. He gave lectures and became a national figure as Americans looked at the pictures and illustrations of the Grand Canyon in amazement. No one had ever seen anything quite like it before. After pauses of hundreds of years between scant visitations, the knowledge of the Grand Canyon was out.

Although Powell brought the Grand Canyon to the nation's attention, it was not immediately brought into the National Park's fold. There was a bill brought forth by U.S. Senator Benjamin Harrison to declare the area a national park in 1887; however, it was never passed. After he became president of the United States, Harrison declared the Grand Canyon to be a National Forest Preserve in 1893. There had been amplified interest in the hopes the area could be mined for lead, asbestos, copper, uranium and zinc in the 1870s and 1880s and while nearly all of the claims proved unprofitable for mining, the number of mining claims tarnished a clean ability to turn the land over to the National Park Service. While the National Forest Preserve status still allowed mining and logging, it paved the way for further protection.

This tee up by Harrison proved to be useful when President Theodore Roosevelt visited the Grand Canyon in 1903. Roosevelt was very passionate about the conservation of the natural gems of the United States and in 1906 established the Grand Canyon Game Preserve. He then added adjacent national forest lands, and on January 11, 1908 re-designated the preserve a U.S. National Monument. This move further protected the area from mining, logging, and cattle grazing in and around the Grand Canyon.

For 11 years, landholders in the area blocked the Grand Canyon from being a National Park, but the National Monument status opened the doors to tourism. Stagecoaches had been offering tours to the Grand Canyon from Flagstaff as early as 1882. By 1901, a rail line had been built to the Grand Canyon Village from Williams, Arizona. This rail line is still in use today and carries the popular Polar Express tours. Back in 1901, the 64-mile (103 km) trip cost $3.95. By 1902 the first car made it the Grand Canyon and while train was the most approachable means of travel to the canyon until the mid-1930s, the ability of travel by either train or car helped expose the merits of the Grand Canyon as a tourist destination over a mining area. On February 26, 1919,

President Woodrow Wilson signed the Grand Canyon into law as the 17th national park. That year it received 44,173 visitors. Today, the Grand Canyon is one of the most popular destinations in the United States and is a required destination for travelers both home and abroad at least once in their lives. As a result, Grand Canyon NP receives nearly 5 million visitors each year.

Things to Do in Grand Canyon NP

The plus for having so many visitors is the park can support a larger variety of programs. The Park Service does a very good job at catering to the broad range of visitors to the area, from casual tourists who are content to step out of their car and look over the edge to hardcore whitewater river rafters and from art enthusiasts to geocaching fans. There is something for just about everybody in the Grand Canyon. The below are a few of the highlighted activities.

South Rim

River Rafting

Rafting down the Colorado is not only a popular activity, for many it is a bucket list item, something they have to do before they head on to the big national park in the sky. As a result, don't expect to show up and get on the river. Rafting is by permit only in the Grand Canyon and, depending on the activity, can take one to two years to receive a permit. The Park has made an effort to streamline the types of trips available and the permitting process for each.

A Dory in Hance Rapid

That said, rafting down the Colorado through the Grand Canyon is truly a defining moment in anyone's life. It is an experience that moves beyond words, resets your definitions of awe and wonder, brings a restful peace to the soul and at times puts you in moments of unholy terror that—on getting to the other side of—help remind you just how awesome it is to be alive. It is worth the planning and the wait.

One Day Commercial River Trips:

Half day and full day smooth water river trips are available through park concessionaire Colorado River Discovery. You can purchase tickets at any of the park's lodges. The smooth water river trips are the only trips that do not require a permit and as the trip never encounters rapids, is open to all ages from four years old and up.

While these trips are gentle and without the excitement of white water, they are a great way to see the park and are highly recommended. Bring food and water, sunscreen, a hat and, of course, your camera. On a side note about the camera, yes, it's okay to bring a camera on the trip that isn't waterproof as it is unlikely you will get wet. That said, use caution. In the summer, you won't need a towel as in the heat of the day you will dry off pretty quickly. In the spring and cooler seasons, bring layers. As you will be entering at the Glen Canyon Dam, which is inside the protection of Homeland Security, you will be checked for weapons, including pepper spray and pocket knives. These will not be allowed, so don't bring them.

Transportation from the lodge to the Dam is included.

3- to 18-Day Commercial River Trips

For those who are looking for white water rapids and adventure, there are hosts of river concessioners that provide full service guided trips. Each company offers its own suite of trips and many cater to the different experiences visitors are looking for. Trips can last for as little as a few days to up to 18 days.

The upside of a guided trip is that, first and foremost, you don't need to become an expert in white water rafting. The domain of the rafter is a world unto itself. They have their own language, and while they are a friendly, tightly knitted group, it's an investment of time and money to enter their world and walk, err—paddle—among them. A guided trip comes with the security that you are riding down the Colorado with an expert at the helm. Plus, the thoughts of where to camp, what to eat, and even where to do your business are pretty much taken care of for you. The downside is the cost and the fact that reservations need to be made one to two years in advance.

Details on what trips are offered, in what type of raft, duration and other amenities are numerous. The best place to start is the Grand Canyon NPS page, which lists all of the river concessionaires. Go to: http://www.nps.gov/grca/planyourvisit/river-concessioners.htm

2- to 5-Day Noncommercial River Trips

Permits are available to the general public starting one year in advance and are assigned on a first come, first served basis. Two noncommercial permits are authorized each day launching from Diamond Creek.

Grand Canyon with Clouds Overhead

Each trip is limited to a maximum of 16 people. There is no fee for the permits and they can be obtained by filling out a permit application and mailing it to the NPS permits department. While the NPS does not charge a fee for the permit, the Hualapai Tribe does charge a fee for crossing their land.

The permit can be found by going to: http://www.nps.gov/grca/planyourvisit/upload/Diamond_Creek_Application.pdf

You can also call directly: (800) 959-9164 or (928) 638-7843.

As mentioned above, you are crossing both National Park Service land and Hualapai tribal land. Hualapai means "people of the tall trees" in reference to the Ponderosa Pine. This small community of about 2,000 individuals primarily bases its economy on tourism. One way they do that is to charge a fee for each person (including drivers) and each vehicle traveling Diamond Creek Road, which they own. Cost is $64.20 for each person and vehicle, (example: 16 passengers, 2 drivers and 2 vehicles will cost $1284 total). Camping on the south side of the river (river left) above the high water mark will also require a permit from the Haulapai. More information can be had by calling the Haulapai directly at (928) 769-2219.

The NPS permits authorize you and your group to travel for 2 to 5 days from Diamond Creek in the Lower Gorge of the Colorado River. This 52-mile (84 km) section is spectacular and includes both smooth water and some decent rapids to shoot as well as culturally significant areas. River users are asked to treat these cultural areas with respect so that future generations can enjoy them. Camping is limited but is free on the north side (river right).

One word of note: acceptance. The river has changed since the days of Powell. You will be sharing the river with many other users, especially at the launch and take-out areas. You will find motorized upstream and downstream travel from Lake Mead and even see a helicopter or two. There will be moments that are all yours, but there will also be moments that are shared with others.

12- to 25-Day Noncommercial River Trips

This type of self-guided river trip travels among the rugged section between Lees Ferry to Diamond Creek and is for those fully experienced in river rafting. The permits are made available through a weighted lottery. For more information, start here: http://www.nps.gov/grca/planyourvisit/overview-lees-ferry-diamond-ck.htm.

Hiking

There are many hiking trails within the South Rim of the Grand Canyon. Hikes range from pleasant to steep and all offer exceptional views. Exploring the canyon from the rim is a very nice way to enjoy the canyon's scenery if you are looking for a non-strenuous hike. Bright Angel Trail is much steeper but gets you down further into the canyon itself. Backpacking is also available via permit.

While you can go down to the river and back in one day, it is an all-day hike and is typically not recommended. The hike down and back up is often underestimated. At the rim, it is pleasantly cool and the distance perception is heavily skewed. Objects don't look that far away and look smaller than they really are. It is only when hikers get to the bottom of the river that they fully understand the enormity of the Grand Canyon. At the river's edge, it is often very hot, and while the water looks tempting, it could carry you away if you get in it, so it doesn't offer the reprieve you hoped to get. From the river's bottom, the rim is a never-ending uphill journey that you will likely feel for a day or so afterwards. If you do go, start early and bring lots of water and pleasant little comfort foods and drinks to help you enjoy the journey.

Rim Trail

Easy – (13 mi / 21 km) one way, time varies

The Rim Trail is great for just strolling in the Grand Canyon with the view slowly changing before you. The trail starts at the South Kaibab Trailhead and extends to Hermit's Rest. It can be picked up from any overlook, and by utilizing the shuttle system one can pick up the trail and drop off it with a great deal of convenience. The trail is mostly paved and well travelled. For quieter moments, try walking it in tune to the sunrise or meander along its route in the late afternoon into dusk.

Bright Angel Trail

Strenuous – (12 mi / 19.3 km), to Plateau Point round trip)

Bright Angel is a very well-defined trail that ultimately leads to the Colorado River itself. While it is possible to do this in one day, as mentioned above, this is an all-day hike and not for the casual hiker. The thing to realize about Bright Angel is it is very inviting and gives wonderful views as you immerse yourself into the depths of the canyon. However, the trail is steep,

View from Bright Angel Trail

which gives you the impression that you are "cooking with gas" as you travel downward. It is only on the return that you realize just how steep this trail is. Allow twice as much time for the return trip and bring twice as much water for this hot, exposed trail.

For groups with small children, going to the first switchback offers a good experience without subjecting little feet to the steeper bits just ahead. For those not looking to do a full 12-mile (19 km) hike, going to Indian Gardens offers great views and a nice stopping point before turning around. There is water to refill your canteen and even a ranger on duty most of the time. Indian Gardens is 9 miles (14.5 km) round trip. If you decide to go the 1.5 miles (2.4 km) farther to Plateau Point, you won't be disappointed. This fairly level trail takes you to a nice viewpoint of the Colorado River and surrounding canyon. This is a great spot to get a good understanding of the immensity, grandeur and beauty of the Grand Canyon. You'll see how far you've traveled, and upon looking at the river below, you'll see how far you would still need to go, which is humbling.

South Kaibab Trail

Strenuous – (6.0 mi / 9.7 km), to Skeleton Point round trip

It is possible to take the South Kaibab Trail to the river and even connect over to Bright Angel, but most people do this as a multiday trip due to the strenuous nature of the journey. Just like Bright Angel Trail, South Kaibab is steep, offers incredible views and is very exposed. The first destination along the trail is Ooh-Ahh Point, which offers an expansive view of the canyon and is less than 2 miles (3.2 km) round trip.

By the way, Ooh-Aah Point gets its name from an uncommon, nearly prehistoric language that is hotly debated by linguists as to its exact meaning. This is a rough translation, but most agree that "Ooh-Ahh" means either "Wow!"

South Kaibab Trail

or "The-Place-of-Amazing-Selfie-with-View-of-Grand-Canyon-About-One-Mile-From-Rim." You decide which translation works best for you.

There is a restroom at Cedar Ridge, but that is the extent of the facilities on the South Kaibab Trail. Cedar Ridge is about 1.5 miles (2.4 km) from the rim. Skeleton Point offers great views of the river and the surrounding area and is the recommended turnaround for day hikers.

On the question of South Kaibab versus Bright Angel, South Kaibab's fewer amenities means it is slightly less traveled than Bright Angel. That said, there are very few hikers on these trails relative to the vast number of people looking over the canyon's edge at the rim. If you are looking to escape into your own personal experience of the canyon, either trail will get you there.

Hermit Trail

Strenuous – (17.8 mi / 28.6 km), to Colorado River round trip

The Hermit Trail begins at Hermit's Rest and, like all the trails described here, is accessed via shuttle. This trail is great for many reasons if you are an experienced hiker looking for something a little more rugged. It was originally built by horse thieves during the nineteenth century and is today considered a threshold trail, which means the National Park doesn't actively maintain it. There is water to be found along the trail, but it needs to be treated. Some of the trail has rutted out in areas and, in some cases, rock slides covering the trail require one to do a little scrambling to navigate around them. The point here is, if you are an experienced hiker, the Hermit Trail offers just about everything,

Hermit Trail

including an endpoint worthy of the journey. It is 8.9 miles (14 km) down to the river, but if you are able to make it, you are rewarded with Hermit Rapids, perhaps the strongest hydraulics and biggest waves of any set of rapids in the canyon. The Hermit Rapids help to greatly motivate any hiker and do not disappoint. You hear them before you see them and in seeing them there is nothing but gushing awe and respect.

It cannot be overstated that this is a trail to be taken seriously. Plan—bring the right gear, including plenty of food and water, and start early if you do plan to take on this all-day hike. There is a primitive campground at the river's edge and most folks do this as an overnight trip.

Grandview Trail

Strenuous – (6.0 mi / 9.7 km), to Horseshoe Mesa/ Toilet Junction round trip

Grandview is one of the quickest ways to get down into the canyon. It is very steep in some places and during the winter is dangerously icy. Crampons or some other means of traction for your footwear is required in winter. The trail offers deep views into the canyon as well as ruins of historic mining structures. Another feature of the trail is the placement of log "cribs" in some of the more vertical sections of the Kaibab/Toroweap section. Many of these log supports were swept away during a landslide in the winter of 2005, but there are a few examples of these historical trail structures still around.

The Grandview Trail is not as well maintained as either Bright Angel or South Kaibab Trails. There are steep drop-offs in some areas. Use caution when hiking this trail.

Mule Trips

The mule rides offered by park concessionaire Xanterra are a classic way of seeing the Grand Canyon. The day trips offered change seasonally, and new offerings open up at the whim of the concessionaire. Most rides are typically 3-hour, 4-mile (6.4 km) rides. You don't need prior experience riding a mule, and your tour will include a fair amount of interesting interpretation about the geology and human history along the trail.

Overnight tours are also offered, and this ride is on par with rafting down the Colorado River in terms of generating incredible memories. You will ride your mule to Phantom Ranch located near the river. Lunch is provided and the steak dinner at the ranch is hearty and very welcome after the day's journey. As with the day trips, the overnight trips are full of interpretive narration on nearly all aspects of the park. The overnight trip to Phantom Ranch has been a high water mark for many visitors.

The downsides to the mule trips are the expense and the fact that you need to reserve the event well in advance. There is a wait list for day-before cancellations;

Mule Parking

however, the chances of people canceling are very slim. As of June 2014, it cost $548.84 for one person or $960.01 for two to ride a mule to Phantom Ranch and spend the night there.

Mule rides from the South Rim can be reserved through:

Xanterra Parks & Resorts (303) 297-2757, (888) 297-2757

Grand Canyon Panorama

Virtual Caching

For those who have never heard of this, virtual caching is the delightful marriage of treasure hunting and technology. Specifically, a "cache" is a term that denotes a bunch of stuff stowed somewhere in the wilderness. With virtual caching, a visitor uses his or her GPS system to find the cache. The reward is in part the journey and in part finding the cache, which— being virtual—means what you find is a cool location.

The National Park Service has done a wonderful job of offering an interesting way to explore the park.

You will need a GPS device (or smart phone with GPS), the park map, which is located inside the park's official newspaper, The Guide, and a copy of the instruction sheet, titled "Story of Grand Canyon." The instructions can be picked up at the Grand Canyon Visitor Center, where different coordinates are listed. Input the coordinates into your GPS device and take the shuttle or walk to the various destinations. None of the virtual caching is done off trail; everything can be found on the paved rim of the park and on the trails. Along the way, the instruction sheet acts as an educational pamphlet on different aspects of the park. Virtual caching is a cool way to discover new things about the park, and if you are navigationally challenged, perhaps a way of discovering a bit about yourself as well!

You will need to keep a record of all your coordinates, which will be necessary to solve the final clue. It takes about 4–6 hours to complete this puzzle, and the tour will take you over a good deal of the park along the way. You can, in the end, receive a certificate of completion. See the visitor center for more details.

Driving Around

Like Zion NP and Bryce NP, Grand Canyon receives too many visitors to make driving around the park practical. The NPS offers a fairly robust shuttle system to get you around, and it is not only highly recommended to use the shuttle system; it is the only method year round for some roads and during peak season for others.

In general, the shuttle system is divided into two loops, the Village Route and Kaibab Rim Route. The Village Route goes to the west and stops at Mather Campground, Trailer Village, Market Plaza, Grand Canyon Visitor Center, Shrine of the Ages, Train Depot, Bright Angel Lodge and Trailhead, and Maswik Lodge. The Village Route also stops at the Hermit's Rest Transfer, which is where you pick up the Hermit's Rest shuttle during peak season.

The Kaibab Route winds to the east and stops at the Grand Canyon Visitor Center, South Kaibab Trailhead, Yaki Point, Pipe Creek Vista, Mather Point and Yavapai Geology Museum.

You can drive on Hermit's Rest Road during the winter months and, to the east, the Desert View is a wonderful drive that ultimately takes you to the East Rim of the Grand Canyon.

Sunset from El Tovar

There is so much to do in the South Rim of the Grand Canyon

There is a tremendous number of things to do and see, more than this little all-inclusive guidebook of seven National Parks can manage to describe in detail. Here are a few places worth exploring further:

Kolb Studio

Art gallery, photo gallery, bookstore and place of historical interest run by the Grand Canyon Association. Near the Bright Angel Lodge

El Tovar Hotel

Built in 1905, this hotel is on the National Register of Historic Places. It is noted for its Arts and Crafts as well as Mission style interior and exterior and is an incredible example of early twentieth century National Park lodge architecture.

Yavapai Geology Museum

A great place to learn everything you wanted to know about the geology of the Grand Canyon. Many exhibits, three dimensional models and photographs along with the outdoor nature and geology "Trail of Time" where each meter traveled on the trail represents one million years of the geology of the Grand Canyon. If you think about it, the "Trail of Time" took about 2 billion years to make, so it is well worth seeing.

Kolb Studio

Desert View Watchtower

Located on the East Rim of the park, the four story, 70-foot-high (21m) stone building was built in 1932 by Fred Harvey Architect Mary Colter. Mary Colter designed many of the buildings in the Grand Canyon, including Hopi House, Lookout Studio, Bright Angel Lodge, the Phantom Ranch buildings and Hermit's Rest (but not El Tovar Lodge). Patterned after the Pueblo kivas and watchtowers, the watchtower has a unique touch in its design.

Skywalk

The Skywalk is managed by the Hualapai Tribe and is located on their tribal lands. It is a horseshoe-shaped walkway securely bolted into the canyon walls such that is juts out over the canyon itself. With the floors and sides made of glass, the structure juts out about 70 feet (21m) from the canyon rim, giving the feeling that you are suspended in air over the canyon. It is one of the most famous attractions within the western portion of the Grand Canyon. There is a separate fee for this attraction. Skywalk reservations: 1-888-868-9378 or 1-928-769-2636

Desert View Watchtower

254

North Rim

If forty is the new twenty, then the North Rim of the Grand Canyon is the new South Rim. It is harder to get to, not open year round and, as a result, it has an energy of peace, tranquility and overall slowness of pace. The North Rim gets a mere 10 percent of the overall visitor traffic to the Grand Canyon, offering more chances to feel you have the park to yourself. On the South Rim, there are more amenities and it is open year-round; however, if you are going during peak season, the North Rim becomes an attractive option if you aren't prepared to share your experience with literally busloads of fellow visitors. It is the view less photographed, the road less traveled and the experience less shared, but it is still everything the Grand Canyon is known for, just from the other side of the river.

Skywalk

There are a couple of other things to know about the North Rim. It is at a higher elevation, ranging from 8,000 to 8,800 feet (2438 to 2682m). This is 1000 to 1800 feet higher than the South Rim. This means the weather will be cooler and the snow deeper, hence the closure of the park in winter. The other thing to note is there are fewer trails going into the canyon on the North Rim and the only one going to the river is longer and thus more strenuous because of the elevation gain.

Hiking

North Kaibab Trail

Strenuous – (14 mi / 22.5 km), one way

The North Kaibab Trail is special be-cause it is starts at a higher elevation than either South Kaibab or Bright Angel trails. The 1000-foot in-crease in elevation is such that a hike down the North Kaibab Trail to the Colorado River means you will pass through every ecosystem found

Grand Canyon View from the North Rim

between Canada and Mexico. It is the least visited of the maintained trails and is also the most strenuous. It is definitely a serious day hike at 28 miles (45 km) round trip and is typically done as a backpacking trip. There are a few restroom facilities and seasonal water available, though the water will need to be treated.

The trail heads steeply down at first until it flattens out a bit as you enter into the base of Bright Angel Canyon. At 5.0 miles (8.0 km), you encounter Roaring Springs, which is a short side trip that is easily visible from the trail. Here you can see water coming directly out of the cliff, typically with a nice flow, creating a little island of moss and ferns within the desert. Roaring Springs flows into Bright Angel Creek as you continue down the trail. This is an important water source, delivering the drinking water for every visitor within Grand Canyon NP. If you make it to the Colorado River, you can see the pipe going over the river on the underside of Bright Angel Trail's Silver Bridge.

North Kaibab Trail

Just a little farther down at 5.4 miles (8.7 km) is a structure known as the Pumphouse Residence, or Aiken Residence. From 1973 to 2006, Bruce Aiken was an artist, NP employee and pump master, overseeing the water supply for the park. He and his wife Mary raised three children at the canyon bottom and lucky hikers were greeted with lemonade from the children from time to time. Aiken's work reflects a fine-tuned harmony with the area of the Grand Canyon. Working mainly in oil, the light, balance and overall portrayal of rock and water are testimonies to living within the Grand Canyon, raising a family and experiencing nearly each day of one's life for 33 years inside its walls.

Another treasure on the North Kaibab is Ribbon Falls (8.5 miles (13.7 km). It is a little grotto in the desert cascading gently on the west side of Bright Angel Creek. It is a great place to get out of the heat of the day, which can be intense in the summer. Between the Cottonwood Campground and Bright Angel Campground you enter the Inner Gorge, which is a narrow canyon of the 2 billion-year-old Vishnu Schist. If you make it this far, you are now walking among rock roughly half as old as the earth itself. You can connect to either the South Kaibab or Bright Angel Trail over the two bridges that cross the Colorado at the canyon bottom.

At this point you may be thinking North Kaibab is a gem of a trail, (which it is), and thus wondering if you could do a rim-to-rim adventure. The good news is you can. Trans Canyon Shuttle offers two rim-to-rim shuttles daily (go to http://www.trans-canyonshuttle.com for more info). The not-so-good news is getting reservations at one of the primitive campgrounds is a challenge. In addition, the shuttles depart early morning and early afternoon, so factor in an overnight stay at the opposing rim or hoofing it out to make the shuttle on the last day.

Bright Angel Point

Easy – (0.5 mi / 0.8 km round trip)

Bright Angel Point is a nice walk from Grand Canyon Lodge and nearby visitor center. There are examples of marine fossils within the rocks along the way. Be sure to pick a park brochure, which shows the location of the fossils and gives a good historical backstory of the lodge and this historic trail.

Transept Trail

Lower Ribbon Falls

Easy – (3.0 mi/ 4.8 km), round trip, allow 90 minutes

The Transept Trail starts at the Grand Canyon Lodge and follows the rim of the canyon to the North Rim Campground. Great views along the way.

Uncle Jim Trail

Moderate – (5.0 mi / 8.0 km), round trip, allow 2 - 3 hours

This trail starts from the same parking lot as the North Kaibab Trailhead and meanders through the Kaibab Plateau forest to Uncle Jim's Point, which overlooks Bright Angel, Roaring Springs and an overall spectacular view of the canyon.

Cape Final Trail

Easy – (4.0 mi / 6.4 km), round trip, allow 2 hours

An easy trail that ends at one of the higher elevation views of the Grand Canyon at Cape Final. As this trail is not often used, it provides good promise if you are looking for a secluded and peaceful hike. Cape Final is at 7,850 feet. Be careful if you decide to go onto the ledge's edge; it's a long way down.

Mule Trips

You can set out on a mule from the North Rim, but none of these trips goes down to the river. These trips are generally available and can be reserved at the Grand Canyon Lodge. There are an hour trip to the rim and two half-day trips to either Uncle Jim's Point or along the North

Kaibab Trail to the Supai Tunnel. Visitors need to be 7–10 years old and weigh less than 220 pounds to ride the mules.

Driving Around

There are two main drives from the visitor center and Grand Canyon Lodge that take you to canyon rim overlooks. The drives are very scenic and offer many pullouts to get out and explore the panorama of the canyon. Visiting both points can take half a day.

Cape Royal

(15 miles / 24.1 km)

Cape Royal is arguably the most panoramic drive in the entire Grand Canyon. It offers views up and down the canyon as well as across, providing ample opportunities for amazing photos or simply breathtaking memories. It is a popular destination both at sunrise and at sunset for this reason. There is a natural arch known as Angels Window, where, from the right angle, one can see through the arch to the Colorado River itself. It is also possible to see the Desert View Watchtower on the South Rim.

Point Imperial

(3 miles / 4.8 km)

Point Imperial is the highest point on the North Rim at 8,803 feet (2,683 meters). From this high vantage point you get an overview of the eastern end of the Grand Canyon, starting as the narrow walls of Marble Canyon and opening up profoundly into the Grand Canyon proper. The Painted Desert lies farther in the distance.

Cape Final

Welcome to the Colorado

Super Mario is a communist ..

[Everest]: Dad, I believe Super Mario is a communist.

[Me]: I've heard this theory. How did you find out about it?

[Everest]: YouTube and the fact he wears red overalls.

[Me]: I'm pretty sure he was just an opportunistic pizza guy or something.

[Everest]: Maybe, but I think the whole pizza thing was just to cover up his communistic tendencies.

[Me]: Son, are you even sure you know what a communist is?

[Everest]: I know red is their color.

[Me]: Ah. Well, this is very useful stuff; thanks for clearing it all up for me. I for one am really glad we had this conversation.

[Everest]: Yeah, me too. Can I watch more YouTube?

[Me]: Absolutely not.

Everest

While we had arrived in the wake of a thunderstorm, the Grand Canyon was no less outstanding. Absent was the normalcy of dreary wetness. Here it was replaced with spectacular awe. Threads of lightning hit the mesa tops in a chorus of visual glory combined with the rolling rumble of deep thunder. Large drops hit the windshield of our RV. The lightning struck the air sideways in almost musical patterns from left to right, randomly and without reason. We pulled the motor home over and just watched this headliner show. After a time the rain finally stopped, lifting the purest and most colorful of rainbows across the canyon. It followed us or perhaps we followed it into the campground. We stepped out with souls refreshed and washed clean from the desert storm. The Colorado far down below changed from green to muddy brownish red. It looked at home and at peace within its rushing torrents and true colors.

With the sun back out, so too came the hordes of people. There were so many tourists here, unlike at any of the other parks. It was easy to reconcile that this was the most popular destination of all the parks we had visited. Some five million tourists a year come to gaze out over the edge. We passed a McDonald's seemingly in the park. It was clear we were too close to civilization. The natural beauty of the Grand Canyon was not mixing well with the darkness of capitalism.

My first thoughts were how to escape the masses of people. So many of them were just looking out over the edge of this vast and amazing place and going no further. Each time I saw the river poke through over a mile underneath us, I felt compelled to head to the banks and greet it. I needed to go up to this natural artist in residence of the past 17 million years and simply throw a nod, a humble little bow of respect to say "Bravo! Well done, river. Well done indeed."

The hike to the Colorado River is not an easy one. It is highly recommended that you get a permit, backpack your way to the banks, and back up. It is highly not recommended that you go to the Colorado as a day hike. There are signs at the trailhead, as big as billboards, that state essentially that you are nuts if you try this as a day hike and downright silly stupid if you think you can attempt it without water.

The hike is a little more than 8 miles downhill, each step down taking the traveler 60,000 years back in geologic time. Then the same 8 miles back up. At the top of the mesa, you are almost 7,000 feet above sea level. The air is refreshingly cool and, as a result, misleading. Down at the river you have dropped to 2,480 feet and the temperatures are oven hot with all that baking rock surrounding you and little relief given by the river itself.

Here is what was going through my head at this point.

Okay, so the park service guides suggest that it would be nuts to do the South Rim to the river and back as a day hike, but completely insane to do it without water. Got it, they are saying brings lots of water…check. The hike is over 16 miles long, so I might want to bring some food. Yep, definitely going to need some food, a few granola bars maybe, well, wait, perhaps I should bring meals. I remember the last time I didn't pack enough food (I thought briefly back to a hike in Death Valley that almost didn't end well).

I should pack in some "just in case" clothing (as in just in case something goes wrong and I have to stay the night). Under the same loosely bound safety-first section of my thought process, I also threw in a lighter, a flashlight, a compass and a pocketknife. Finally, the map was added to the daypack.

"Okay, now only one thing to do," I said out loud to no one, "is convince my wife." I had no real strategy there. The hike would take all day, certainly. It would rob a day's vacation of family time and devote it instead to an incredibly selfish endeavor. I looked down at the Colorado River again. "Bring it" was all it seemed to say. "I'm not going anywhere." The river was calling me, so against all that marriage had taught me over those past 14 years, I approached Angela, daypack and hat in hand.

There is really no need to describe the gentle influence and suave nature in which I handled the situation, mainly because I utterly lack these characteristics. No, I usually go with some variant of dense male approach. I fall on my sword, make an argument loosely based on the wonderful attributes of pity and somehow manage to convince my wife that while yes, she probably could have done better in marriage, she did pick me knowing full well my preponderance for hiking and thus should save us the trouble and just let me go. Perhaps the only argument that had any merit involved the question,

"When will I ever be back this way again?" The rest of my rationale for going was completely indefensible and could have been stopped in its tracks with ease on her part.

In the end, despite myself, she did let me go on the condition that I went as soon as I could in the morning, not dawdle on the trail, didn't wake her in leaving, and took Everest with me. (Everest had lobbied to be included as part of the negotiation early in the talks). Given I would have bought her a nice dinner and some jewelry just to go on this hike; I think I got off pretty easy.

I woke Ev up at 6 a.m. and while we made every attempt to be quiet, the reality of our packing up was loud enough to garner a few mumblings and resettling of the sleeping occupants. It was a quick hike from the campground to Kolb Studio and the beginning of Bright Angel Trailhead. We met a few likeminded hikers and exchanged the usual banter about the length and strenuousness of the hike. Some folks pointed out the young age of Everest.

After we were alone I asked him, "Do you think you are too young to go on this long of a hike, Ev?"

"Mm...I don't know" followed by the word "shrugs" while shrugging his shoulder. "I think I'll be fine, but this will be the longest hike I've ever done."

"I think you'll make it, but you will certainly feel it toward the end of the hike, guaranteed."

"Shrugs," Ev grinned. "I'm sure you will feel it too, Old Hinges."

"Old Hinges? Does that mean I can call you Young Hinges?"

"No, sorry. That just doesn't sound right. Everest works, though!" he beamed.

The first part of the hike descends steeply, and we made good time, eating granola bars while we walked. The trail started to lighten a bit in its severity and we settled into a cadence that took us to Indian Gardens, the main resting spot, primitive campground and watering hole for the weary traveler. We were hardly weary just yet and decided we should continue the final three miles to the river without further hesitation.

The second leg didn't go quite as fast as the first. The sun no longer hidden by the canyon walls, it now beat down upon us. I looked at the time and realized it was already well into midmorning. It was hot but not completely unbearable, and the downhill trend helped immensely. We heard the river long before we reached it, but reach it we did. Everest detoured to the nearby pit toilet while I walked toward the banks of the Colorado. It was a raging young vibrant thing, all red and muddy from the recent rains. As I approached the water's edge, I saw two rafts coming down. One rafter oared close to shore, waved and yelled out with exuberance, "Welcome to the Colorado!" He then threw out two cans of Budweiser, held together by their plastic ring. The beers landed on the sand right at my feet. I grinned ear to ear at this wondrous synchronicity and waved back a big, "Thanks!" The river continued to roar as the oarsman sat back into place to navigate further onward as they traveled out of site.

"What are those, Dad?"

"Beers!" I exclaimed.

"Seriously? Where did you get them"?

I pointed at the nearly vanished rafters and said, "Those guys."

"Wow," Ev said, looking at the rafters. "That's really cool." He paused for a moment, looking at the beers. "You know, we made it. We're here, Dad! This would be a great time to have that iconic father-son first beer moment, right?"

"I'll tell you what. Let's do this hike again when you are 21 and if someone throws a couple of beers at my feet, I'll be happy to share them with you. Until then, that's a big fat no on the beer moment."

Ev remained ever nonplussed as he released a drab felt, "Lolz."

After the two beers landing at my feet in the middle of the desert, at the shores of the Colorado River no less, I felt pretty good. I couldn't help but draw a correlation that I had come down to pay tribute to the river and it had in its own way paid tribute back. That made these beers special and I wanted to have one, but I knew if I did, I'd be in for a head pounding in that heat. I put them in my pack to save for when I got back up.

As I put away the beers, I noticed that a couple was eyeing us with some insistence. I pretended to not notice that they were watching us, but after the sixth glance over and meeting with eye contact, the woman decided to come over.

It was clear from her accent she was from Germany. "Pardon us. We came down the trail and did not bring enough water. We were thinking maybe you could sell us some water or a can of soda or something."

I thought about the huge billboard-like sign that warned against doing this hike without water—that serious illness can occur, even death. The warning is printed in several languages and shows a man holding his head in a near death posture. It is impossible to miss, which led me to one singular conclusion: my own stubborn obstinacy toward such warning signs obviously comes from the Germanic side of my heritage.

The husband didn't look like he was doing well at all. There was a hot sun baking down on us at this point, and it was definitely having an effect on the man. I opened up my daypack and handed them my second water bottle, which was untouched at this point as we had refilled at Indian Gardens.

"Here, drink as much as you want. How much water did you bring with you?"

"How much? None."

"You didn't bring any?" I asked in disbelief and then caught myself. I was shocked. It was then I noticed they didn't even carry a daypack. For whatever reason, they thought this hike was a casual stroll. It was clear the park service needed a bigger warning billboard.

They both drank a little and then tried to hand the water bottle back. I pushed it back toward them, shaking my head.

"Feel free to drink the whole bottle. We can get more in 3 miles at Indian Gardens. Did you get water there on the way down?" Everest handed them his spare water bottle. The couple would now have two quarts of water in them.

"No", the woman said. "We didn't see any water coming down."

"Which way did you come down?" I asked.

"We came down South Kaibab Trail."

The husband said something. "Fragen Sie ihn, ob er uns zu einem der Biere geben. "

"Sorry, my husband doesn't speak English. He was wondering if you have more water that you can sell or have a container we can buy."

I thought about the beers and handed one can to them. The man looked a little better but it was obvious he would need more water to get to the top.

"Here, take this can. Now it's beer, so don't drink it! It will dehydrate you more if you do. The best thing is to carry this with you to Indian Gardens and then pour out the beer and use the container to fill it with water. Indian Gardens is 3.2 miles up from here on the Bright Angel Trail. I highly recommend you take that trail out as it has good water whereas South Kaibab has no water."

I debated giving them my spare water bottle but decided against it. My son and I needed a good deal of water to get back. The beer can would have to get them back up. I knew there was typically a ranger at Indian Gardens and told them that, explaining that the ranger could help them further.

The woman nodded and took the can and then handed it to her husband. He looked at the can and went to open it. I warned her again about not drinking the beer, that drinking it wouldn't help, that it would only dehydrate them more. She nodded vaguely at me while the husband continued to look drained and gruff.

We parted ways after showing them where Bright Angel Trail was and repeating my advice several times as if repetition would help. Everest and I sat at the river's edge and ate lunch, pondering how many people come down this way completely unprepared, despite the rather obvious signs the park service put up warning people not to do stupid things. We stopped giving stupid people a hard time for being stupid when we came full circle to the fact that we ourselves were ignoring the park's warnings. A sixteen-mile hike was not for the beginner, to be sure. Above all things, water is the single most important item one should bring. Common sense, planning for shade optimization and plenty of food were up there at the top as well.

The hike back was as expected, a thoroughly strenuous and exhausting trek. The first jaunt back to Indian Gardens, however, was easy enough. We refilled our water bottles and asked fellow resting hikers about the Germans we had met. I told them about the can of beer we gave them.

"Yeah, we heard about these guys. I heard the husband drank the beer shortly after they got the can. They found the ranger and he helped them out I think."

I laughed. I guess it was too much to ask. Of course, they drank the beer! What was I thinking?

From Indian Gardens, I was reminded of another sign posted on Bright Angel Trail. It said, "Caution! Down is Optional. UP IS MANDATORY." The remainder of the trail was grueling. It started uphill and didn't let up, with the final 1.6 miles being the steepest. You climb a full 1300 vertical feet in that last mile and a half. Still, what choice was there? Up was mandatory. The sign made perfect sense. We couldn't stay where we are, we couldn't stay down at the river; we needed to go up. The sun fell low enough to provide shade for the remaining few miles. A train of pack mules shared the journey with us for a short while, looking as excited as we were to be climbing the steep incline. Finally, as with all hikes, we made it back to the top and paused to look back at what we had accomplished. It was late afternoon and the Grand Canyon was lit with magnificent sunshine contrasting with darkness of shadow. Families and couples, young and old, were at the canyon's edge, just taking in the grandeur. The Grand Canyon, no matter how one enjoys it, has a way of settling any restlessness of soul, removing if only for a moment the dark buildup on one's spirit. It is the magnum opus for the Colorado River in a gallery of natural masterpieces strung along its banks.

I sat at the rim and gazed out at this wonder immersed in thoughts, lost in quiet wonder of the river's long journey.

At its birth in the quiet green valley of the Southern Rocky Mountains, just below the La Poudre Pass, the Colorado River trickles like a cooing infant. The water is clear and crisp, reflecting sunlight in prisms of clean light. It gathers in abundance as it travels, and by the time it leaves its namesake state, it is still just as pure but now gushing with abundance of whitewater, rushing as a boy sprinting in play. There are moments of stillness intertwined here and there, at times the river slows down to take note of its surroundings before rushing further downstream.

By the time it meets the confluence of the Green River, the largest tributary of the Colorado, it has reached a manner not unlike a young adult. It bucks and bubbles, flowing through the Cataract Canyon in the Canyonlands with a sense of immortality, roiling with energy and at times with bullheaded stubbornness. Here the river is met with a true adversary, solid rock. It cuts through in a tormented agreement between the centuries of stone, deter-mined and with a sense that nothing can stand in its way.

Then the river enters the Grand Canyon. The Colorado continues to cut through stone unabated, carving its way over a mile deep into the bedrock of Earth. If we were to continue with the analogy of the Colorado as an anthropomorphism, then here as a fully formed adult the river created its legacy. The Grand Canyon stands as no other. More than merely grand, more than just a canyon, it is a work of natural art, a dedication of the life's work of one river given tremendous blocks of stone to mold.

The Colorado then leaves its Grand Canyon of a legacy and continues downstream, winding downwards in energy, becoming stiller, ending as a quiet tinkering, a river delta spread wide as fingers of soft dying water into the Gulf of Mexico. Here it is but a shadow of its sturdier self, gasping a presence more like its origin than its heyday. It silently returns into the grander oceans, its individuality lost and absorbed in the union. The Colorado River is much like life itself, starting out so pure, finding wonder in its innocence and with a small amount of wisdom, performing feats that amaze and at times strike fear.

Then in adulthood it finds its way, makes a lasting impression, a contribution to mankind before whiling its last days as only a shadow of what it once was. The Colorado's 1,450-mile journey alone is a lesson.

Then, however, there is another lesson within the river, that in place, it is timeless. When you gaze out on the flowing waters, you are seeing something that has never been seen before, maybe similar but not exactly the same. The water flowing upstream toward you is in the future. The water that has passed and is no longer in view is the past. The river that lies inside your field of vision is therefore the constant present. It is always now at the banks of the Colorado, no matter what bank you happen to be on. Never before has this scene before you been witnessed. Perhaps scenes similar, sure, but not this one, not the very one that passes before you. The sight before you has been building up, building for centuries just waiting to display itself at this moment. With that in mind, each viewing of the Colorado is special. The mighty Colorado, always changing, yet seemingly eternal. We take this grand design of nature for granted all too often, but the fact remains that you can never step twice on the same piece of water. Each moment is evidence of renewal.

I gazed out at the river below us with those thoughts in the back of my mind. Ev and I took one last look and then headed back toward our home. The shuttle bus arrived, and we boarded it as outsiders. We were dirty, tired and sun baked specters in a bus full of clean and eager tourists. In the RV, we showered, we ate, we satiated our thirst, and at night I dreamt of the hike we had lived out during the day.

In my dream, the rafter who had thrown me the keepsake cans of beer pulled over to allow Everest and me to get in. We floated downstream as a team, hungry for wonder. We joined in their madcap adventures of white water rafting, side canyon explorations and sleeping under the dark canopy of touchable stars. In this dream, new stories are told, new books are written, lives are lived—a world within a world existing eternally along the banks of the Colorado.

Then, without pause or notice, the dream flowed around a bend into the unknowable realm of deep unconsciousness. Untethered to our wants and struggles, we floated into the currents of shared emptiness. The Milky Way passed above us in silence once again. The moon, too, rose high and over. Nocturnal animals patrolled while other animals slept in cuddled burrows. And inside the RV, we slept as well, the canvas of our thoughts wiped clean for the next day to draw upon.

Conclusion

For me, both the visitation of these parks and the writing of this book has been a mixture of adventure and reflection, a personal journey that has at times been both spiritual and fulfilling. The Colorado Plateau offers a lifetime of exploration and the national parks that have been set aside for all of us to enjoy are without a doubt some of the most amazing places in the world to visit. It is a bit of a conflict to say you could spend decades here when most of us get only 2–3 weeks, but even if that is all the time you are able to carve out to explore these great lands, it will be time that imprints upon your soul and sticks with you as one of the fonder memories in your life.

Zion with its massively tall red rock walls, Bryce and its fruit loop charms, the peaceful magic of Capitol Reef, the immensity of Canyonlands and the overwhelming number of rings and windows of Arches. All are unique, amazing and quite honestly beyond any language to fully describe. They aid us in defining majesty and grandeur, challenge our limits of wonder, help us to understand and find a deeper connection with ourselves. I continue to be amazed by the fact that each of these gems was created by nothing more than the humble drops of water, the gentle caress of air and simple tenacity.

The trip to Mesa Verde is different, it is cultural, it takes you back historically and it leaves you with a respect that you have journeyed not through the caves of savages but through the hewn walls of an advanced civilization. If you remove the electronics and the improvements of technology, you come to realize these people loved, suffered, held hands, nurtured their young and lived together with a sophistication that is equal to our lifestyles today.

Then there is the Grand Canyon. Your vacation has come to an end and you look out at this wonder with a sense of peace. You are somehow a different person—at peace with yourself, at peace with your loved ones, at peace with the gift of light, rock and color before you. It is okay, it is enough, to just gaze, to do nothing more, for what lays before you is that magnificent. The Grand Canyon crowns and encapsulates everything that you have seen on this trip. It is, therefore, quite possible that you will come to realize that the canyon is as much at peace with you as you are with it. You realize that it wants nothing from you, that it is exactly where it should be. If you are lucky, that thought will extend to *everything* in your life. In that moment, it's all good; there is nothing more that life can give you that will make you any more content and perfect than you are right now. This is the secret of the Grand Circle, and it gives of its secret easily and freely. You need do nothing to obtain it. It will find you at one point or another along your travels.

View from Yavapai Point on the South Rim

Sources and Recommended Readings

Grand Circle

- Grand Circle.org: http://www.grandcircle.org/

Las Vegas

- A site that is all things Vegas. This is a good site to find all the contact information not listed for Vegas attractions plus the 100's of other attractions not listed in this book: http://www.vegas.com/attractions/attractions-for-kids/
- Mandalay Bay: www.mandalaybay.com
- Monte Carlo: www.montecarlo.com
- The Mirage: www.mirage.com
- Golden Nugget: www.goldennugget.com
- The Flamingo: www.flamingolasvegas.com
- RV Rental
- Apollo RV: www.apollorv.com
- Cruise America: www.cruiseamerica.com
- El Monte RV: www.elmonterv.com
- Road Bear RV: http://www.roadbearrv.com/
- Sarah RV Center: www.sahararv.com

Zion National Park

- Zion Canyon Campground and RV Resort: http://www.zioncamp.com/
- Zion National Park Service site: http://www.nps.gov/zion/
- Zion-Mt. Carmel Tunnel: http://www.nps.gov/zion/historyculture/zmchighway.htm
- Zion History: http://home1.nps.gov/zion/historyculture/index.htm
- Zion History: http://www.utahsdixie.com/zion_national_park.html
- Zion History – Gilbert Stanley Underwood: http://www.cr.nps.gov/history/online_books/sontag/underwood.htm
- Zion History – Angels Landing: http://www.zionnational-park.com/zion-national-park-landmarks.htm
- Zion Trail – Archeology Trail: http://bforist.blogspot.com/2011/07/twelve-great-things-about-archeology.html
- Zion Geology: http://www.nature.nps.gov/Geology/parks/zion/index.cfm
- Zion Geology: http://www.nps.gov/zion/naturescience/geologicformations.htm
- Zion Geology: Biek, R.F., Willis, G.C., Hylland, M.D., and Doelling, H.H., 2000, Geology of Zion National Park, Utah, in D.A. Sprinkel, T.C. Chidsey, Jr., and P.B. Anderson, eds., Geology of Utah's Parks and Monuments: Utah Geological Association Publication 28, p. 107- 138.

Bryce National Park

- Ruby's Inn: www.rubysinn.com
- Bryce Canyon National Park Service site: http://www.nps.gov/brca
- Bryce Canyon History: http://www.nps.gov/brca/historyculture/index.htm
- Bryce Canyon History: http://brycecanyonforever.com/bryce-history
- Bryce Canyon History: http://www.zionnational-park.com/bhistory.htm
- Bryce Canyon Geology: http://www.nps.gov/brca/naturescience/geologicformations.htm

Capitol Reef National Park

- Sunset Magazine: www.sunset.com
- Wonderland RV Park: www.capitolreefrvpark.com
- Capitol Reef National Park Service site: http://www.nps.gov/care
- Capitol Reef Geology: http://www.nps.gov/care/naturescience/geology.htm
- Ann G. Harris, Esther Tuttle, Sherwood D., Tuttle, Geology of National Parks: Fifth Edition (Iowa, Kendall/Hunt Publishing; 1997) ISBN 0-7872-5353-7
- John C. Fremont: http://historytogo.utah.gov/people/johncharlesfremont.html

- Memoirs of My Life, By John Charles Fremont 1886: https://archive.org/stream/memoir-sofmylifei00frrich#page/n7/mode/2up
- Capitol Reef History: http://www.nps.gov/care/historyculture/index.htm
- Atlatl History and Physics, Tasigh.org.: http://www.tasigh.org/ingenium/atlatl.html
- Hiking: http://www.utah.com/hike/golden-throne-trail

Canyonlands National Park

- Canyonlands National Park Service site: http://www.nps.gov/cany
- Canyonlands History: http://www.nps.gov/cany/historyculture/index.htm
- Canyonlands Geology: http://www.nps.gov/cany/naturescience/geologicformations.htm
- Moab Rafters and Links: http://www.moab-utah.com/
- Needles Outpost: http://www.canyonlandsneedlesoutpost.com/

Arches National Park

- Arches National Park Service site: http://www.nps.gov/arch
- Arches History: http://www.nps.gov/arch/historyculture/index.htm
- Arches Geology: http://www.nps.gov/arch/naturescience/geologicformations.htm
- Research: http://www.nps.gov/arch/naturescience/research.htm
- Excellent video on arch formation: http://www.nps.gov/arch/photosmultimedia/geologyvideo.htm
- Edward Abbey, Desert Solitaire
- Wolfe Ranch History: http://pubs.usgs.gov/bul/1393/report.pdf
- More Wolfe History: http://www.noehill.com/ut_grand/nat1975000167.asp

Mesa Verde National Park

- Mesa Verde National Park Service site: http://www.nps.gov/meve
- Nicoles, Francis S. (1919). Biography and Bibliography of Jesse Waher Fewkes
- Park History: Would There Have Been a Mesa Verde National Park Without Virginia Mc-Clurg?: http://www.nationalparktraveler.com/2008/06/park-history-would-there-have-been-mesa-verde-national-park-without-virginia-mcclurg
- The Cliff Dwellings of the Cañons of the Mesa Verde: Publisher(s): American Geographical Society; Author(s): W. R. Birdsall; Source: Journal of the American Geographical Society of New York, Vol. 23, (1891), pp. 584–620
- General Mesa Verde History: http://www.nps.gov/meve/historyculture/index.htm
- Mesa Verde Geology: http://www.nps.gov/meve/naturescience/geology.htm

Grand Canyon National Park

- Grand Canyon National Park Service site: http://www.nps.gov/grca
- Grand Canyon History: http://www.nps.gov/grca/historyculture/index.htm
- Grand Canyon Geology: http://www.nature.nps.gov/views/layouts/Main.html#/GRCA/geology/
- Powell, J. W. (1875). The Exploration of the Colorado River and Its Canyons. New York: Dover Press. ISBN 0-486-20094-9 (and other reprint editions).
- Dolnick, Edward (2002). Down the Great Unknown: John Wesley Powell's 1869 Journey of Discovery and Tragedy Through the Grand Canyon (Paperback). Harper Perennial. ISBN 0-06-095586-4.
- Thomas Moran National Gallery of Art Site: http://www.nga.gov/feature/moran/moranhome.shtm
- Pro Shuttles: http://www.proriver.com/frame_main_shuttles.html

Photo Attributes

Attributions and permissions given where indicated.

Front Cover

- Virign River at Zion National Park, by David Scarbrough, CC-BY-SA-2.0

Back Cover

- (Top): Grand Canyon Panorama, by Chensiyuan, CC-BY-SA-3.0,2.5,2.0,1.0
- (Bottom): Horseriders, by NPS, PD US NPS

Title Page

- Mesa Arch, sunrise, by John Fowler, CC-BY-2.0

In order of appearance.

Introduction to the Grand Circle

- Grand Circle Overview, copyright Gone Beyond Guides

First Stop Las Vegas

- Panoramic shot of Las Vegas from the Paris hotel, lauralyluis, CC-BY-SA-3.0-migrated, CC-BY-SA-2.5,2.0,1.0
- Mandalay Bay, by Erin Khoo, CC-BY-2.0
- The Mirage, by Ronnie Macdonald, CC-BY-2.0
- Monte Carlo, by Antoine Taveneaux, CC-BY-SA-3.0
- The Golden Nugget, by tboard, CC-BY-2.0
- The Flamingo, by Rob Young, CC-BY-2.0
- Excalibur Hotel, by Antoine Taveneaux, CC-BY-SA-3.0
- M&M's World Las Vegas, by Josh Truelson, CC-BY-SA-2.0
- Titanic Exhibition, by InSapphowetrust, CC-BY-SA-2.0
- Adventuredome, by ZooFari, PD-user
- The Mirage Hotel, by Antoine Taveneaux, CC-BY-SA-3.0
- Bellagio fountain from Paris Hotel, by chensiyuan, CC-BY-SA-3.0,2.5,2.0,1.0

Just Park it Anywhere

- Vegas from distance, David Vasquez, CC-BY-SA-3.0-migrated

Oh Blackwater

- Still Life with Bacon, by Eric Henze

Zion National Park

- Grand Circle Overview, copyright Gone Beyond Guides
- Zion National Park Overview Map, Gone Beyond Guides
- The Subway, by God of War, CC-BY-3.0
- Kolob Canyon, by Gmhatfield, CC-Zero
- Tour Buses at Zion Lodge in 1929, by NPS, PD US NPS
- Mt Carmel Tunnel through Zion National Park, by Alex Proimos, CC-BY-2.0
- Temples and Towers of the Virgin, by John Fowler, CC-BY-2.0
- 1938 Poster for Zion National Park, by NPS, PD US NPS
- Crawford Ranch in Zion Canyon, by NPS, PD-US
- Climbing up Angels Landing, by Alex Proimos, CC-BY-2.0
- Waterfall at Emerald Pools in Zion National Park, by Stuart Seeger, CC-BY-2.0

- The Narrows, by Christian Schirm, PD-self
- Narrows, by John Fowler, CC-BY-2.0
- Zion Canyon at Sunset from Angels Landing, by Diliff, CC-BY-SA-3.0,2.5,2.0,1.0
- Shuttle bus, by Ciar, CC-BY-SA-3.0-migrated
- Zion Lodge, by Tomdonohue1, PD-user

The Triple H

- Bug tracks at Coral Pink Sand Dunes State Park, by Eric Henze
- Early on Angels Landing Trail, by Ronnie Macdonald, CC-BY-2.0
- Final ascent Angels Landing, by Roman Fuchs, CC-BY-SA-3.0
- View from top of Angels Landing, by Tobias Alt, CC-BY-SA-4.0,3.0,2.5,2.0,1.0
- From top of Angels Landing, by Tobias Alt, CC-BY-SA-4.0,3.0,2.5,2.0,1.0

Bryce Canyon National Park

- Grand Circle Overview, copyright Gone Beyond Guides
- Bryce National Park Overview Map, Gone Beyond Guides
- Bryce Canyon at Sunrise, by Chris Huck, CC-BY-SA-3.0
- Bryce Canyon panorama, by Julien Narboux, CC-BY-SA-2.5
- Grand Staircase, by NPS, PD US NPS
- Ebenezer Bryce's cabin circa 1881, courtesy National Archives and Records Administration , PD US
- Bryce Canyon Douglas Fir, by selbst gemacht, CC-BY-SA-3.0-migrated
- "Wall Street", by Brian Dunaway, CC-BY-SA-3.0-migrated
- From Bryce Point, by Jean-Christophe Benoist, CC-BY-3.0
- Horseriders, by NPS, PD US NPS
- Bryce Canyon Lodge, by NPS, PD US NPS

Where's Bryce?

- Bryce's first view of Bryce Canyon, at Bryce Point, Eric Henze
- Navajo Loop Trail, Jesper Rautell Balle, CC-BY-SA-3.0
- Bryce Panorama, by Tobi 87, CC-BY-SA-4.0,3.0,2.5,2.0,1.0

Capitol Reef National Park

- Grand Circle Overview, copyright Gone Beyond Guides
- Capitol Reef National Park Overview Map, Gone Beyond Guides
- View near Fruita by Campground, by J Brew, CC-BY-SA-2.0
- Fruita Orchards, by NPS, PD US NPS
- Waterpocket Fold, by NPS, PD-USGOV-INTERIOR-NPS; PD-USGOV-NPS
- Waterpocket Fold from Stike Valley Overlook, by USGS, PD US Government
- Atlatl, by NPS, PD US NPS
- Petroglyphs in Capitol Gorge, by Axcordion, PD-user
- In narrows of Capitol Gorge, circa 1935, by George A. Grant. PD US NPS
- Pie tin recycling barrel, Gifford House, by Eric Henze
- Panorama north and east from Capitol Reef Scenic Drive 4.0 miles from Utah State Route 24, by Famartin, CC-BY-SA-3.0
- The Golden Throne, by Qfl247, CC-BY-SA-3.0

The Speed Queen

- Our RV parked in no name town, by Eric Henze
- Gifford Barn, NPS Photo, PD US NPS
- Hickman Bridge, Paul Hermans, CC-BY-SA-3.0,2.5,2.0,1.0

Canyonlands National Park

- Grand Circle Overview, copyright Gone Beyond Guides
- Canyonlands National Park, Island in the Sky Overview Map, Gone Beyond Guides
- Canyonlands National Park, Needles and The Maze Overview Map, Gone Beyond Guides

The Photographer's Wife

Arches National Park

Hopi Prophecy

Mesa Verde National Park

- Cliff Palace circa 1891, NPS, US-PD
- Cliff Palace, Mesa Verde, Ben FrantzDale, CC-BY-SA-3.0,2.5,2.0,1.0
- Square Tower House, Ben FrantzDale, CC-BY-SA-3.0,2.5,2.0,1.0
- Balcony House ladder, Ken Lund, CC-BY-SA-2.0
- Emmett Harryson, a Navajo, in doorway. 1929, George A. Grant (1929-1954), PD-USGOV-IN-TERIOR-NPS
- Spruce Tree House, CC-BY-SA-3.0,2.5
- Far View Site, Don Graham, CC-BY-SA-2.0
- Wetherill Mesa Road, Ken Lund, CC-BY-SA-2.0
- Step House, Ken Lund, CC-BY-SA-2.0
- House of Many Windows, Axcordion, CC-BY-SA-3.0,2.5,2.0,1.0
- Petroglyph Point, Adam Baker, CC-BY-2.0
- First Glimpse of Spruce Tree House from the Bottom of Spruce Tree Canyon, Ken Lund, CC-BY-SA-2.0
- Weatherill Mesa, Ken Lund, CC-BY-SA-2.0

The Challenge of Fuzzling
- The results of fuzzling, by Eric Henze

Grand Canyon National Park
- Grand Circle Overview, copyright Gone Beyond Guides
- Grand Canyon National Park Overview Map, Gone Beyond Guides
- Grand Canyon, by NPS Digital Image Archives, PD US NPS
- El Tovar, by Wolfgang Moroder, CC-BY-SA-3.0
- Grand Canyon rock layers, by Dept of Interior, PD-USGov
- Portrait of J. W. Powell with Indian," black-and-white photograph, presumably by explorer Frederick Samuel Dellenbaugh, a member of John Wesley Powell's second Colorado River expedition. PD-US
- Colorado River, by Tenji, CC-BY-SA-3.0-migrated
- Nankoweap Creek, Grand Canyon, by Drenaline, CC-BY-SA-3.0
- A Grand Canyon Dory maneuvers through Hance Rapid, NPS Photo by Kristen M. Caldon, PD US NPS
- Grand Canyon taken from Bright Angel, by Tomas Castelazo, CC-BY-SA-3.0
- Grand Canyon switchbacks, by NPS Digital Image Archives, PD US NPS
- This sunrise view is looking north as the Hermit Trail begins to climb the west side of Cope Butte, NPS Photo by Michael Quinn, PD US NPS
- Grand Canyon panorama, by chensiyuan, CC-BY-SA-3.0,2.5,2.0,1.0
- The Grand Canyon South Rim, by Sebastian Toncu, CC-BY-SA-3.0-migrated, CC-BY-SA-2.5,2.0,1.0
- Grand Canyon panorama, by Roger Bolsius, CC-BY-SA-3.0
- Kolb Studio, by NPS, PD US NPS
- Sunset from El Tovar Hotel, by NPS, PD US NPS
- Desert View Watchtower, by Kevin A. Trostle, CC-BY-SA-3.0
- Skywalk, by Jonas.tesch, CC-BY-SA-3.0
- Canyon View from the North Rim, by Khlnmusa, CC-BY-SA-3.0
- North Kaibab Trail, by NPS, PD US NPS
- Ribbon Falls, North Kaibab trail, PD-self
- Cape Final trail sunrise, by Notary137, PD-user

Welcome to the Colorado
- Everest in Antelope Canyon, by Eric Henze
- Bright Angel Canyon, by Tenji, CC-BY-SA-3.0-migrated
- Colorado River, by NPS, PD US NPS
- Ruins on Bright Angel Trail, Fredlyfish, CC-BY-SA-4.0

Conclusion
- View from Yavapai Point on the South Rim, NPS photo by M. Quinn, PD US NPS